Garfield

CAUTION:
WIDE LOAD

BY JIM DAVIS

Ballantine Books • **New York**

A Ballantine Books Trade Paperback Original

Published in the United States by Ballantine Books, an imprint of The Random House Publishing Group,
a division of Random House, Inc., New York.

BALLANTINE and colophon are registered trademarks of Random House, Inc.

ISBN 978-0-345-52596-3
eBook ISBN 978-0-345-54561-9

Printed in the United States of America

www.ballantinebooks.com

9 8 7 6 5 4 3 2 1

NOT-SO-SUPER SUPERHEROES

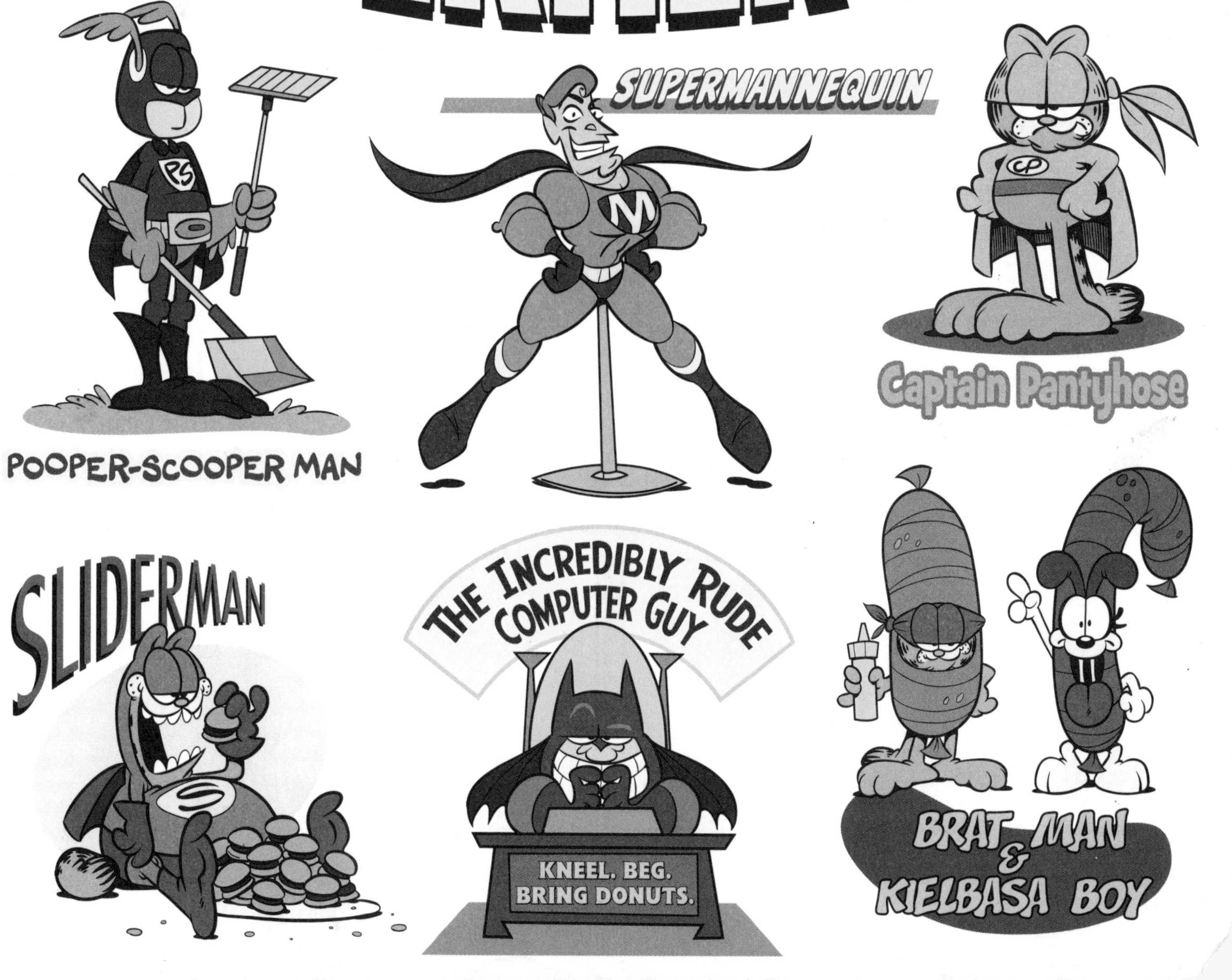
SUPERMANNEQUIN
POOPER-SCOOPER MAN
Captain Pantyhose
SLIDERMAN
THE INCREDIBLY RUDE COMPUTER GUY
KNEEL. BEG. BRING DONUTS.
BRAT MAN & KIELBASA BOY

Garfield®
www.garfield.com
© 2010 PAWS, INC. All Rights Reserved.
UGH
IT'S TOO HOT IN HERE TO NAP
JIM DAVIS 8-15
Distributed by Universal Uclick
Z

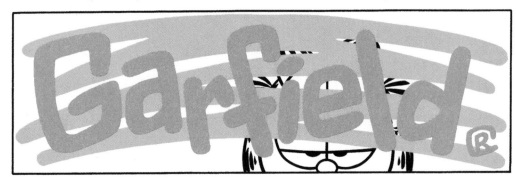

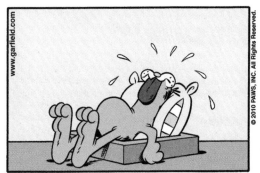

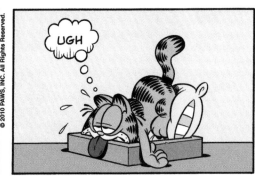

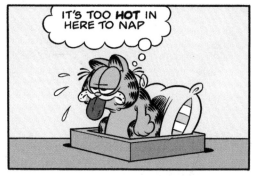

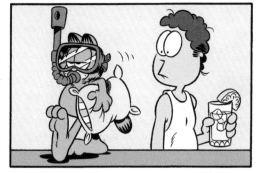

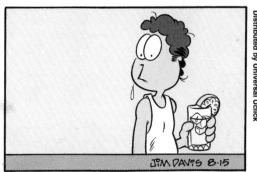

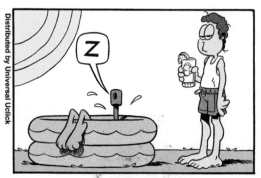

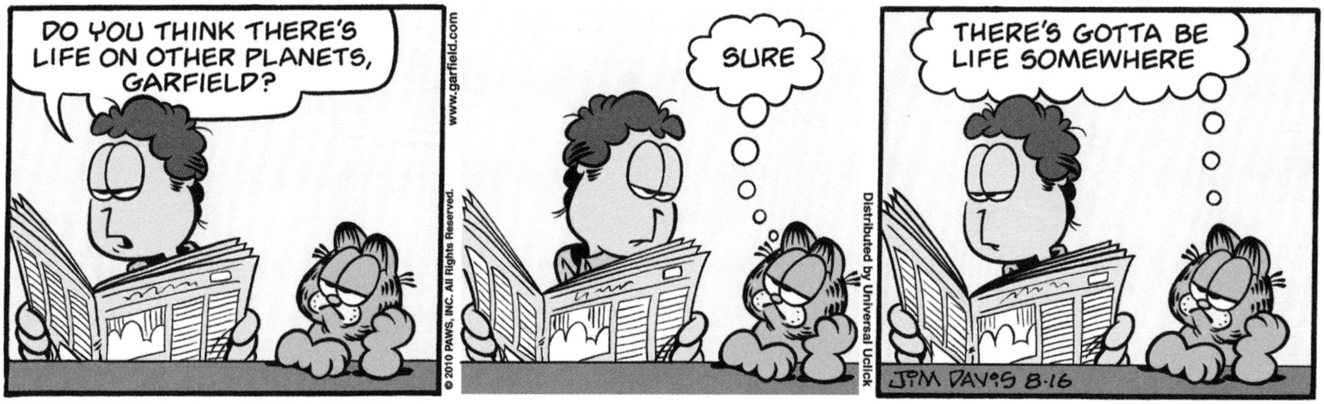
DO YOU THINK THERE'S LIFE ON OTHER PLANETS, GARFIELD?
© 2010 PAWS, INC. All Rights Reserved. www.garfield.com
SURE
Distributed by Universal Uclick
THERE'S GOTTA BE LIFE SOMEWHERE
JIM DAVIS 8-16

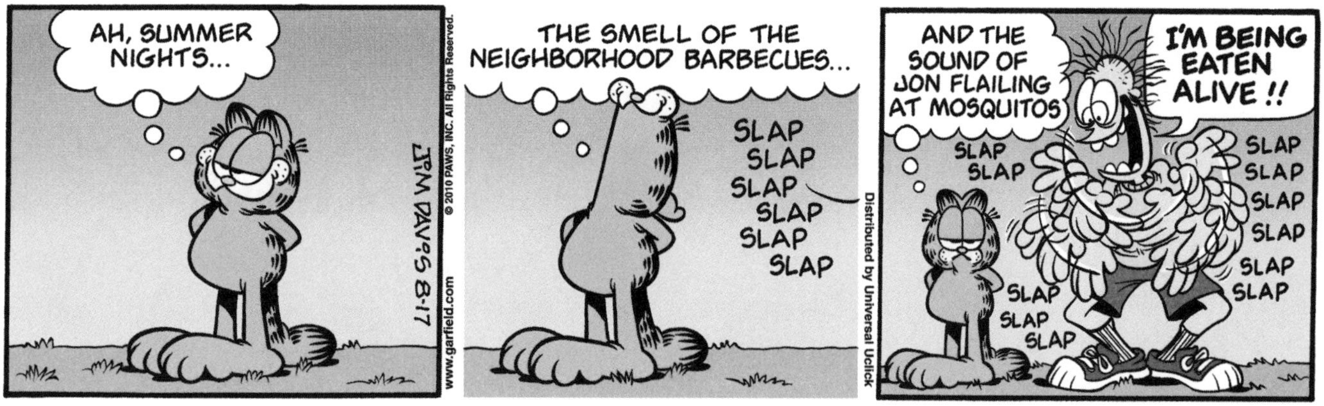
AH, SUMMER NIGHTS...
JIM DAVIS 8-17
© 2010 PAWS, INC. All Rights Reserved. www.garfield.com
THE SMELL OF THE NEIGHBORHOOD BARBECUES...
SLAP SLAP SLAP SLAP SLAP SLAP
Distributed by Universal Uclick
AND THE SOUND OF JON FLAILING AT MOSQUITOS
I'M BEING EATEN ALIVE !!
SLAP SLAP
SLAP SLAP SLAP SLAP SLAP SLAP
SLAP SLAP SLAP

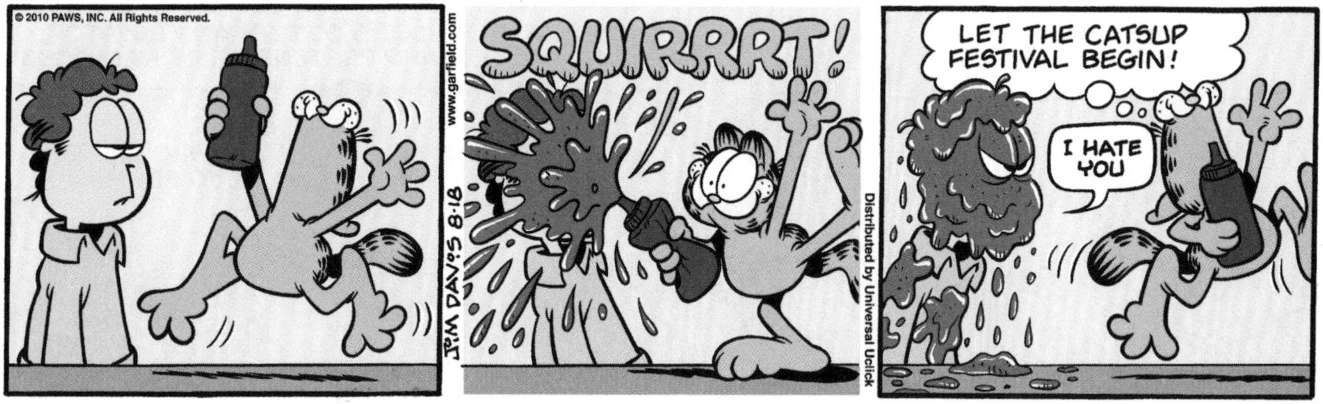
© 2010 PAWS, INC. All Rights Reserved.
www.garfield.com
JIM DAVIS 8-18
SQUIRRRT!
Distributed by Universal Uclick
LET THE CATSUP FESTIVAL BEGIN!
I HATE YOU

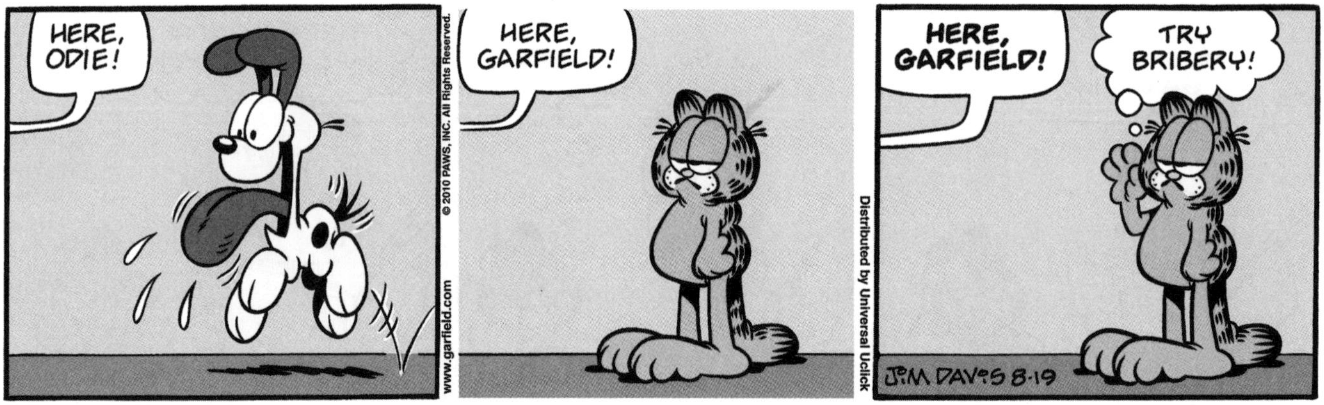
HERE, ODIE!
HERE, GARFIELD!
HERE, GARFIELD!
TRY BRIBERY!
JIM DAVIS 8-19
© 2010 PAWS, INC. All Rights Reserved.
www.garfield.com
Distributed by Universal Uclick

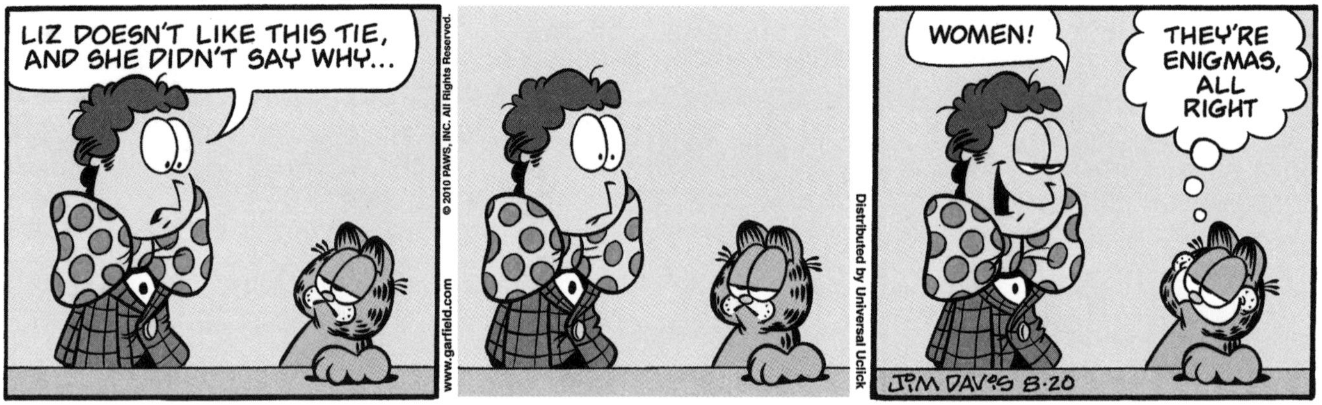
LIZ DOESN'T LIKE THIS TIE, AND SHE DIDN'T SAY WHY...
WOMEN!
THEY'RE ENIGMAS, ALL RIGHT
JIM DAVIS 8-20
© 2010 PAWS, INC. All Rights Reserved.
www.garfield.com
Distributed by Universal Uclick

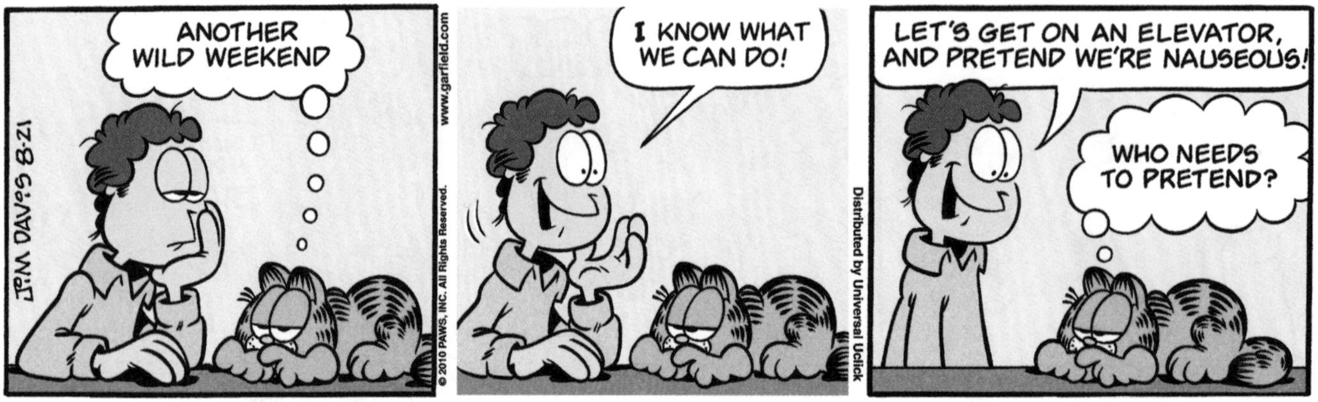
ANOTHER WILD WEEKEND
I KNOW WHAT WE CAN DO!
LET'S GET ON AN ELEVATOR, AND PRETEND WE'RE NAUSEOUS!
WHO NEEDS TO PRETEND?
JIM DAVIS 8-21
© 2010 PAWS, INC. All Rights Reserved.
www.garfield.com
Distributed by Universal Uclick

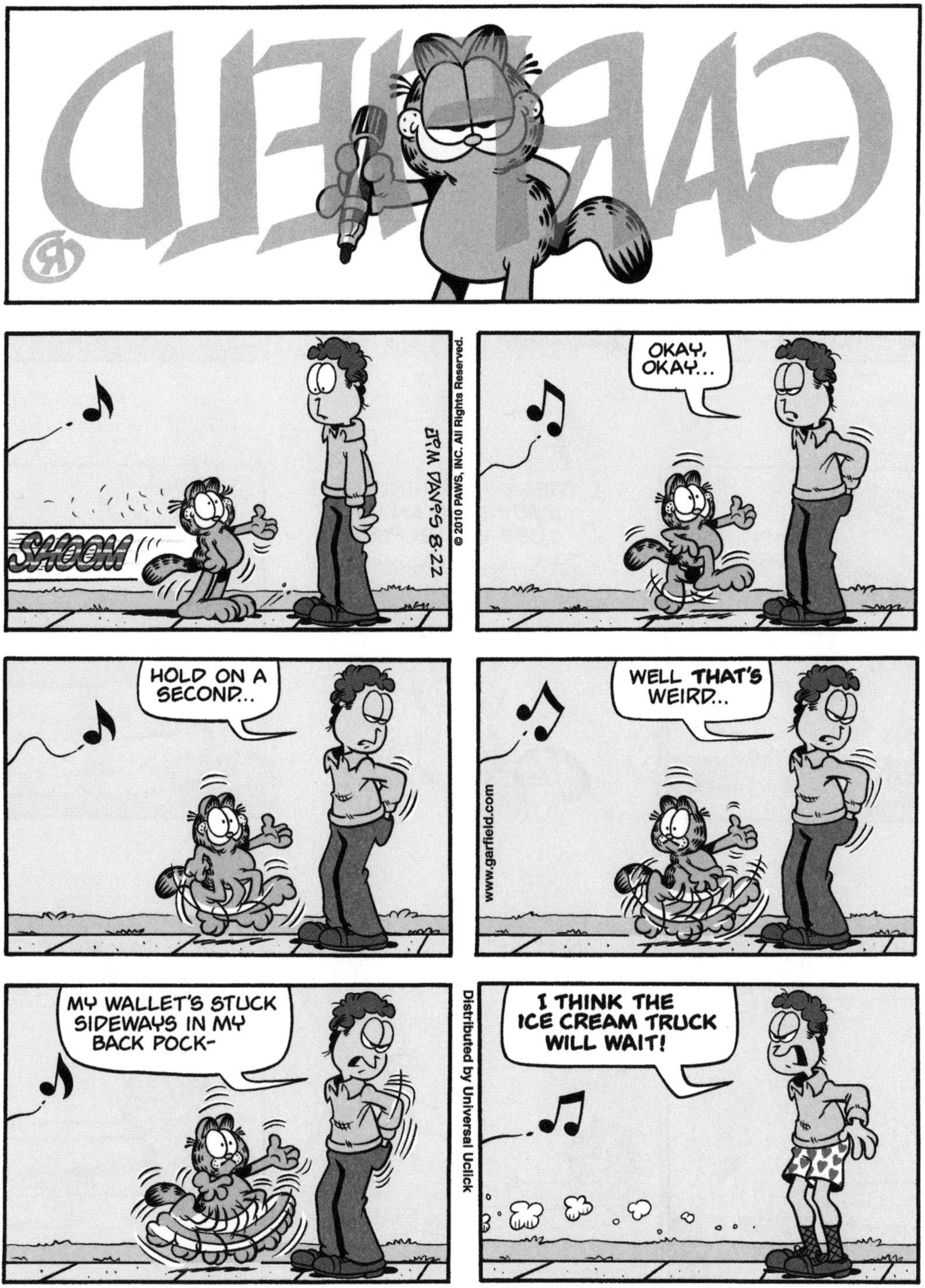
GARFIELD
SHOOM
JIM DAVIS 8-22
© 2010 PAWS, INC. All Rights Reserved.
OKAY, OKAY...
HOLD ON A SECOND...
WELL THAT'S WEIRD...
www.garfield.com
MY WALLET'S STUCK SIDEWAYS IN MY BACK POCK-
Distributed by Universal Uclick
I THINK THE ICE CREAM TRUCK WILL WAIT!

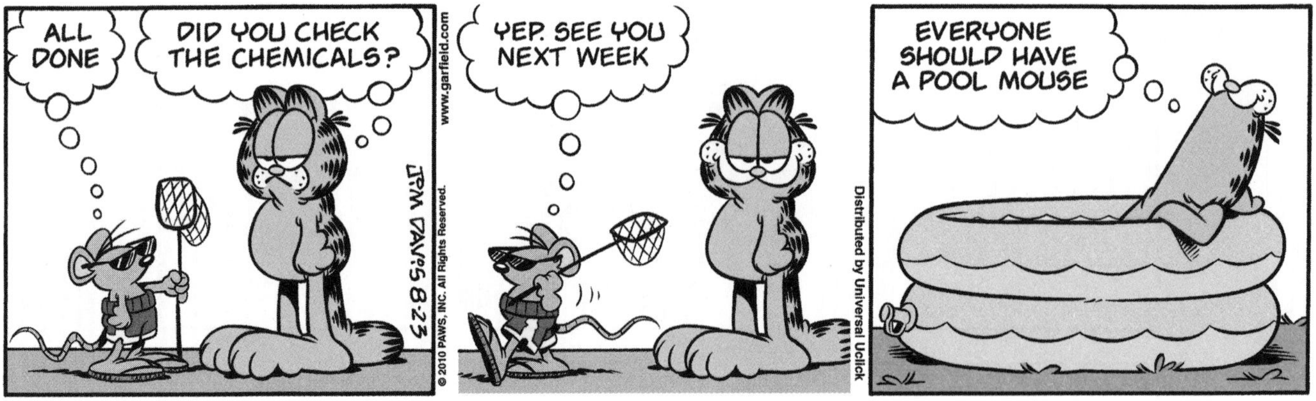
ALL DONE
DID YOU CHECK THE CHEMICALS?
YEP. SEE YOU NEXT WEEK
EVERYONE SHOULD HAVE A POOL MOUSE
JPM DAVPS 8-23
© 2010 PAWS, INC. All Rights Reserved.
www.garfield.com
Distributed by Universal Uclick

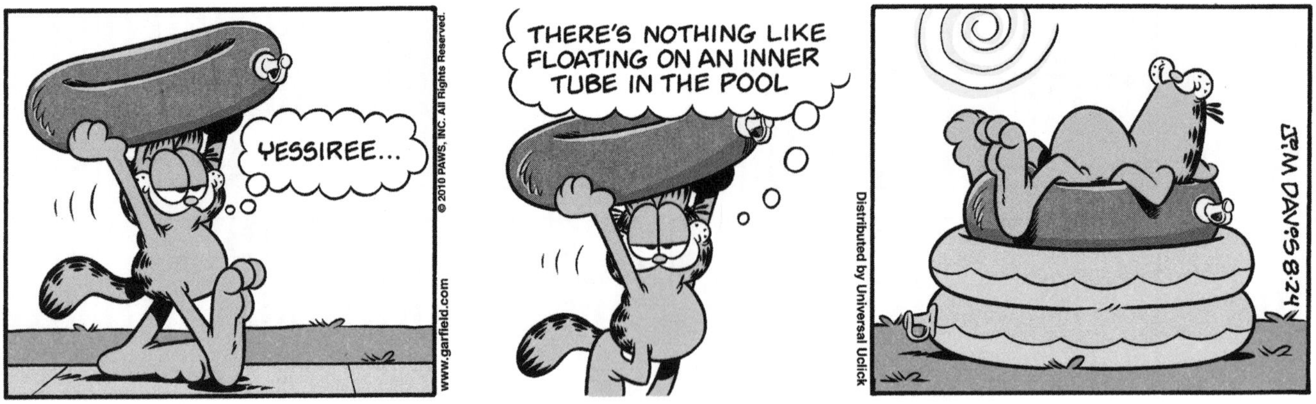
YESSIREE...
THERE'S NOTHING LIKE FLOATING ON AN INNER TUBE IN THE POOL
JPM DAVPS 8-24
© 2010 PAWS, INC. All Rights Reserved.
www.garfield.com
Distributed by Universal Uclick

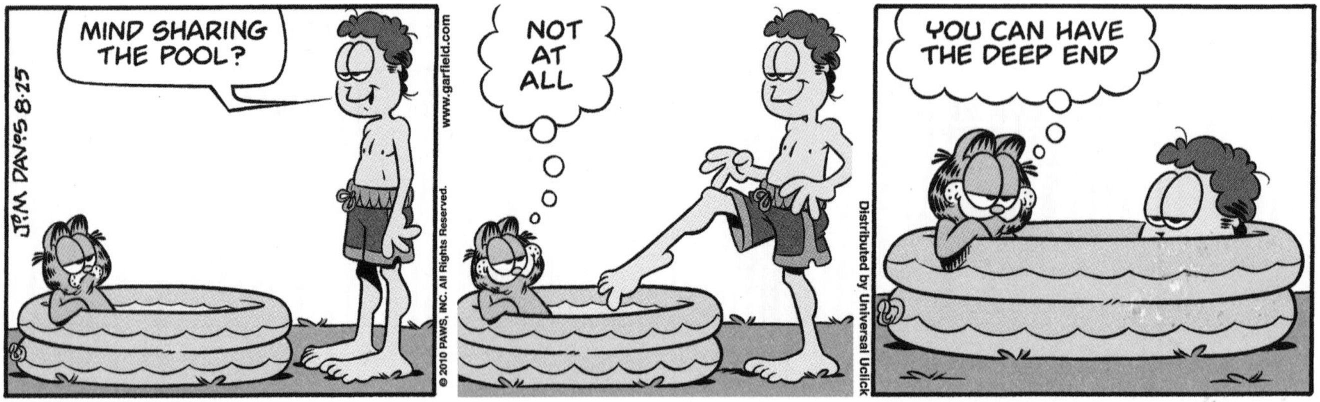
MIND SHARING THE POOL?
NOT AT ALL
YOU CAN HAVE THE DEEP END
JPM DAVPS 8-25
© 2010 PAWS, INC. All Rights Reserved.
www.garfield.com
Distributed by Universal Uclick

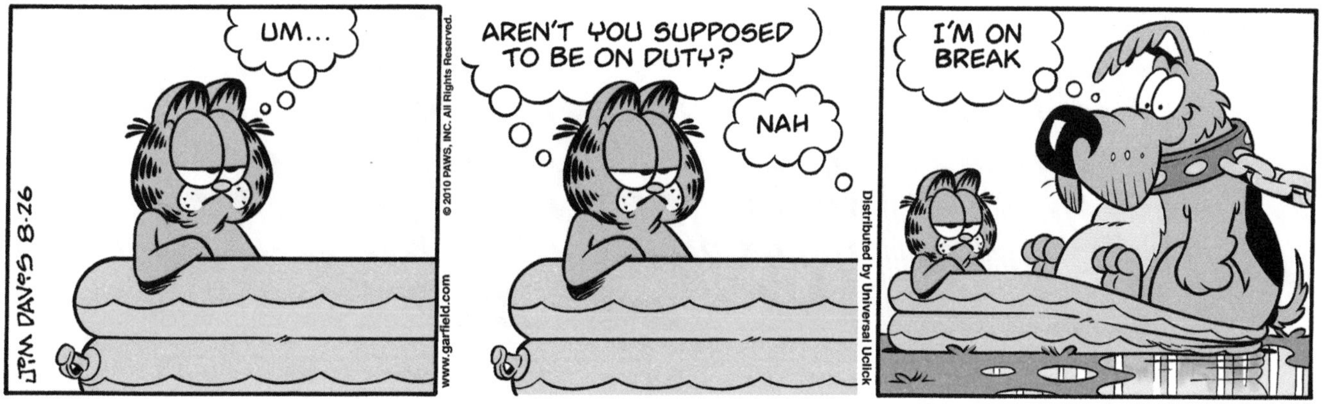
JIM DAVIS 8-26
UM...
© 2010 PAWS, INC. All Rights Reserved.
www.garfield.com
AREN'T YOU SUPPOSED TO BE ON DUTY?
NAH
Distributed by Universal Uclick
I'M ON BREAK

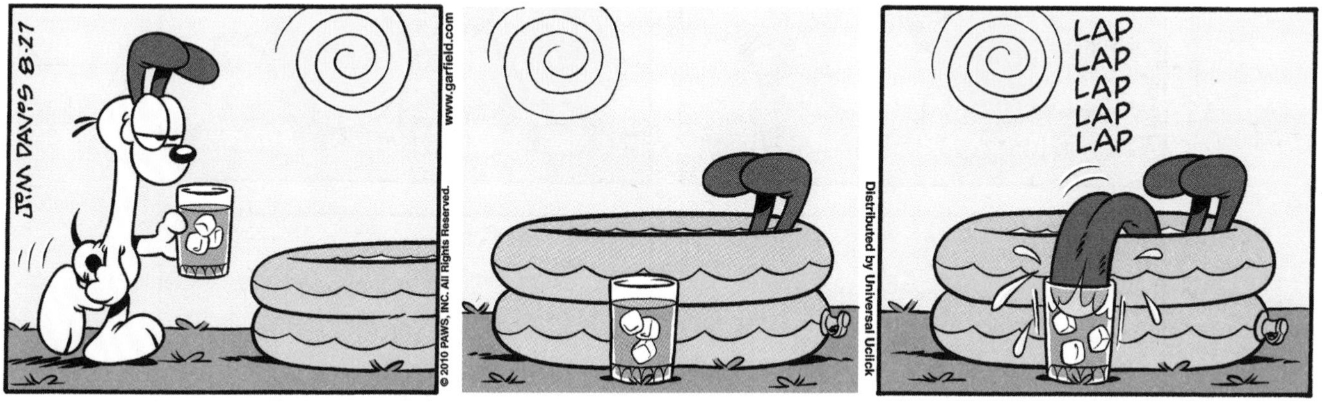
JIM DAVIS 8-27
www.garfield.com
© 2010 PAWS, INC. All Rights Reserved.
Distributed by Universal Uclick
LAP
LAP
LAP
LAP
LAP

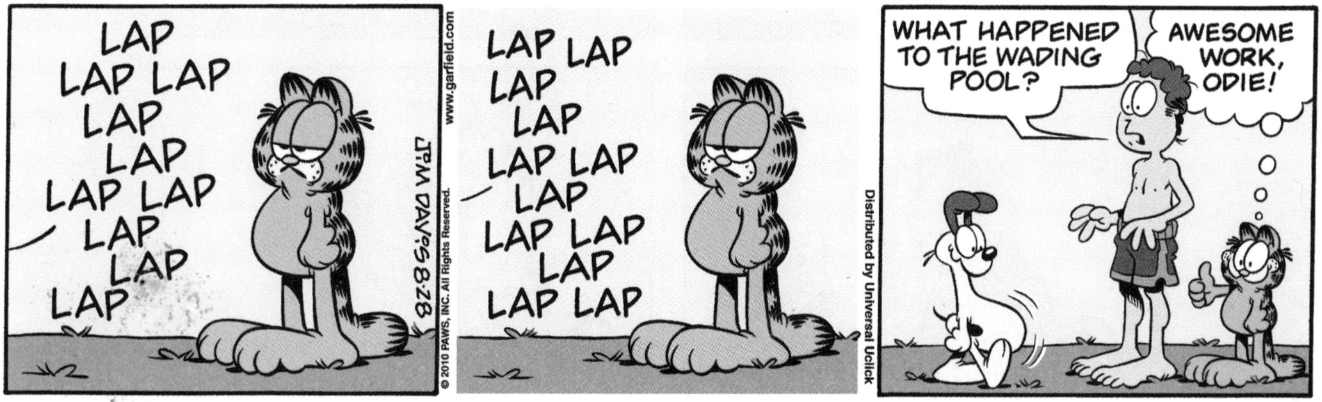
LAP
LAP LAP
LAP
LAP
LAP LAP
LAP
LAP
LAP
JIM DAVIS 8-28
www.garfield.com
© 2010 PAWS, INC. All Rights Reserved.
LAP LAP
LAP
LAP
LAP LAP
LAP
LAP LAP
LAP
LAP LAP
Distributed by Universal Uclick
WHAT HAPPENED TO THE WADING POOL?
AWESOME WORK, ODIE!

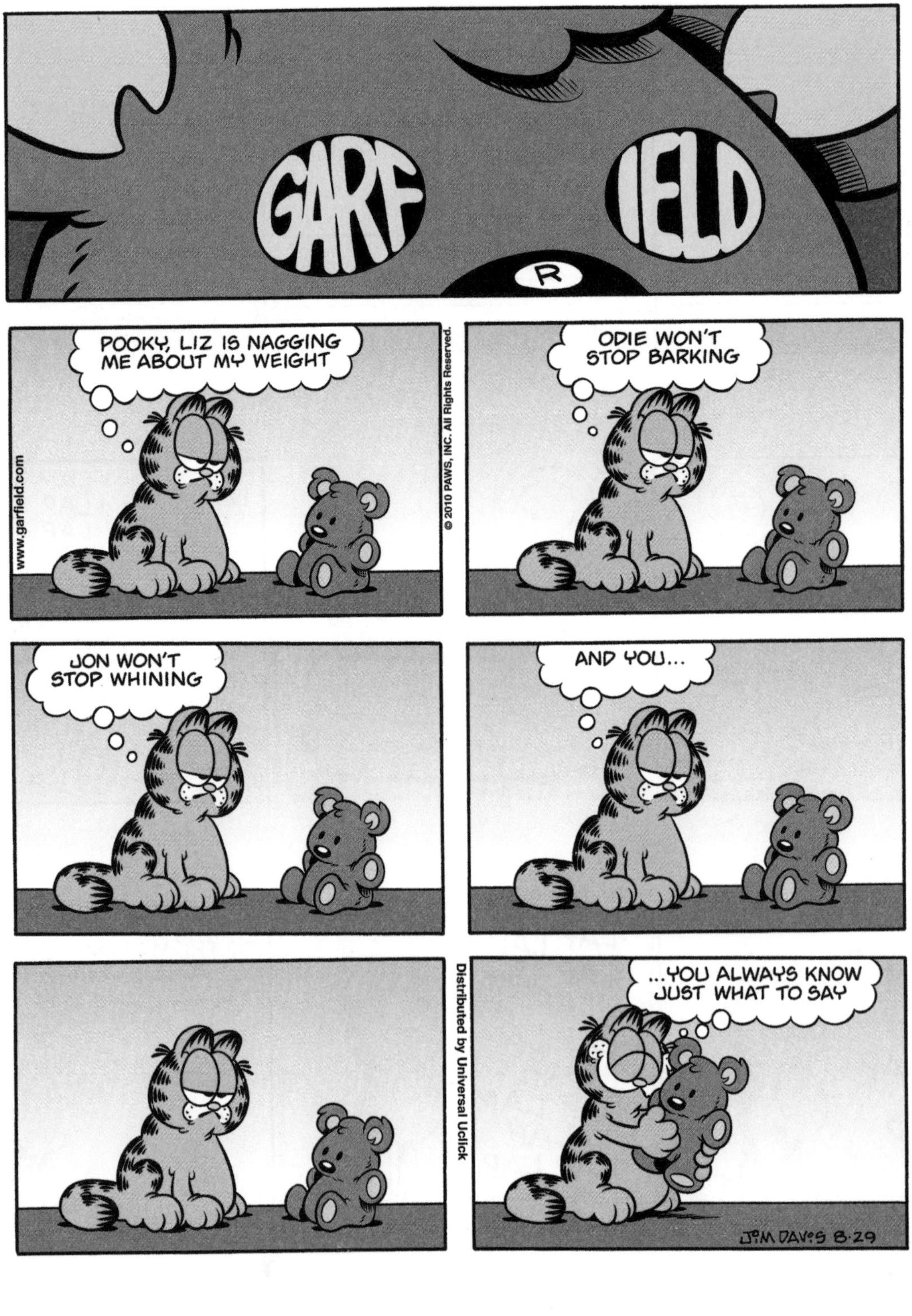
GARFIELD
R
POOKY, LIZ IS NAGGING ME ABOUT MY WEIGHT
ODIE WON'T STOP BARKING
JON WON'T STOP WHINING
AND YOU...
...YOU ALWAYS KNOW JUST WHAT TO SAY
JIM DAVIS 8-29
www.garfield.com
© 2010 PAWS, INC. All Rights Reserved.
Distributed by Universal Uclick

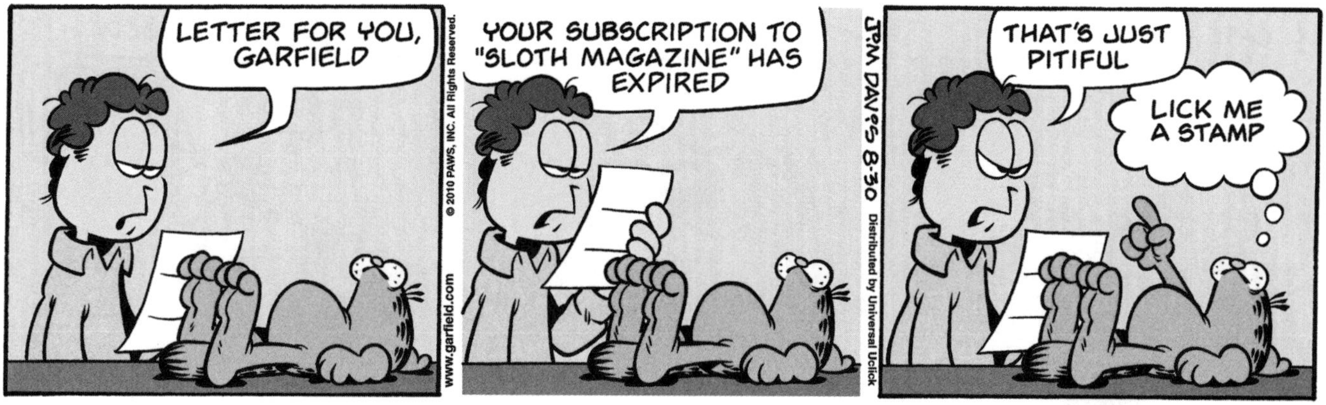
LETTER FOR YOU, GARFIELD
YOUR SUBSCRIPTION TO "SLOTH MAGAZINE" HAS EXPIRED
THAT'S JUST PITIFUL
LICK ME A STAMP
JIM DAVIS 8-30
© 2010 PAWS, INC. All Rights Reserved.
www.garfield.com
Distributed by Universal Uclick

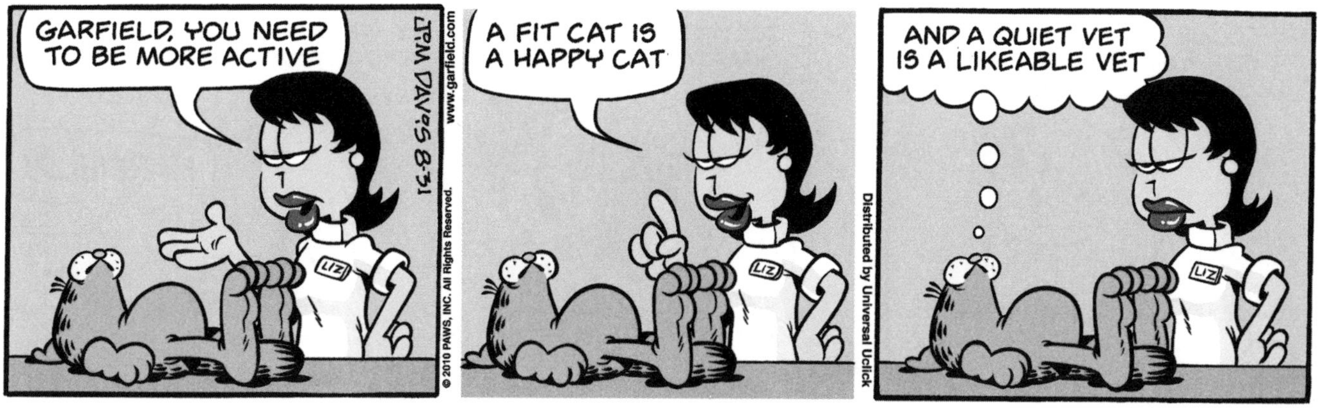
GARFIELD, YOU NEED TO BE MORE ACTIVE
A FIT CAT IS A HAPPY CAT
AND A QUIET VET IS A LIKEABLE VET
LIZ
JIM DAVIS 8-31
© 2010 PAWS, INC. All Rights Reserved.
www.garfield.com
Distributed by Universal Uclick

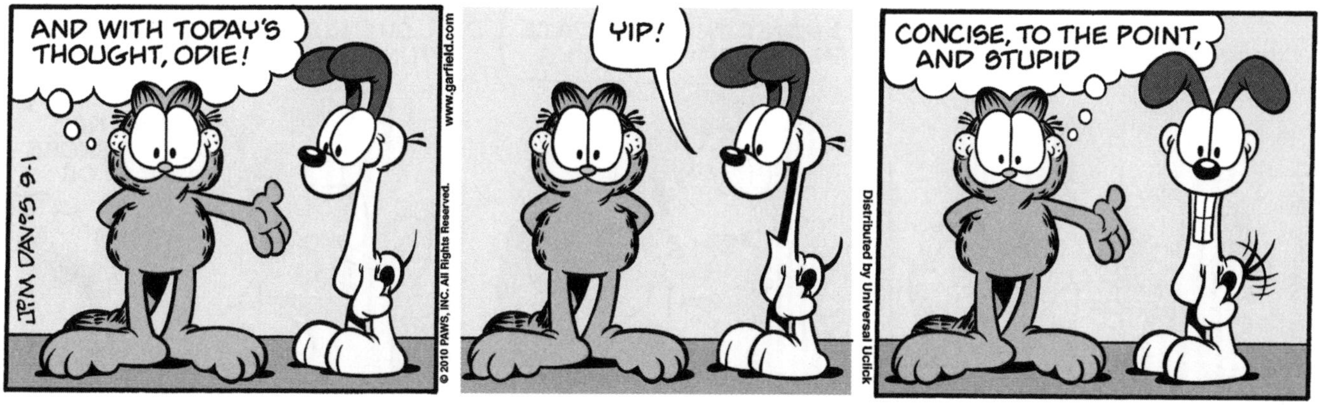
AND WITH TODAY'S THOUGHT, ODIE!
YIP!
CONCISE, TO THE POINT, AND STUPID
JIM DAVIS 9-1
© 2010 PAWS, INC. All Rights Reserved.
www.garfield.com
Distributed by Universal Uclick

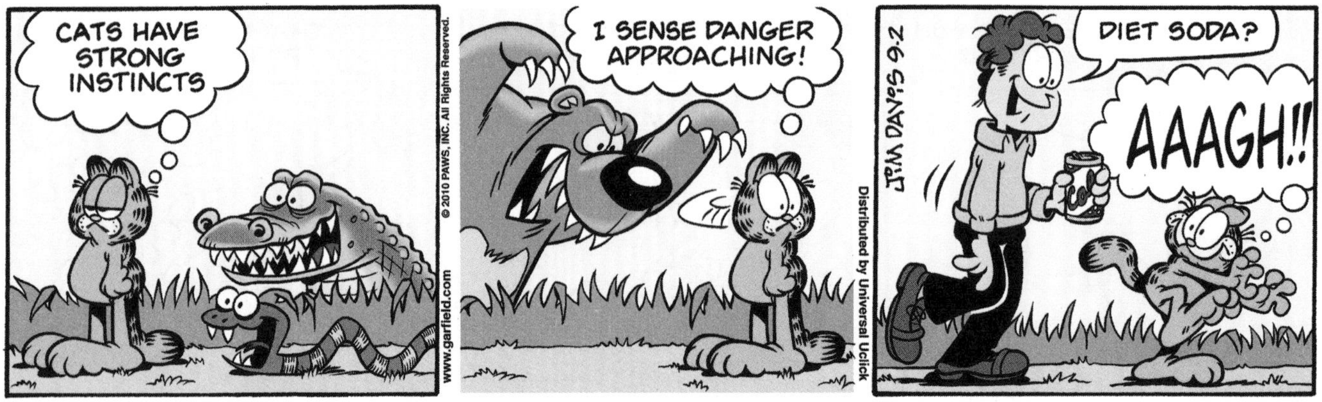
CATS HAVE STRONG INSTINCTS
I SENSE DANGER APPROACHING!
DIET SODA?
AAAGH!!!
JIM DAVIS 9-2
© 2010 PAWS, INC. All Rights Reserved. www.garfield.com
Distributed by Universal Uclick

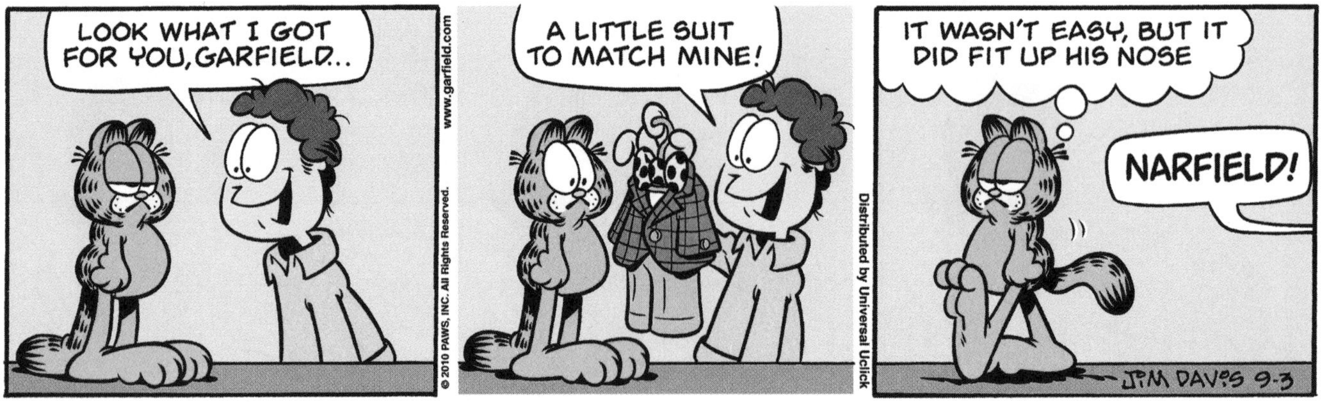
LOOK WHAT I GOT FOR YOU, GARFIELD...
A LITTLE SUIT TO MATCH MINE!
IT WASN'T EASY, BUT IT DID FIT UP HIS NOSE
NARFIELD!
JIM DAVIS 9-3
© 2010 PAWS, INC. All Rights Reserved. www.garfield.com
Distributed by Universal Uclick

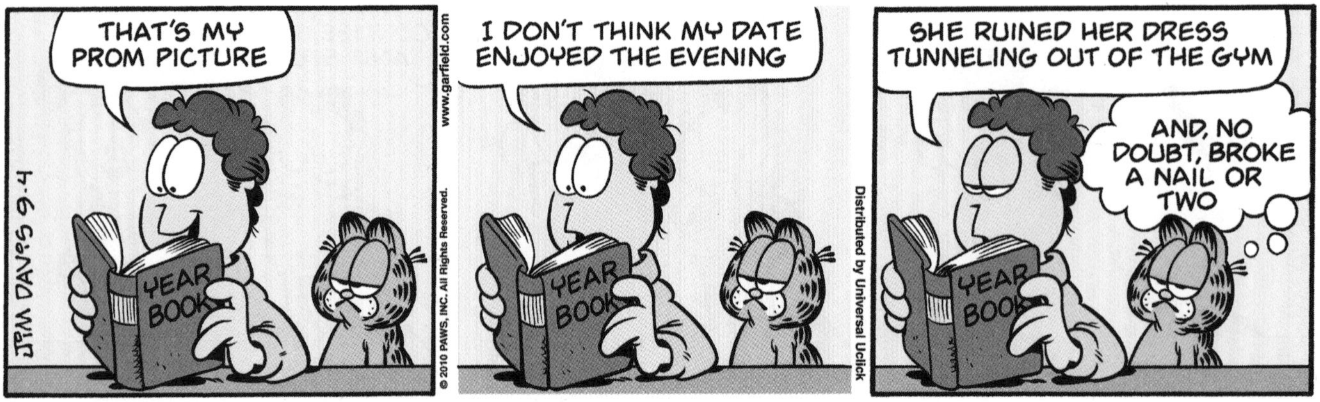
THAT'S MY PROM PICTURE
YEAR BOOK
I DON'T THINK MY DATE ENJOYED THE EVENING
SHE RUINED HER DRESS TUNNELING OUT OF THE GYM
AND, NO DOUBT, BROKE A NAIL OR TWO
JIM DAVIS 9-4
© 2010 PAWS, INC. All Rights Reserved. www.garfield.com
Distributed by Universal Uclick

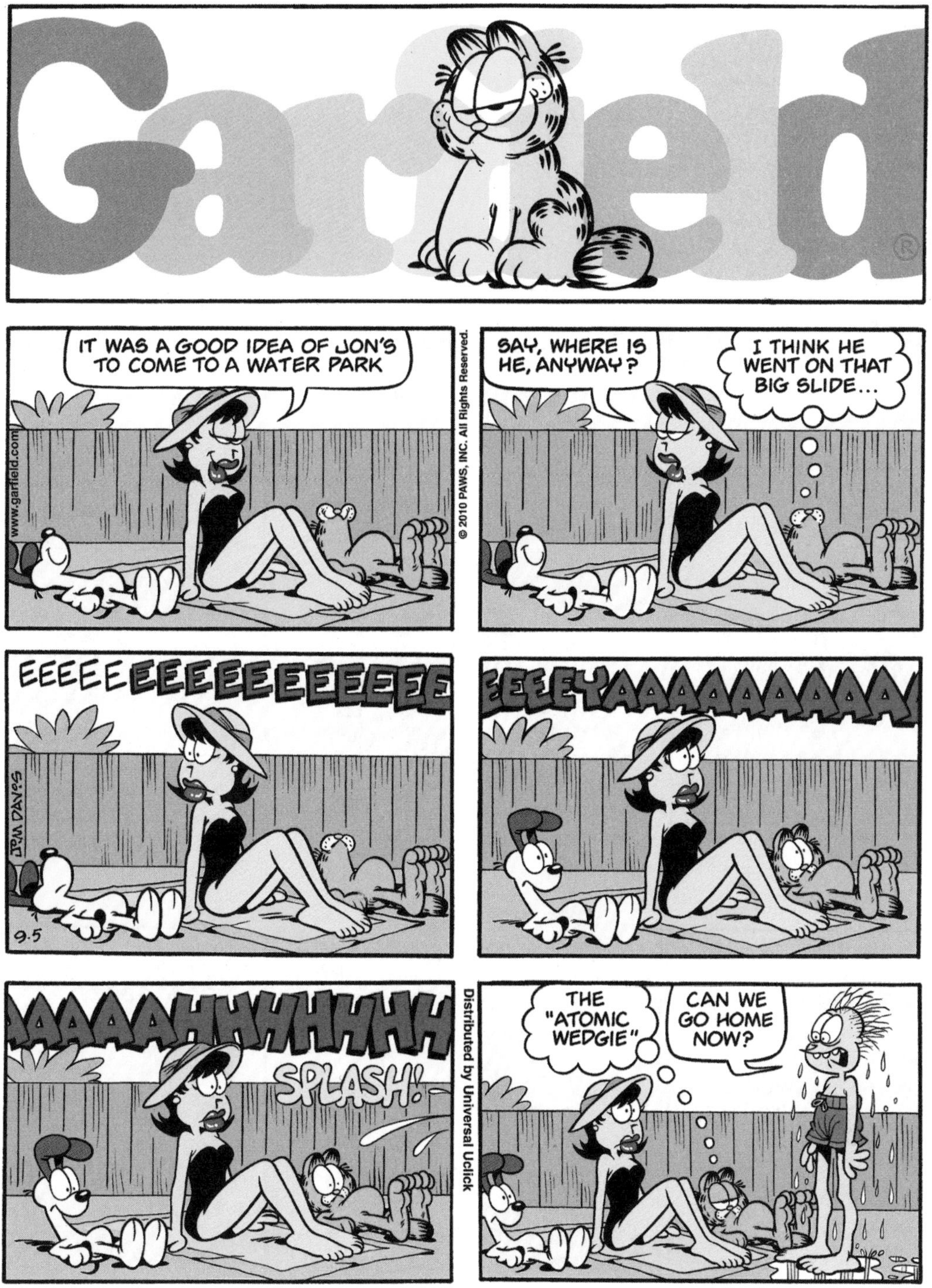
Garfield®
IT WAS A GOOD IDEA OF JON'S TO COME TO A WATER PARK
www.garfield.com
© 2010 PAWS, INC. All Rights Reserved.
SAY, WHERE IS HE, ANYWAY?
I THINK HE WENT ON THAT BIG SLIDE...
EEEEEEEEEEEEEEEEE
JPM DAVIS
9-5
EEEEYAAAAAAAAAAA
AAAAAHHHHHHH
SPLASH!
Distributed by Universal Uclick
THE "ATOMIC WEDGIE"
CAN WE GO HOME NOW?

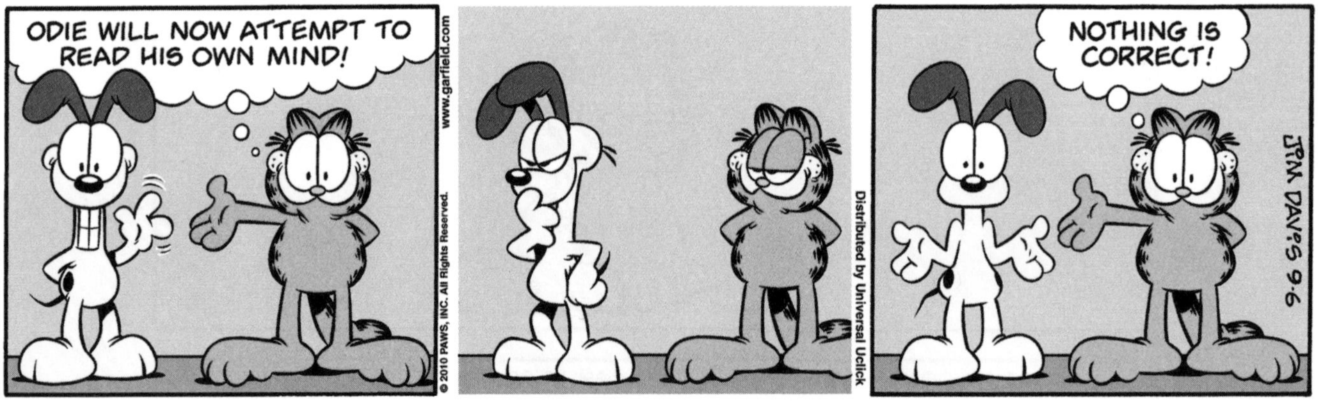
ODIE WILL NOW ATTEMPT TO READ HIS OWN MIND!
NOTHING IS CORRECT!
JIM DAVIS 9-6
© 2010 PAWS, INC. All Rights Reserved.
www.garfield.com
Distributed by Universal Uclick

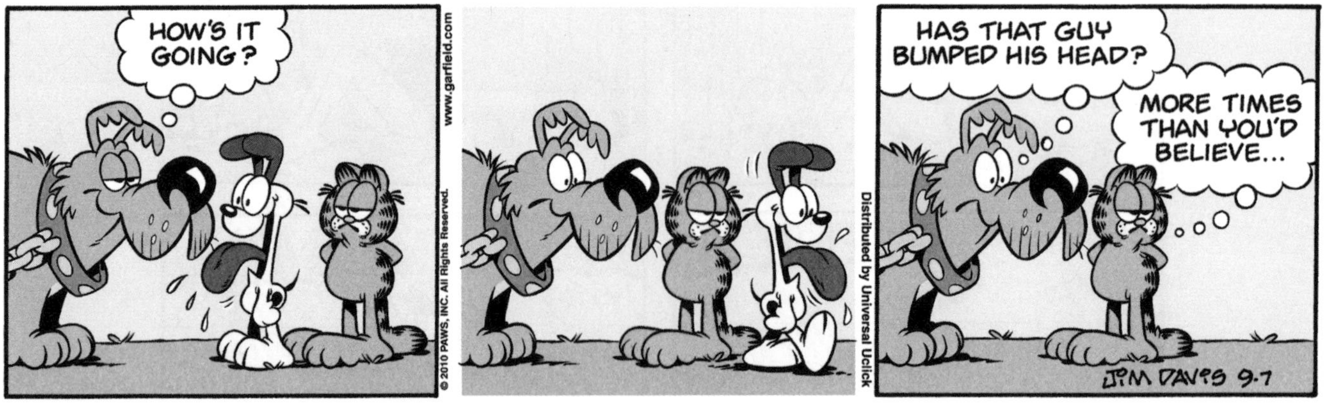
HOW'S IT GOING?
HAS THAT GUY BUMPED HIS HEAD?
MORE TIMES THAN YOU'D BELIEVE...
JIM DAVIS 9-7
© 2010 PAWS, INC. All Rights Reserved.
www.garfield.com
Distributed by Universal Uclick

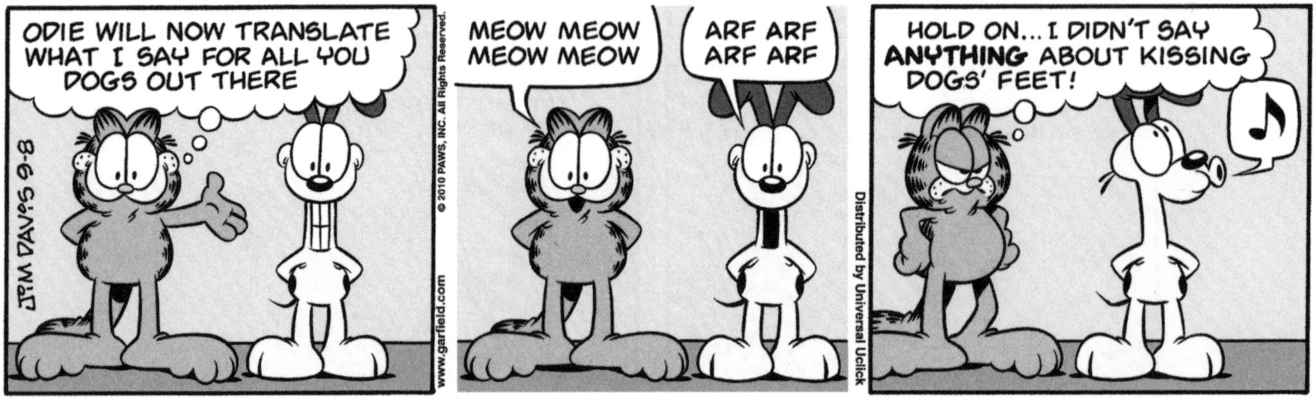
ODIE WILL NOW TRANSLATE WHAT I SAY FOR ALL YOU DOGS OUT THERE
JIM DAVIS 9-8
MEOW MEOW MEOW MEOW
ARF ARF ARF ARF
HOLD ON... I DIDN'T SAY **ANYTHING** ABOUT KISSING DOGS' FEET!
© 2010 PAWS, INC. All Rights Reserved.
www.garfield.com
Distributed by Universal Uclick

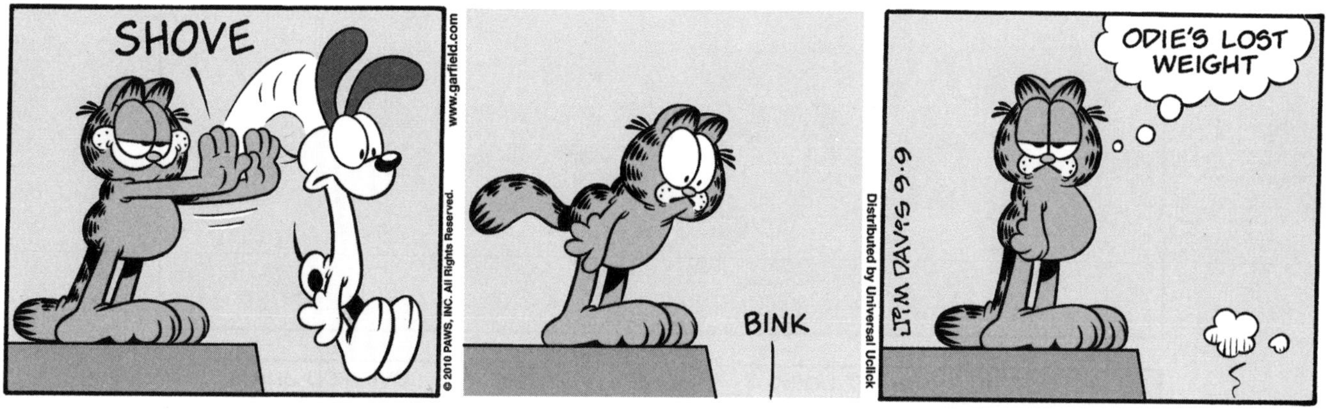
SHOVE
© 2010 PAWS, INC. All Rights Reserved.
www.garfield.com
BINK
JIM DAVIS 9-9
Distributed by Universal Uclick
ODIE'S LOST WEIGHT

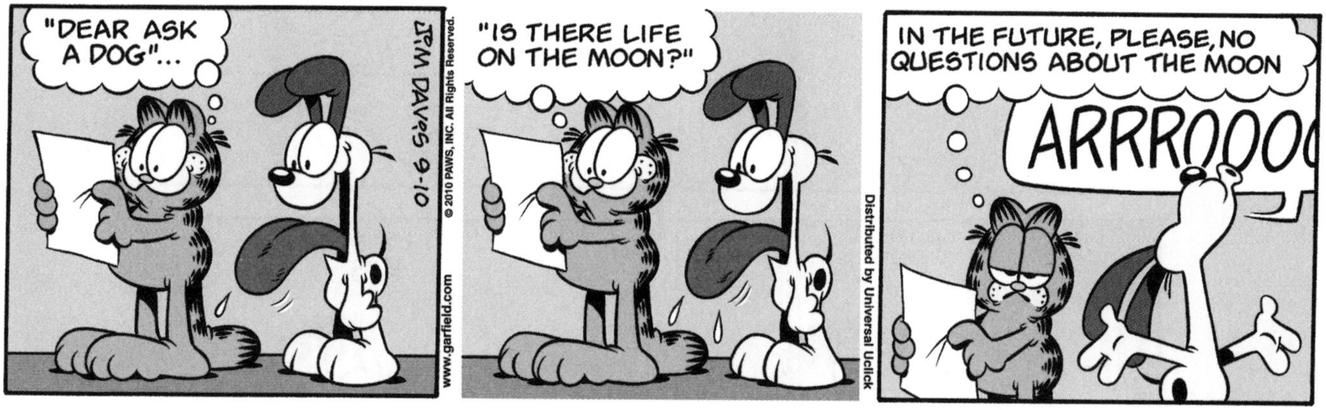
"DEAR ASK A DOG"...
JIM DAVIS 9-10
© 2010 PAWS, INC. All Rights Reserved.
www.garfield.com
"IS THERE LIFE ON THE MOON?"
Distributed by Universal Uclick
IN THE FUTURE, PLEASE, NO QUESTIONS ABOUT THE MOON
ARRROOOO

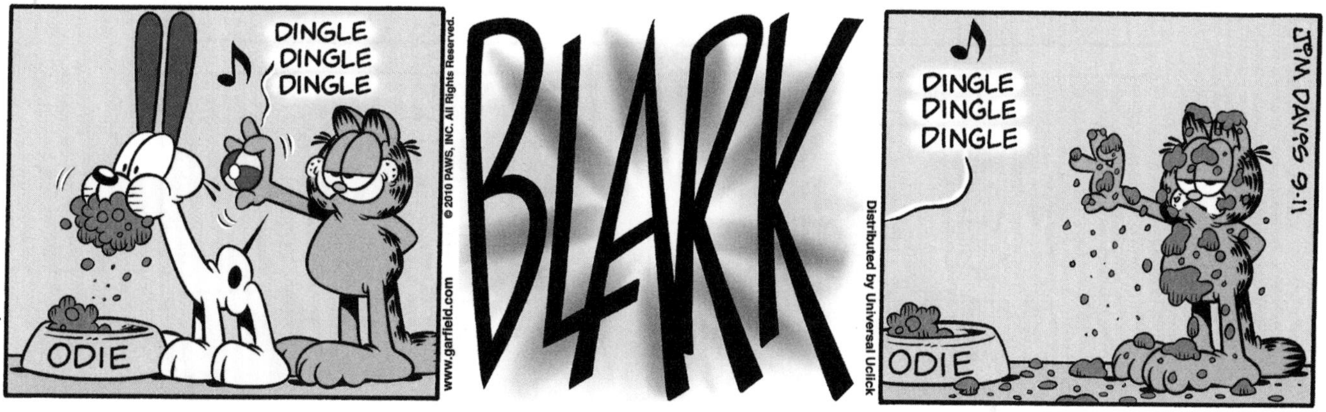
DINGLE DINGLE DINGLE
ODIE
© 2010 PAWS, INC. All Rights Reserved.
www.garfield.com
BLARK
Distributed by Universal Uclick
DINGLE DINGLE DINGLE
ODIE
JIM DAVIS 9-11

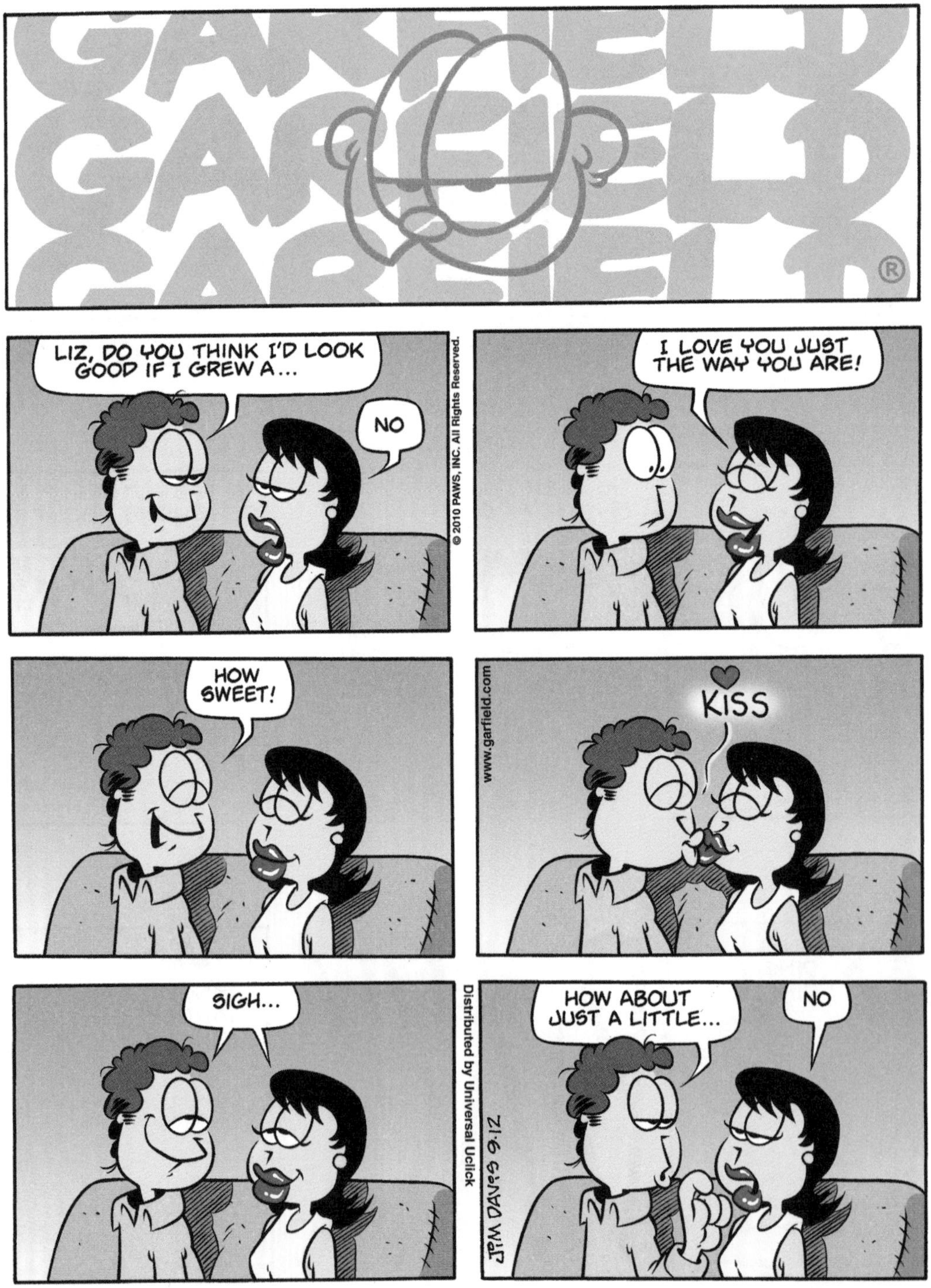
GARFIELD
LIZ, DO YOU THINK I'D LOOK GOOD IF I GREW A...
NO
I LOVE YOU JUST THE WAY YOU ARE!
HOW SWEET!
KISS
SIGH...
HOW ABOUT JUST A LITTLE...
NO
JPM DAVIS 9.12

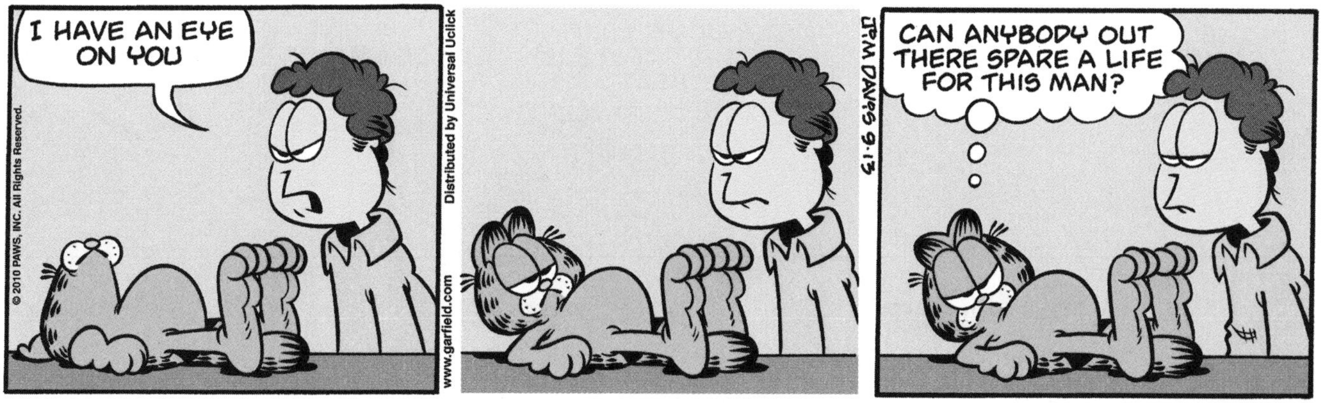
I HAVE AN EYE ON YOU
CAN ANYBODY OUT THERE SPARE A LIFE FOR THIS MAN?
JIM DAVIS 9·13
© 2010 PAWS, INC. All Rights Reserved.
www.garfield.com
Distributed by Universal Uclick

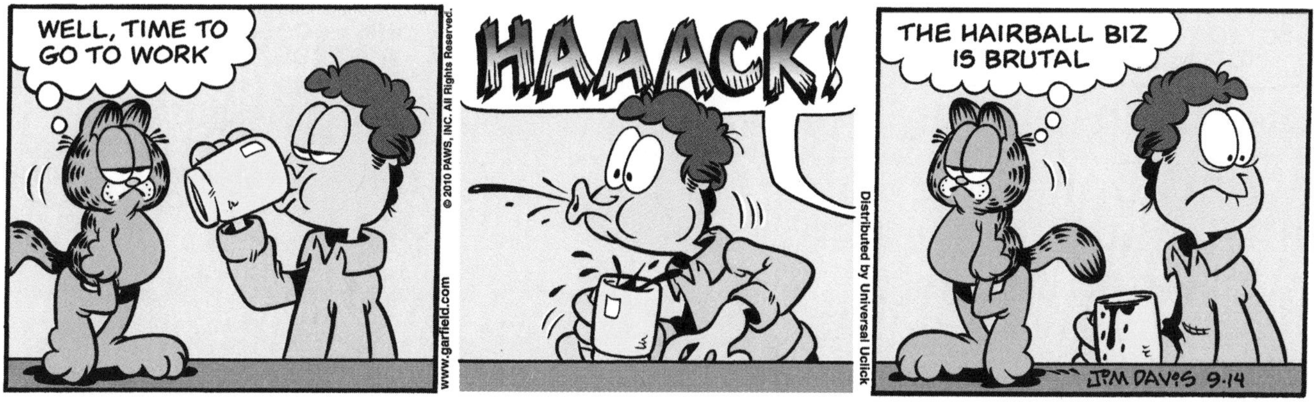
WELL, TIME TO GO TO WORK
HAAACK!
THE HAIRBALL BIZ IS BRUTAL
JIM DAVIS 9·14
© 2010 PAWS, INC. All Rights Reserved.
www.garfield.com
Distributed by Universal Uclick

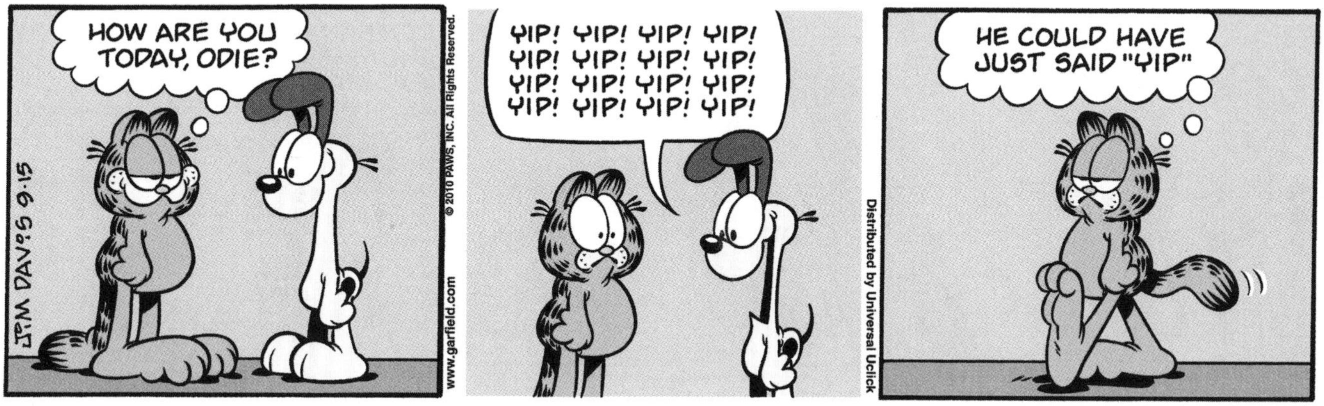
HOW ARE YOU TODAY, ODIE?
YIP! YIP! YIP! YIP! YIP! YIP! YIP! YIP! YIP! YIP! YIP! YIP! YIP! YIP! YIP! YIP!
HE COULD HAVE JUST SAID "YIP"
JIM DAVIS 9·15
© 2010 PAWS, INC. All Rights Reserved.
www.garfield.com
Distributed by Universal Uclick

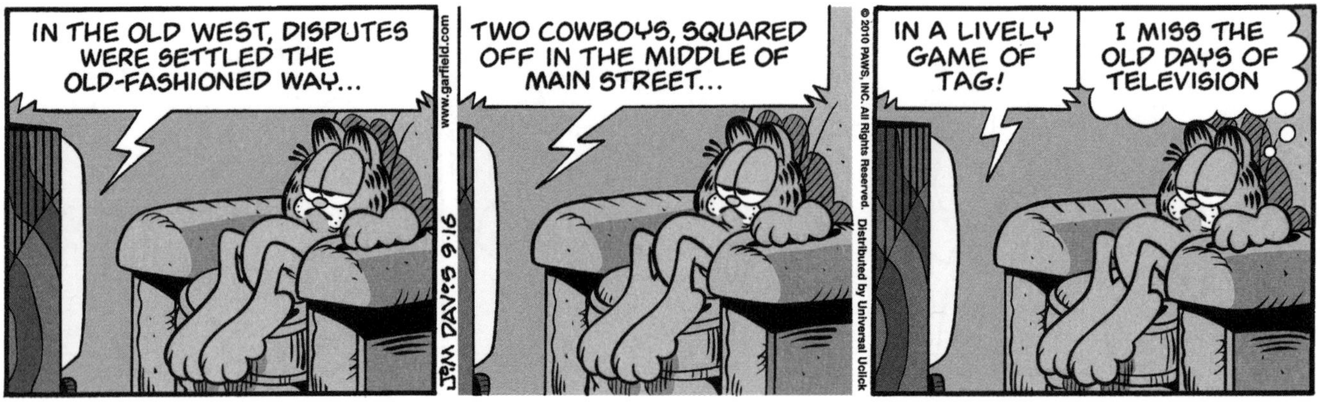
IN THE OLD WEST, DISPUTES WERE SETTLED THE OLD-FASHIONED WAY...
TWO COWBOYS, SQUARED OFF IN THE MIDDLE OF MAIN STREET...
IN A LIVELY GAME OF TAG!
I MISS THE OLD DAYS OF TELEVISION
JIM DAVIS 9·16
www.garfield.com
© 2010 PAWS, INC. All Rights Reserved. Distributed by Universal Uclick

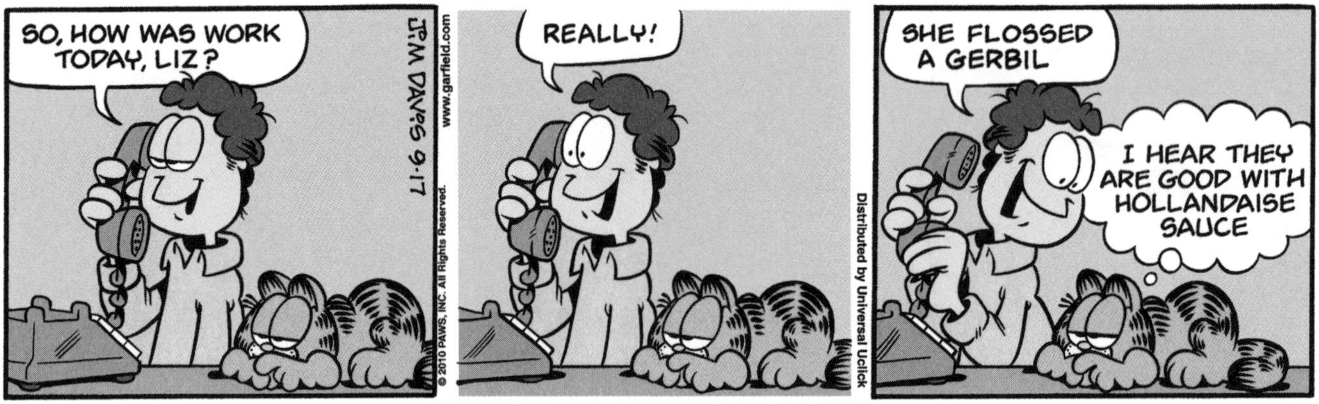
SO, HOW WAS WORK TODAY, LIZ?
REALLY!
SHE FLOSSED A GERBIL
I HEAR THEY ARE GOOD WITH HOLLANDAISE SAUCE
JIM DAVIS 9·17
www.garfield.com
© 2010 PAWS, INC. All Rights Reserved.
Distributed by Universal Uclick

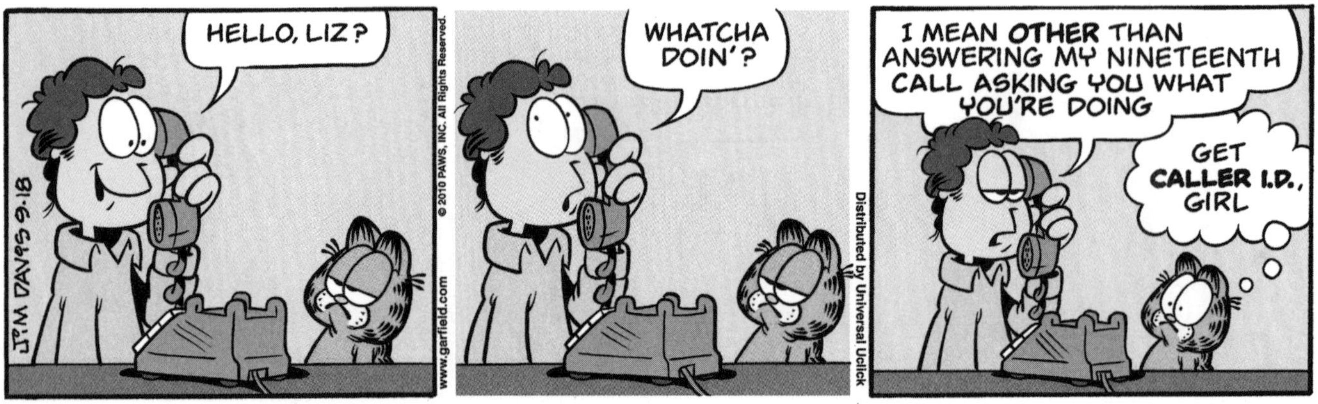
HELLO, LIZ?
WHATCHA DOIN'?
I MEAN **OTHER** THAN ANSWERING MY NINETEENTH CALL ASKING YOU WHAT YOU'RE DOING
GET **CALLER I.D.**, GIRL
JIM DAVIS 9·18
www.garfield.com
© 2010 PAWS, INC. All Rights Reserved.
Distributed by Universal Uclick

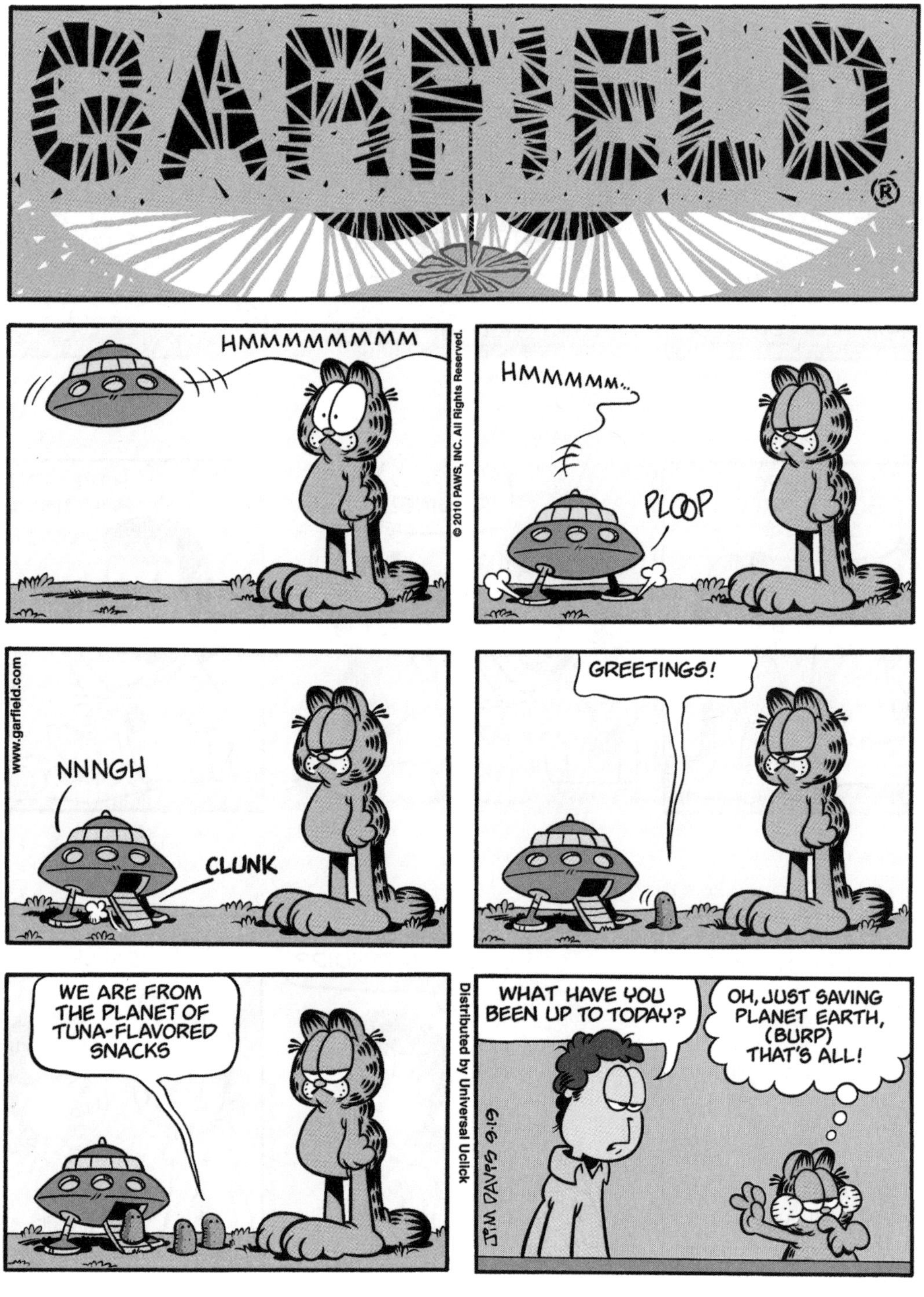
GARFIELD
HMMMMMMMMM
© 2010 PAWS, INC. All Rights Reserved.
HMMMMM...
PLOOP
www.garfield.com
NNNGH
CLUNK
GREETINGS!
WE ARE FROM THE PLANET OF TUNA-FLAVORED SNACKS
Distributed by Universal Uclick
WHAT HAVE YOU BEEN UP TO TODAY?
OH, JUST SAVING PLANET EARTH, (BURP) THAT'S ALL!
JPM DAVPS 9-19

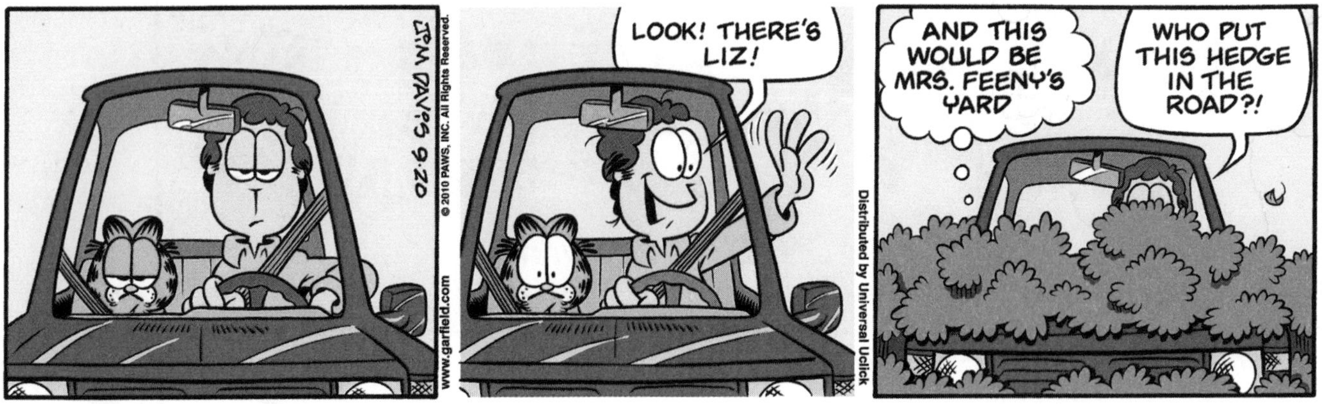
JIM DAVIS 9.20
© 2010 PAWS, INC. All Rights Reserved.
www.garfield.com
LOOK! THERE'S LIZ!
Distributed by Universal Uclick
AND THIS WOULD BE MRS. FEENY'S YARD
WHO PUT THIS HEDGE IN THE ROAD?!

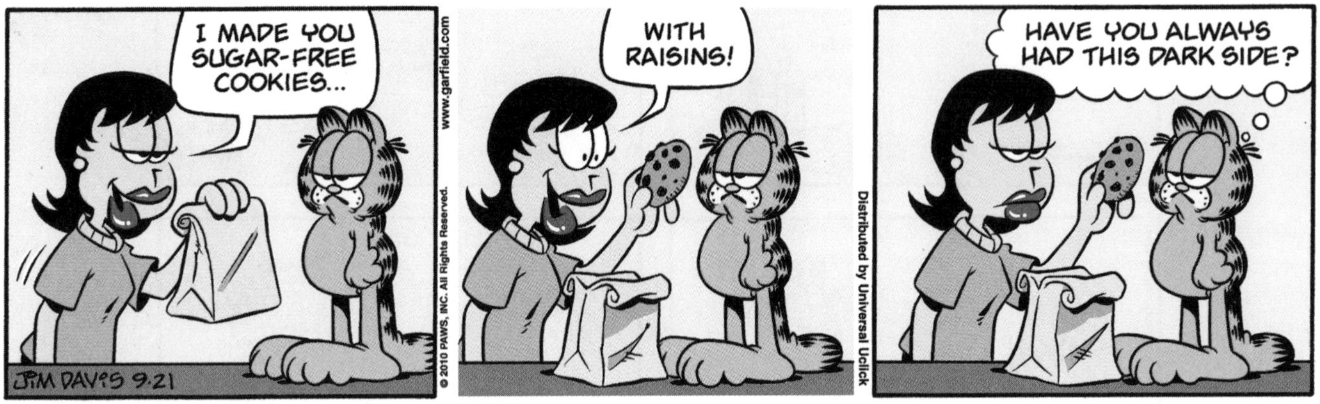
I MADE YOU SUGAR-FREE COOKIES...
JIM DAVIS 9.21
www.garfield.com
© 2010 PAWS, INC. All Rights Reserved.
WITH RAISINS!
Distributed by Universal Uclick
HAVE YOU ALWAYS HAD THIS DARK SIDE?

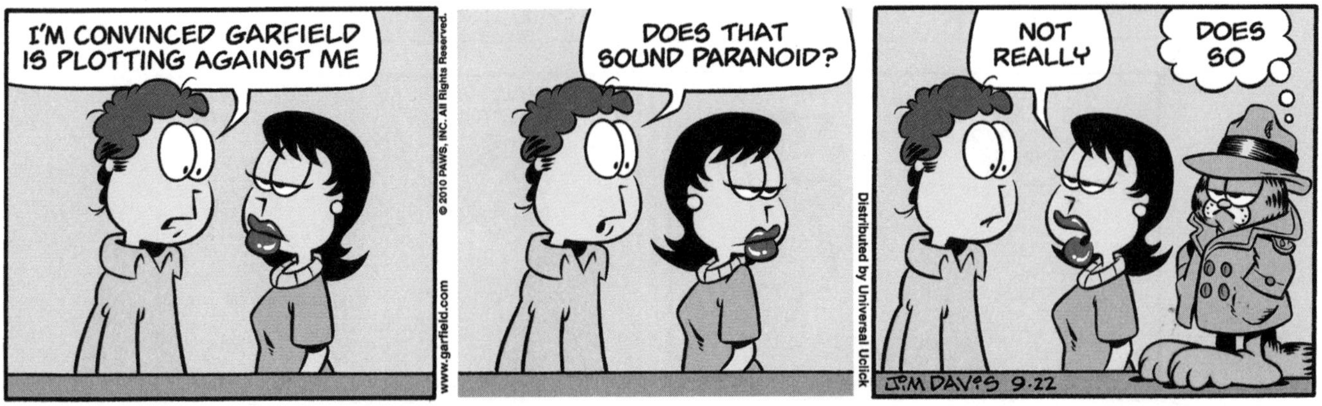
I'M CONVINCED GARFIELD IS PLOTTING AGAINST ME
© 2010 PAWS, INC. All Rights Reserved.
www.garfield.com
DOES THAT SOUND PARANOID?
Distributed by Universal Uclick
NOT REALLY
DOES SO
JIM DAVIS 9.22

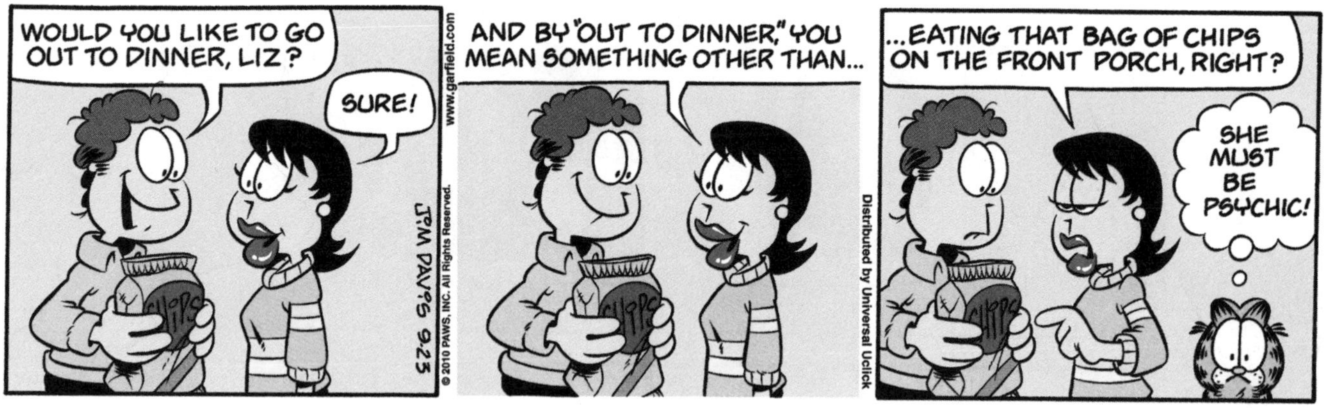
WOULD YOU LIKE TO GO OUT TO DINNER, LIZ?
SURE!
JIM DAVIS 9.23
© 2010 PAWS, INC. All Rights Reserved.
www.garfield.com
AND BY "OUT TO DINNER," YOU MEAN SOMETHING OTHER THAN...
Distributed by Universal Uclick
...EATING THAT BAG OF CHIPS ON THE FRONT PORCH, RIGHT?
SHE MUST BE PSYCHIC!

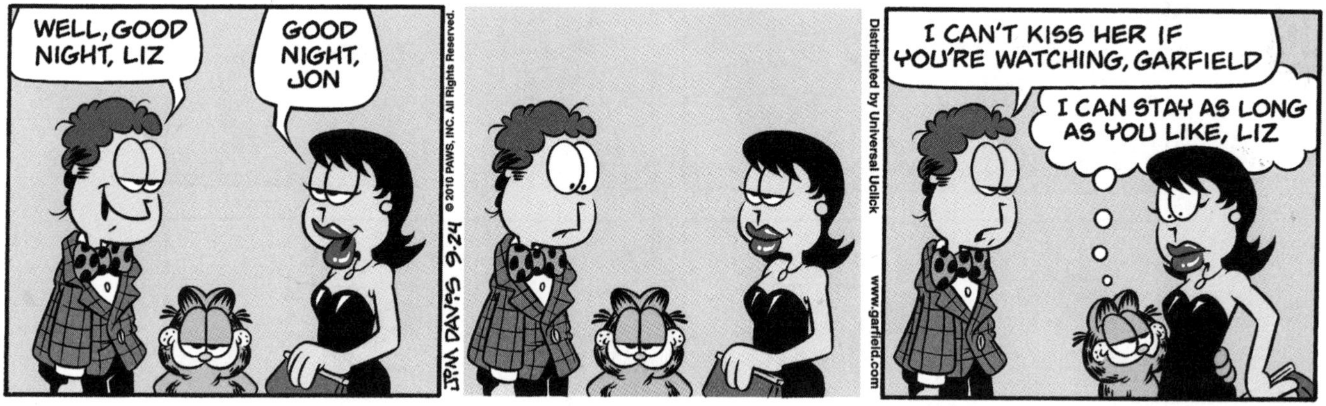
WELL, GOOD NIGHT, LIZ
GOOD NIGHT, JON
JIM DAVIS 9.24
© 2010 PAWS, INC. All Rights Reserved.
Distributed by Universal Uclick
www.garfield.com
I CAN'T KISS HER IF YOU'RE WATCHING, GARFIELD
I CAN STAY AS LONG AS YOU LIKE, LIZ

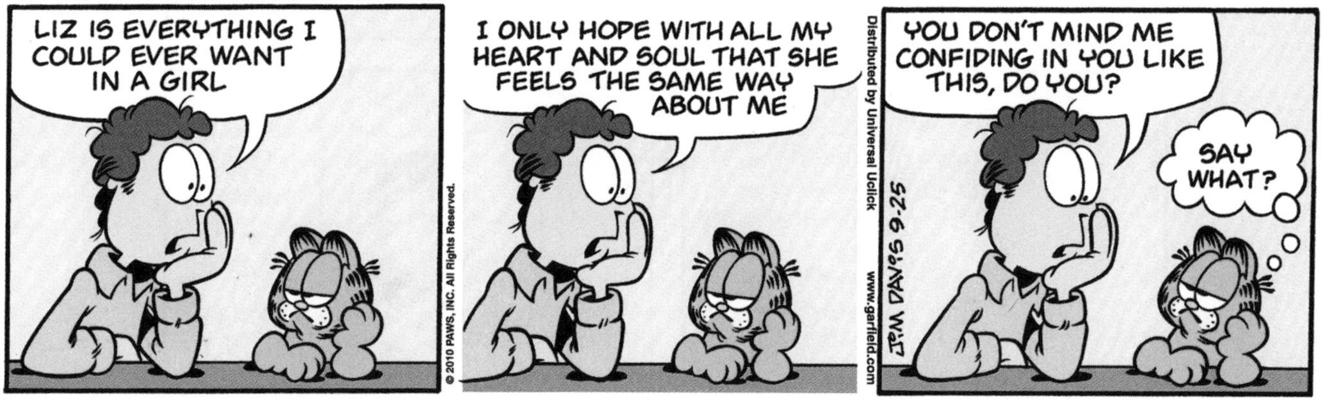
LIZ IS EVERYTHING I COULD EVER WANT IN A GIRL
© 2010 PAWS, INC. All Rights Reserved.
I ONLY HOPE WITH ALL MY HEART AND SOUL THAT SHE FEELS THE SAME WAY ABOUT ME
Distributed by Universal Uclick
JIM DAVIS 9.25
www.garfield.com
YOU DON'T MIND ME CONFIDING IN YOU LIKE THIS, DO YOU?
SAY WHAT?

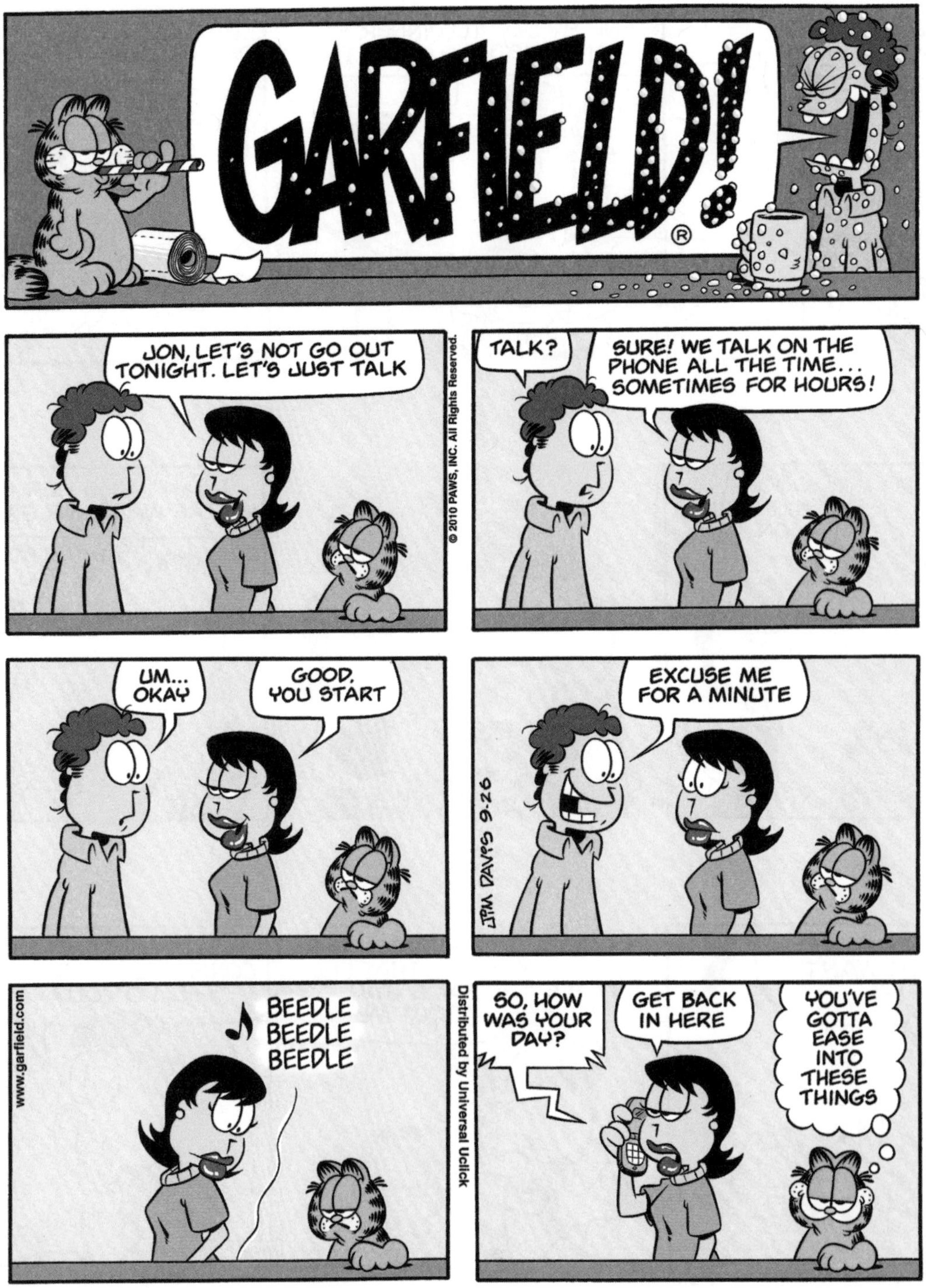
GARFIELD!
JON, LET'S NOT GO OUT TONIGHT. LET'S JUST TALK
© 2010 PAWS, INC. All Rights Reserved.
TALK?
SURE! WE TALK ON THE PHONE ALL THE TIME... SOMETIMES FOR HOURS!
UM... OKAY
GOOD. YOU START
EXCUSE ME FOR A MINUTE
JIM DAVIS 9-26
www.garfield.com
BEEDLE BEEDLE BEEDLE
Distributed by Universal Uclick
SO, HOW WAS YOUR DAY?
GET BACK IN HERE
YOU'VE GOTTA EASE INTO THESE THINGS

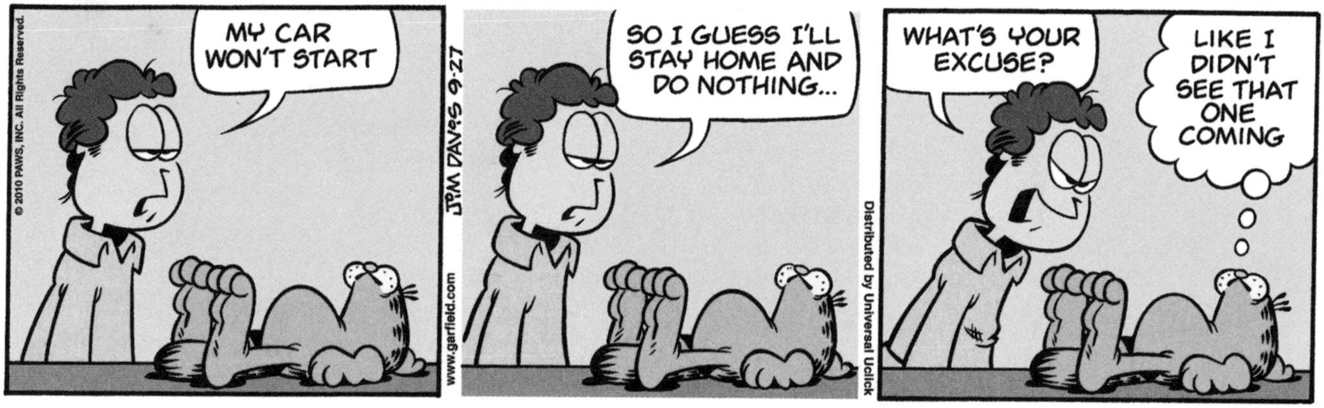
MY CAR WON'T START
SO I GUESS I'LL STAY HOME AND DO NOTHING...
WHAT'S YOUR EXCUSE?
LIKE I DIDN'T SEE THAT ONE COMING
JIM DAVIS 9-27
© 2010 PAWS, INC. All Rights Reserved.
www.garfield.com
Distributed by Universal Uclick

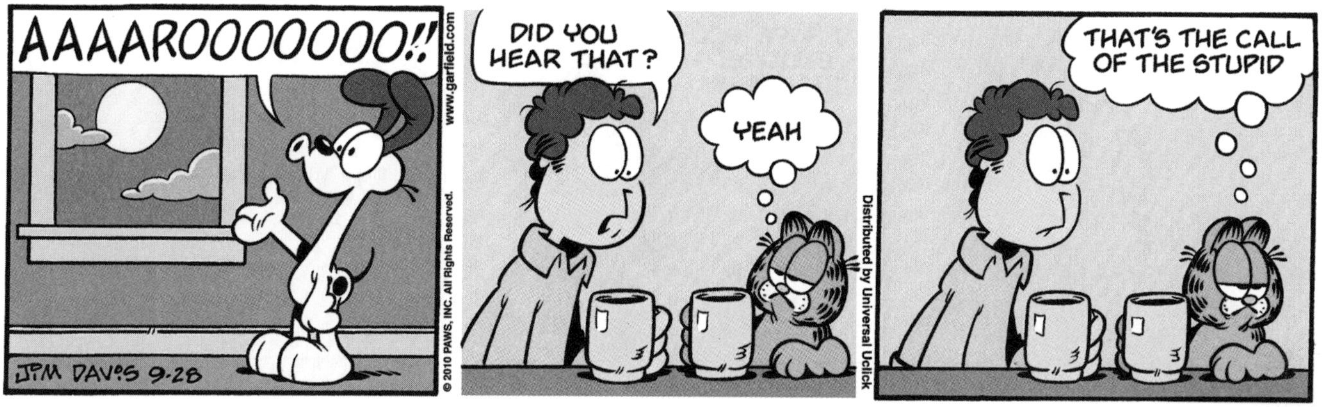
AAAAROOOOOOOO!!
JIM DAVIS 9-28
DID YOU HEAR THAT?
YEAH
THAT'S THE CALL OF THE STUPID
www.garfield.com
© 2010 PAWS, INC. All Rights Reserved.
Distributed by Universal Uclick

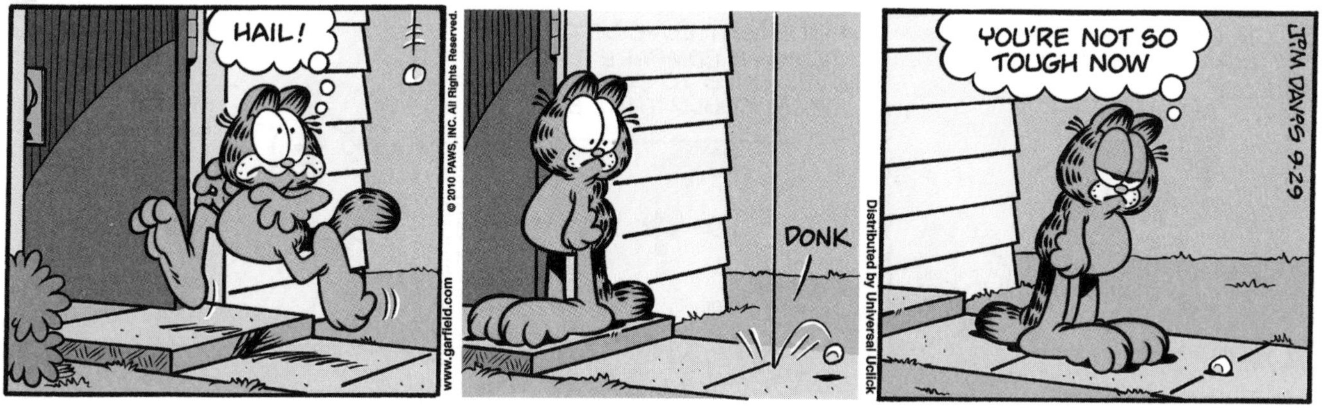
HAIL!
DONK
YOU'RE NOT SO TOUGH NOW
JIM DAVIS 9-29
© 2010 PAWS, INC. All Rights Reserved.
www.garfield.com
Distributed by Universal Uclick

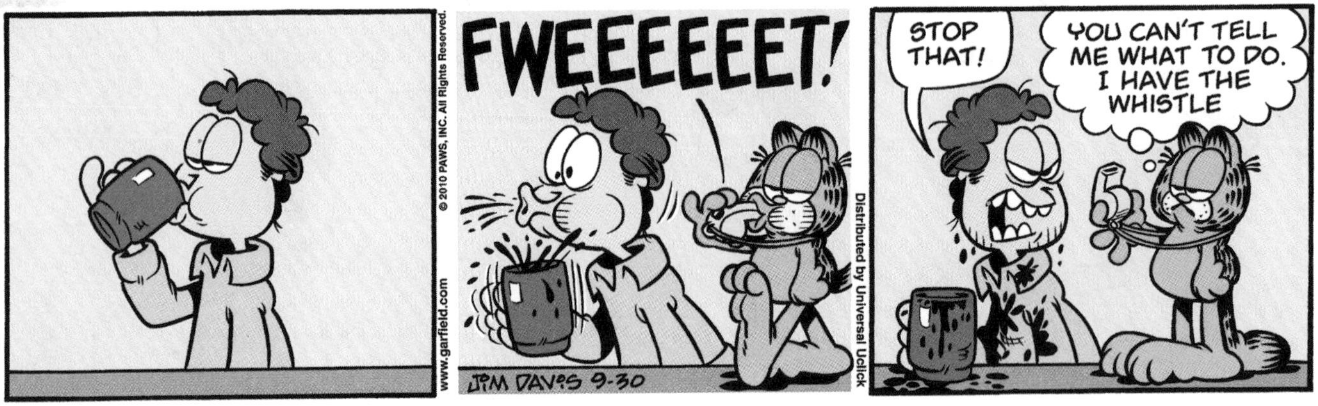
FWEEEEEET!
STOP THAT!
YOU CAN'T TELL ME WHAT TO DO. I HAVE THE WHISTLE
JIM DAVIS 9-30

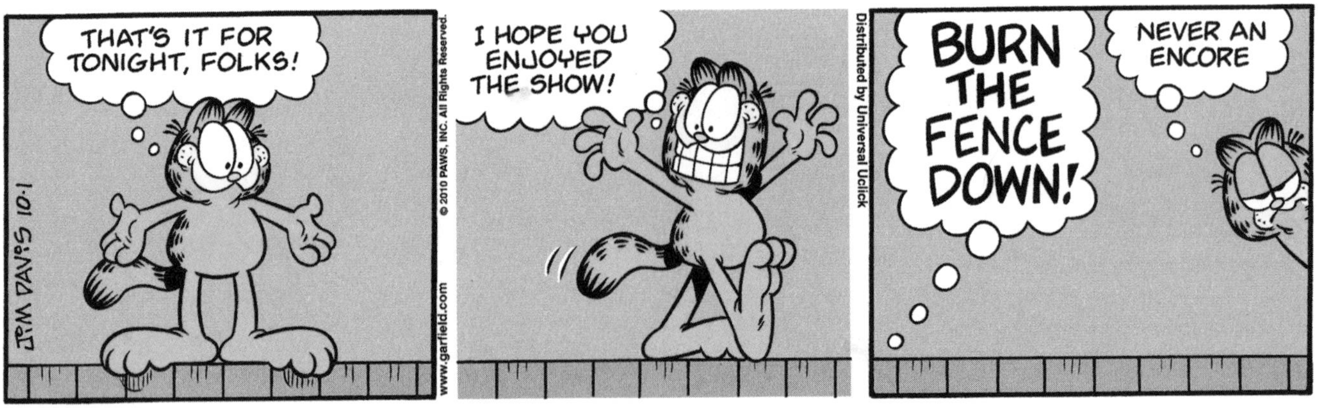
THAT'S IT FOR TONIGHT, FOLKS!
JIM DAVIS 10-1
I HOPE YOU ENJOYED THE SHOW!
BURN THE FENCE DOWN!
NEVER AN ENCORE

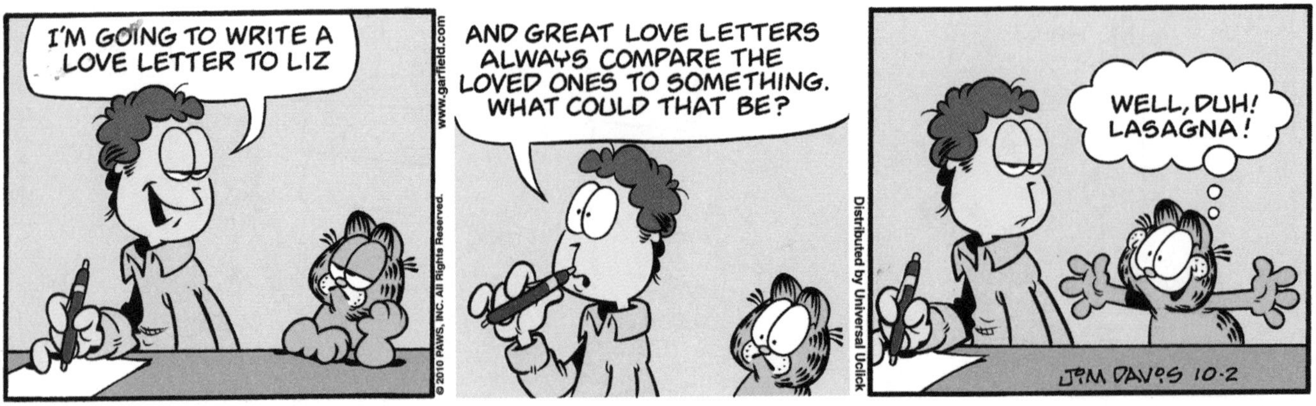
I'M GOING TO WRITE A LOVE LETTER TO LIZ
AND GREAT LOVE LETTERS ALWAYS COMPARE THE LOVED ONES TO SOMETHING. WHAT COULD THAT BE?
WELL, DUH! LASAGNA!
JIM DAVIS 10-2

FOOF FOOF FOOF FOOF

FOOF FOOF FOOF FOOF
FOOF FOOF FOOF FOOF
FOOF F__OOF FOOF

HUUUHHH

JIM DAVIS 10-3

FOOOOOF

LIZ! I FINALLY GOT THE COALS STARTED!

PIZZA'S HERE

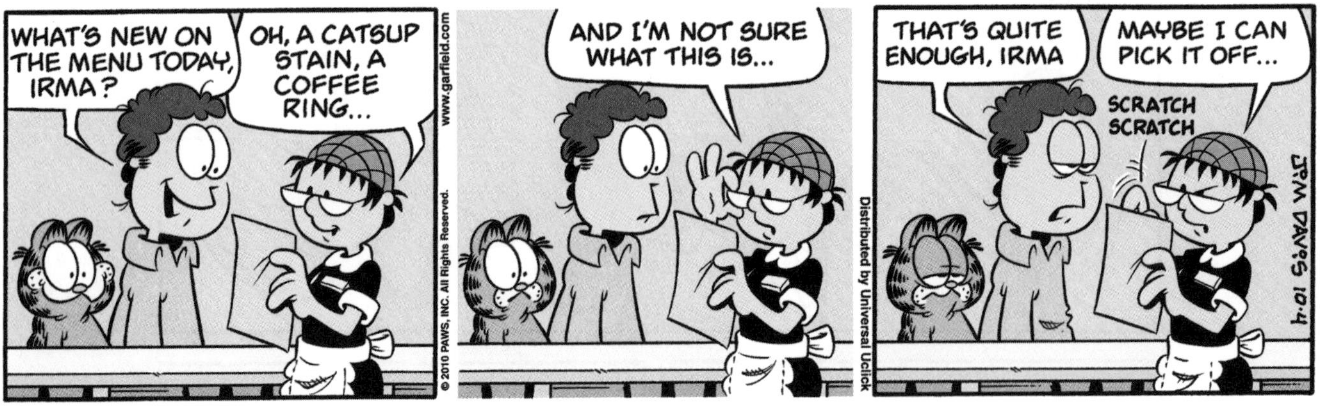
WHAT'S NEW ON THE MENU TODAY, IRMA?
OH, A CATSUP STAIN, A COFFEE RING...
AND I'M NOT SURE WHAT THIS IS...
THAT'S QUITE ENOUGH, IRMA
MAYBE I CAN PICK IT OFF...
SCRATCH SCRATCH
JIM DAVIS 10-4
© 2010 PAWS, INC. All Rights Reserved. www.garfield.com
Distributed by Universal Uclick

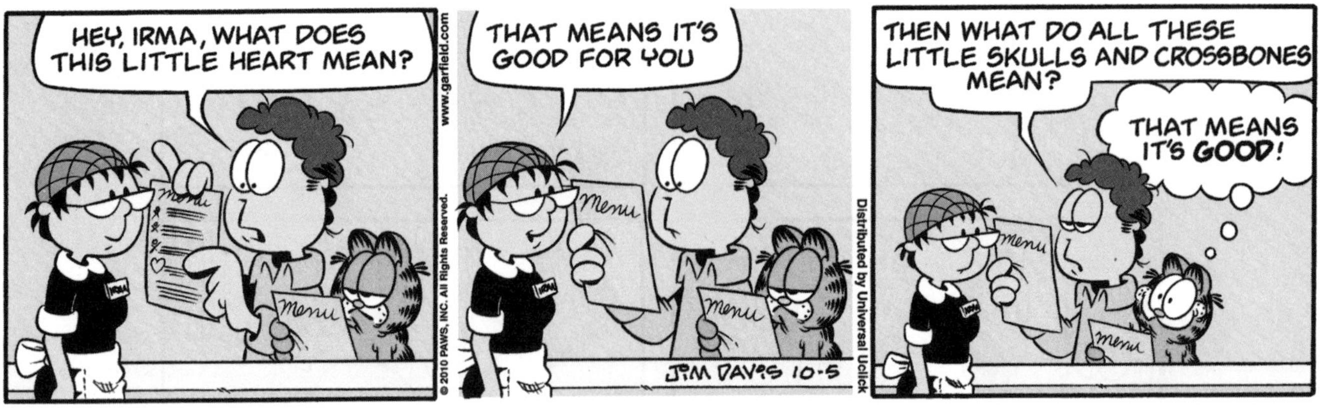
HEY, IRMA, WHAT DOES THIS LITTLE HEART MEAN?
THAT MEANS IT'S GOOD FOR YOU
THEN WHAT DO ALL THESE LITTLE SKULLS AND CROSSBONES MEAN?
THAT MEANS IT'S **GOOD**!
JIM DAVIS 10-5
© 2010 PAWS, INC. All Rights Reserved. www.garfield.com
Distributed by Universal Uclick

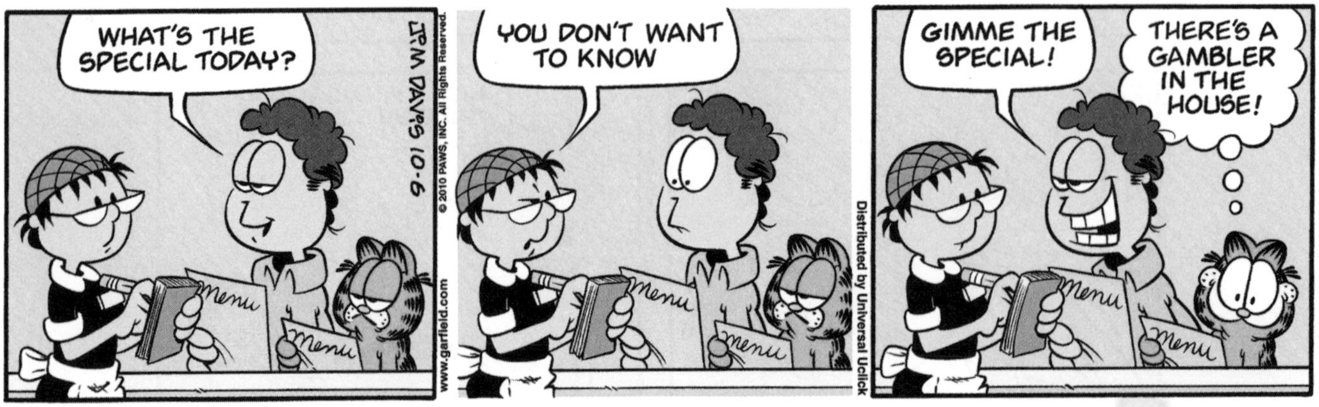
WHAT'S THE SPECIAL TODAY?
YOU DON'T WANT TO KNOW
GIMME THE SPECIAL!
THERE'S A GAMBLER IN THE HOUSE!
JIM DAVIS 10-6
© 2010 PAWS, INC. All Rights Reserved. www.garfield.com
Distributed by Universal Uclick

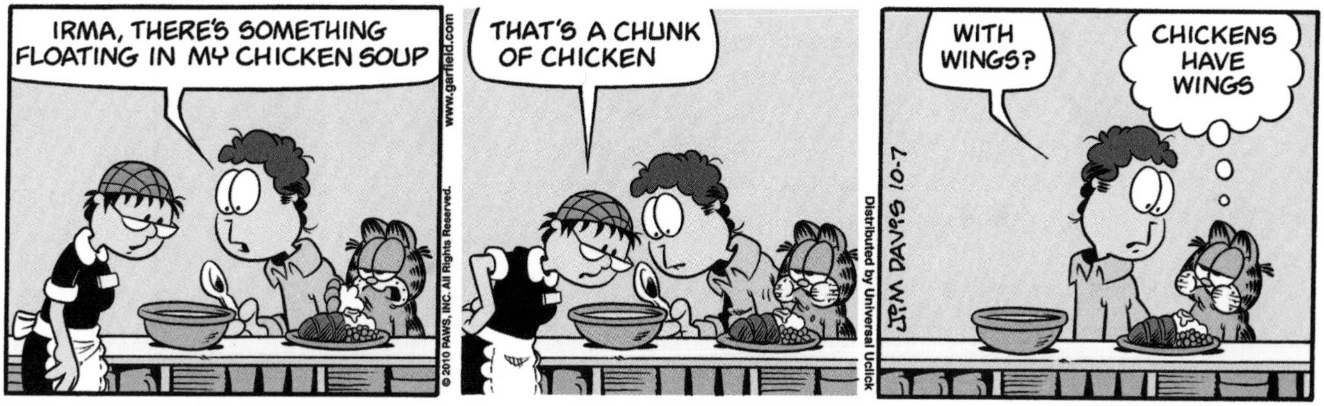
IRMA, THERE'S SOMETHING FLOATING IN MY CHICKEN SOUP
THAT'S A CHUNK OF CHICKEN
WITH WINGS?
CHICKENS HAVE WINGS
JIM DAVIS 10-7
© 2010 PAWS, INC. All Rights Reserved.
www.garfield.com
Distributed by Universal Uclick

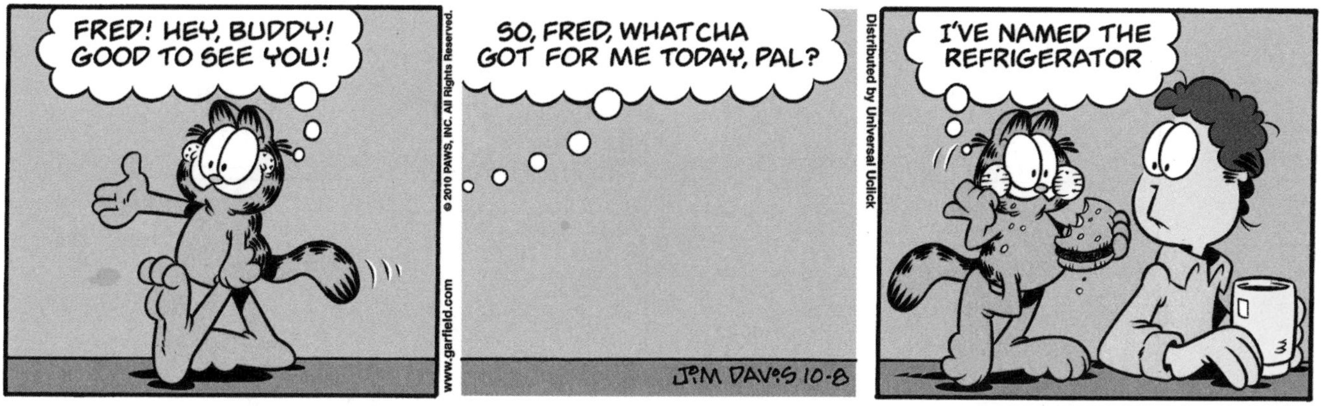
FRED! HEY, BUDDY! GOOD TO SEE YOU!
SO, FRED, WHATCHA GOT FOR ME TODAY, PAL?
I'VE NAMED THE REFRIGERATOR
JIM DAVIS 10-8
© 2010 PAWS, INC. All Rights Reserved.
www.garfield.com
Distributed by Universal Uclick

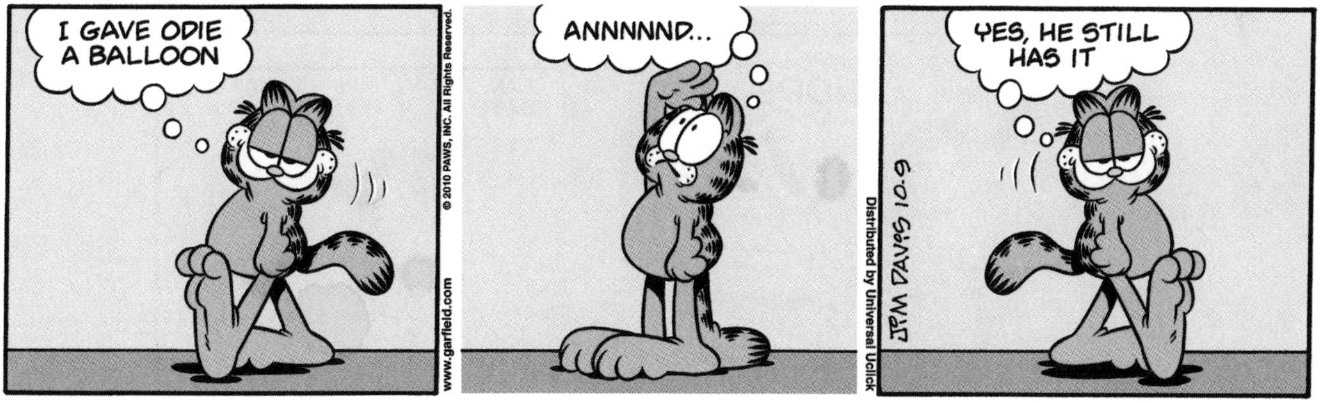
I GAVE ODIE A BALLOON
ANNNNND...
YES, HE STILL HAS IT
JIM DAVIS 10-9
© 2010 PAWS, INC. All Rights Reserved.
www.garfield.com
Distributed by Universal Uclick

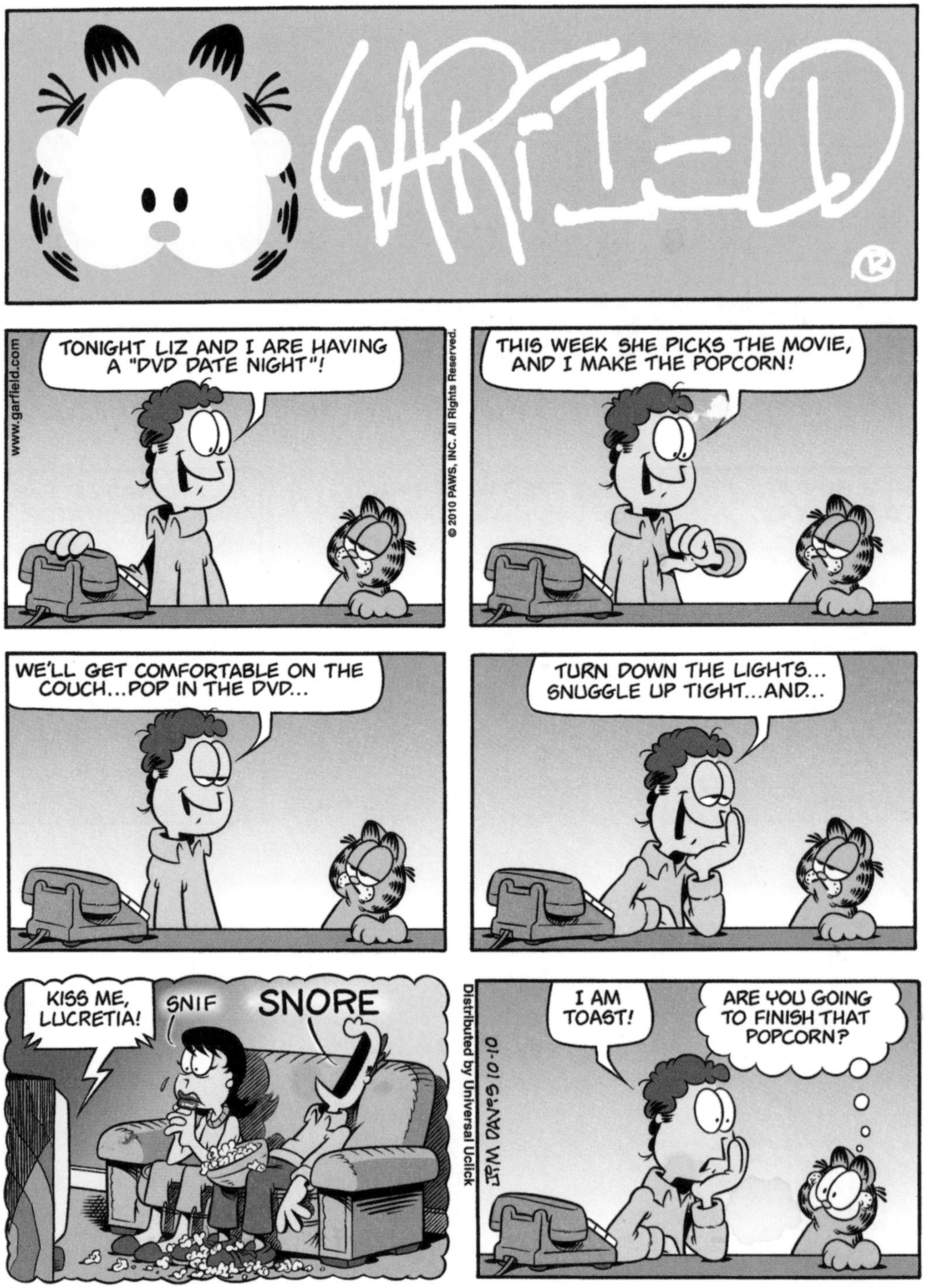
GARFIELD
www.garfield.com
TONIGHT LIZ AND I ARE HAVING A "DVD DATE NIGHT"!
© 2010 PAWS, INC. All Rights Reserved.
THIS WEEK SHE PICKS THE MOVIE, AND I MAKE THE POPCORN!
WE'LL GET COMFORTABLE ON THE COUCH...POP IN THE DVD...
TURN DOWN THE LIGHTS... SNUGGLE UP TIGHT...AND...
KISS ME, LUCRETIA!
SNIF
SNORE
Distributed by Universal Uclick
I AM TOAST!
ARE YOU GOING TO FINISH THAT POPCORN?

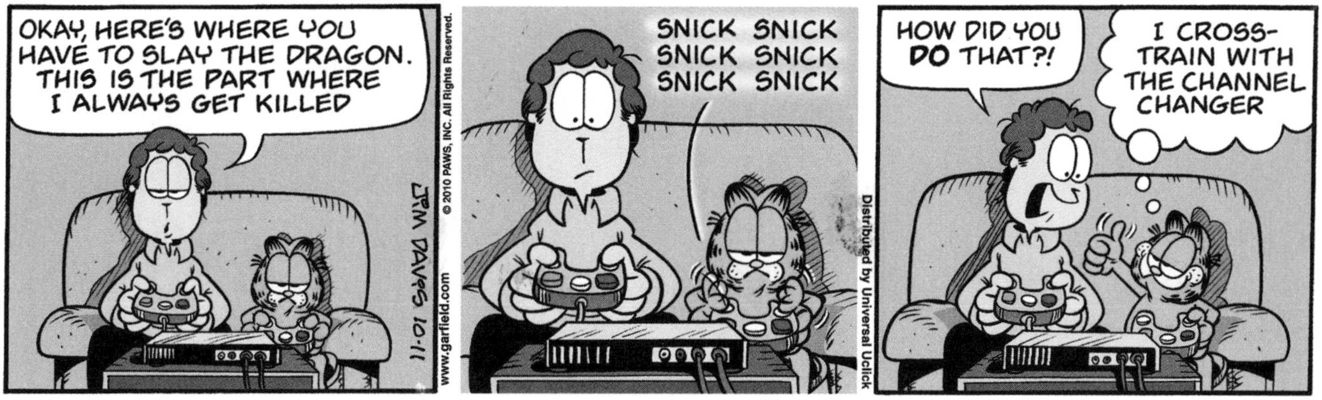
OKAY, HERE'S WHERE YOU HAVE TO SLAY THE DRAGON. THIS IS THE PART WHERE I ALWAYS GET KILLED
JIM DAVIS 10-11
© 2010 PAWS, INC. All Rights Reserved.
www.garfield.com
SNICK SNICK SNICK SNICK SNICK SNICK
Distributed by Universal Uclick
HOW DID YOU **DO** THAT?!
I CROSS-TRAIN WITH THE CHANNEL CHANGER

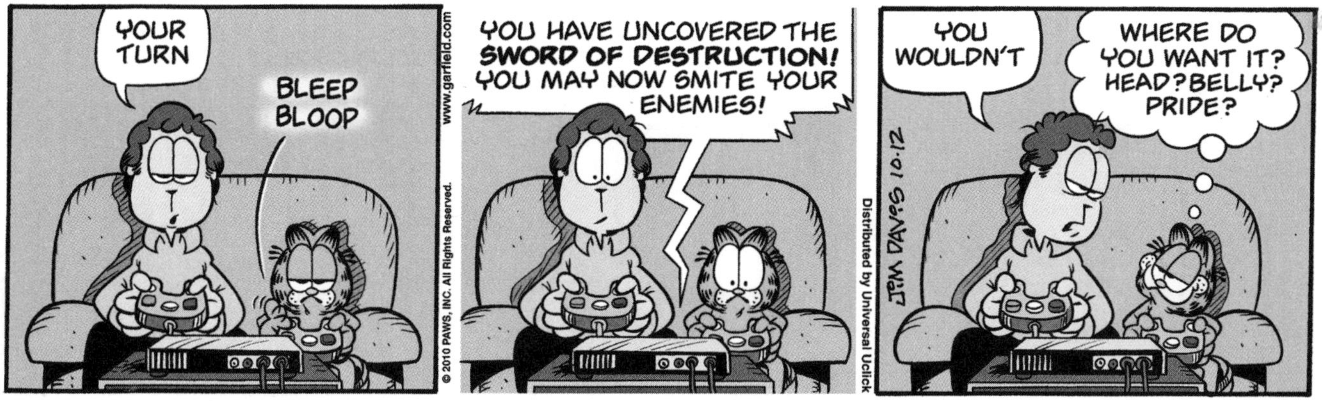
YOUR TURN
BLEEP BLOOP
www.garfield.com
© 2010 PAWS, INC. All Rights Reserved.
YOU HAVE UNCOVERED THE **SWORD OF DESTRUCTION!** YOU MAY NOW SMITE YOUR ENEMIES!
Distributed by Universal Uclick
YOU WOULDN'T
WHERE DO YOU WANT IT? HEAD? BELLY? PRIDE?
JIM DAVIS 10-12

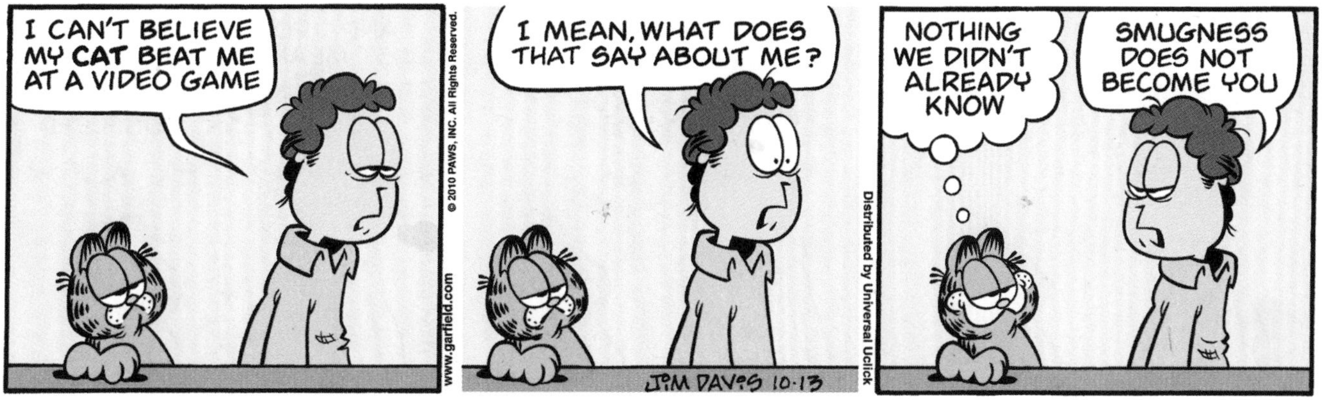
I CAN'T BELIEVE MY **CAT** BEAT ME AT A VIDEO GAME
© 2010 PAWS, INC. All Rights Reserved.
www.garfield.com
I MEAN, WHAT DOES THAT SAY ABOUT ME?
JIM DAVIS 10-13
Distributed by Universal Uclick
NOTHING WE DIDN'T ALREADY KNOW
SMUGNESS DOES NOT BECOME YOU

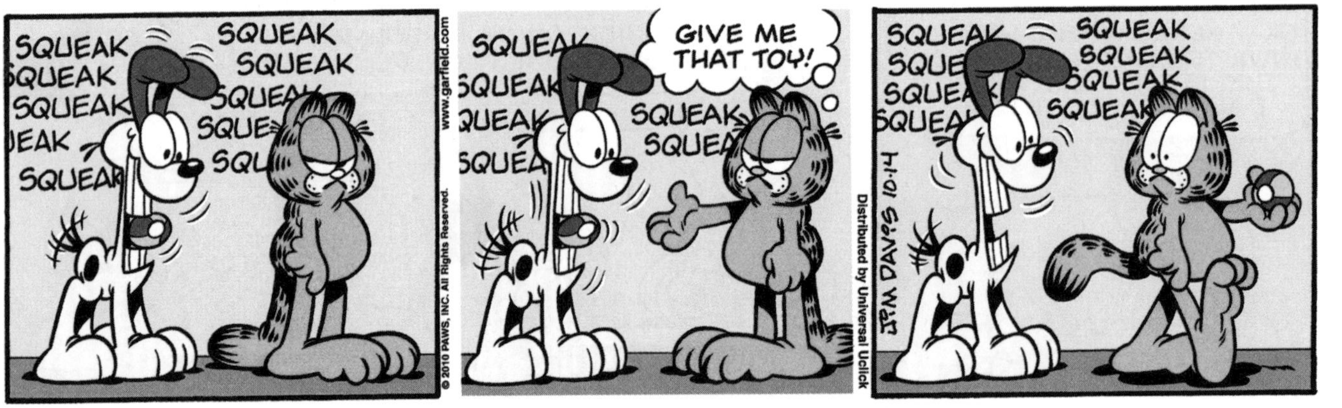
SQUEAK
SQUEAK
SQUEAK
SQUEAK
SQUEAK
SQUEAK
SQUEAK
GIVE ME THAT TOY!
SQUEAK
SQUEAK
SQUEAK
SQUEAK
SQUEAK
SQUEAK
© 2010 PAWS, INC. All Rights Reserved. www.garfield.com
Distributed by Universal Uclick
JPM DAVIS 10-14

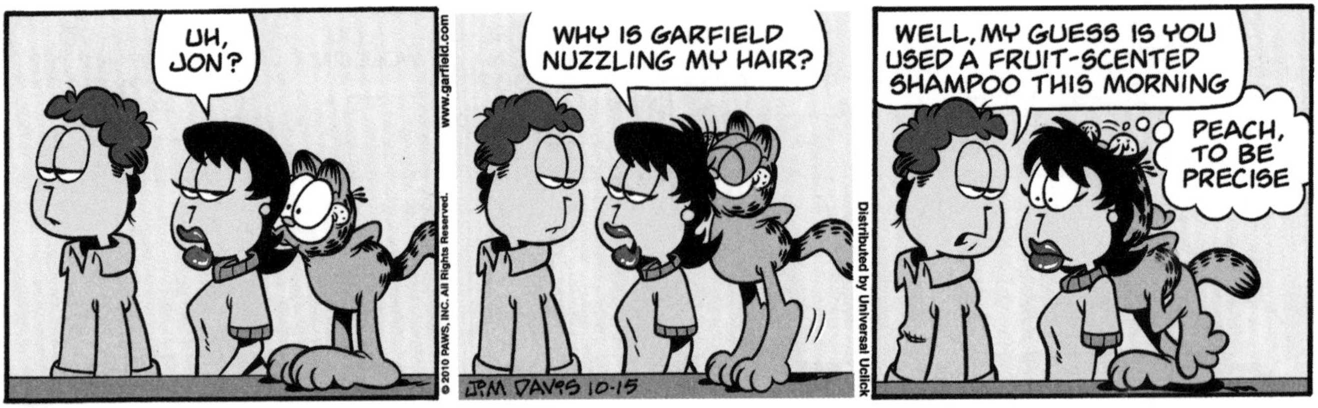
UH, JON?
WHY IS GARFIELD NUZZLING MY HAIR?
WELL, MY GUESS IS YOU USED A FRUIT-SCENTED SHAMPOO THIS MORNING
PEACH, TO BE PRECISE
© 2010 PAWS, INC. All Rights Reserved. www.garfield.com
Distributed by Universal Uclick
JPM DAVIS 10-15

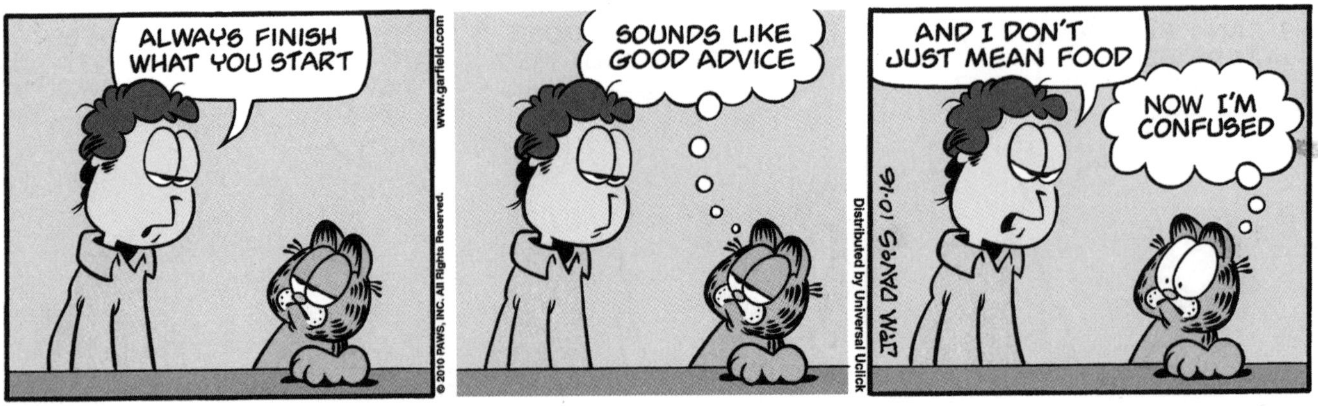
ALWAYS FINISH WHAT YOU START
SOUNDS LIKE GOOD ADVICE
AND I DON'T JUST MEAN FOOD
NOW I'M CONFUSED
© 2010 PAWS, INC. All Rights Reserved. www.garfield.com
Distributed by Universal Uclick
JPM DAVIS 10-16

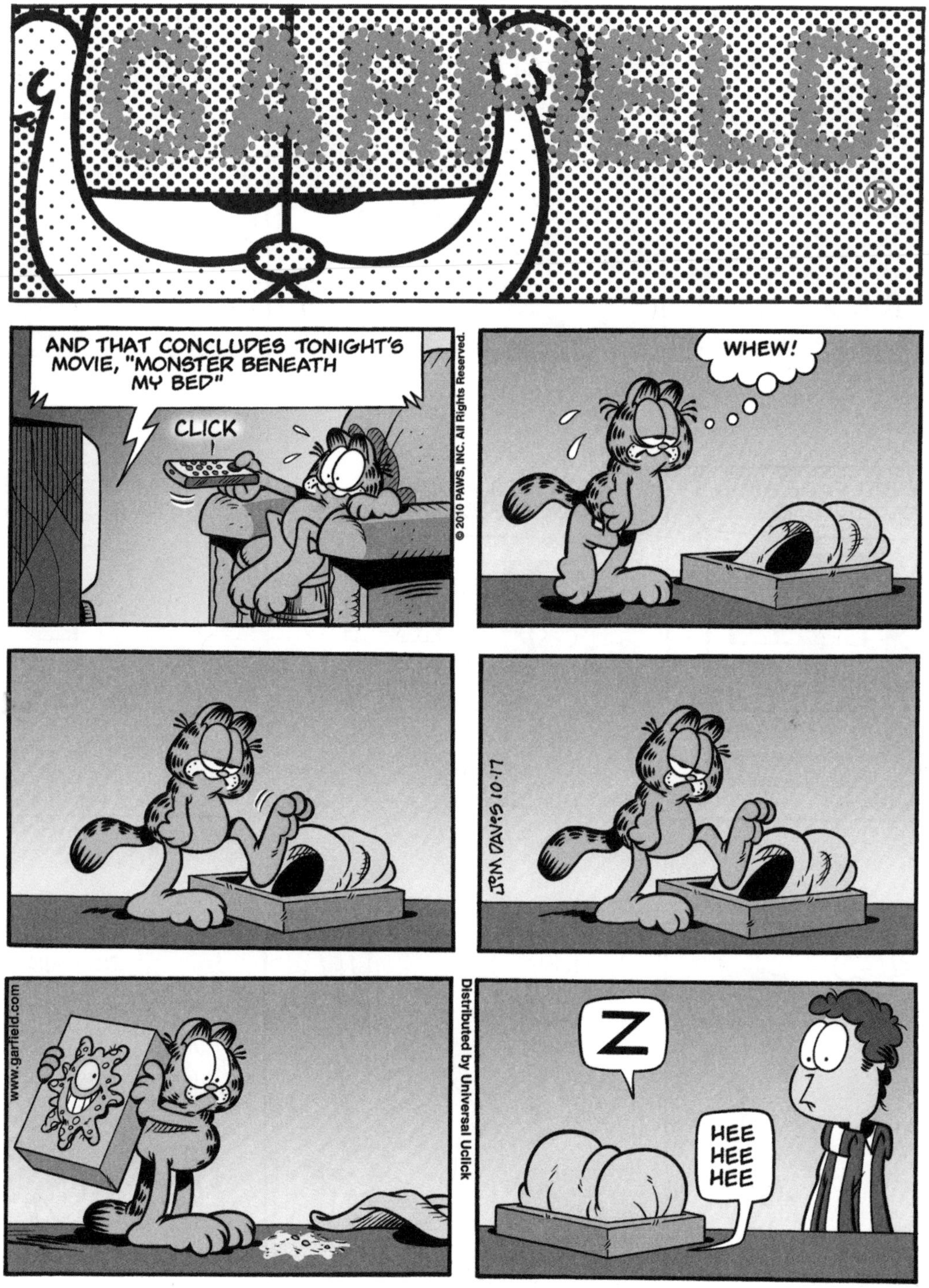
GARFIELD
AND THAT CONCLUDES TONIGHT'S MOVIE, "MONSTER BENEATH MY BED"
CLICK
© 2010 PAWS, INC. All Rights Reserved.
WHEW!
JPM DAVPS 10-17
www.garfield.com
Distributed by Universal Uclick
Z
HEE HEE HEE

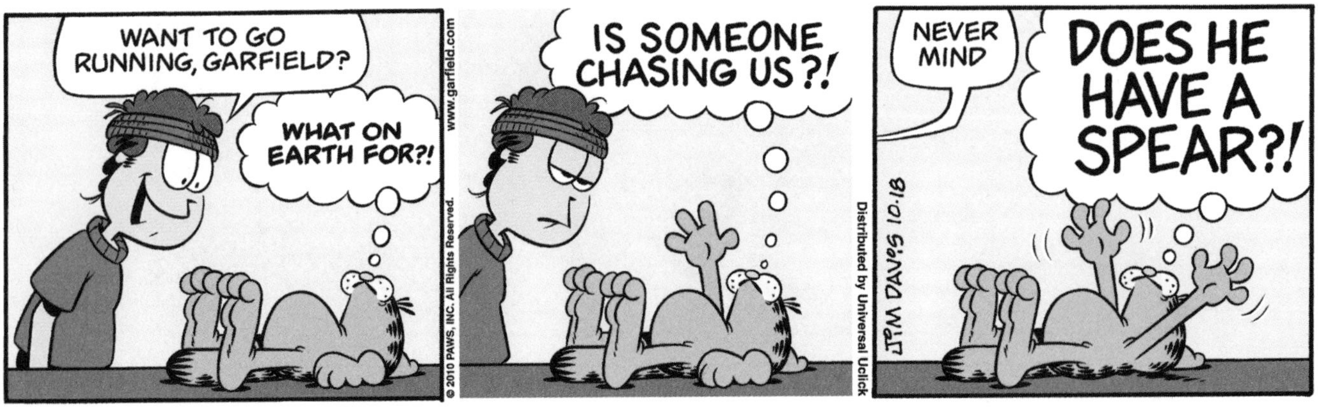
WANT TO GO RUNNING, GARFIELD?
WHAT ON EARTH FOR?!
© 2010 PAWS, INC. All Rights Reserved.
www.garfield.com
IS SOMEONE CHASING US?!
Distributed by Universal Uclick
NEVER MIND
DOES HE HAVE A SPEAR?!
JIM DAVIS 10-18

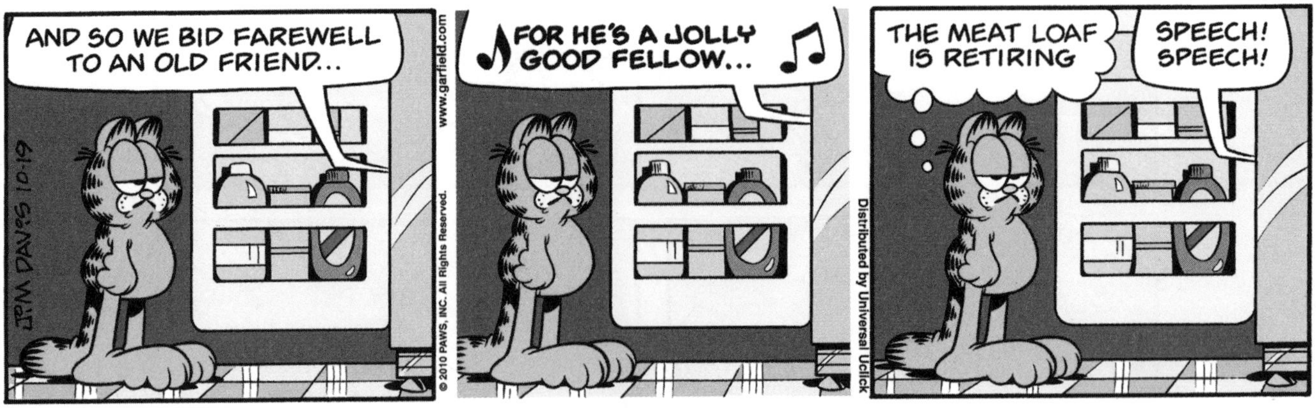
AND SO WE BID FAREWELL TO AN OLD FRIEND...
JIM DAVIS 10-19
www.garfield.com
© 2010 PAWS, INC. All Rights Reserved.
FOR HE'S A JOLLY GOOD FELLOW...
Distributed by Universal Uclick
THE MEAT LOAF IS RETIRING
SPEECH! SPEECH!

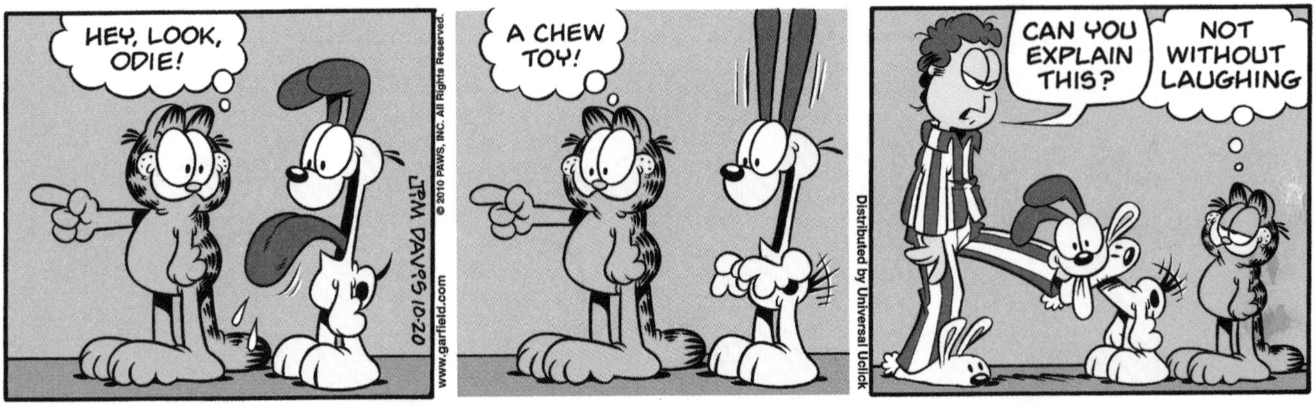
HEY, LOOK, ODIE!
© 2010 PAWS, INC. All Rights Reserved.
JIM DAVIS 10-20
www.garfield.com
A CHEW TOY!
Distributed by Universal Uclick
CAN YOU EXPLAIN THIS?
NOT WITHOUT LAUGHING

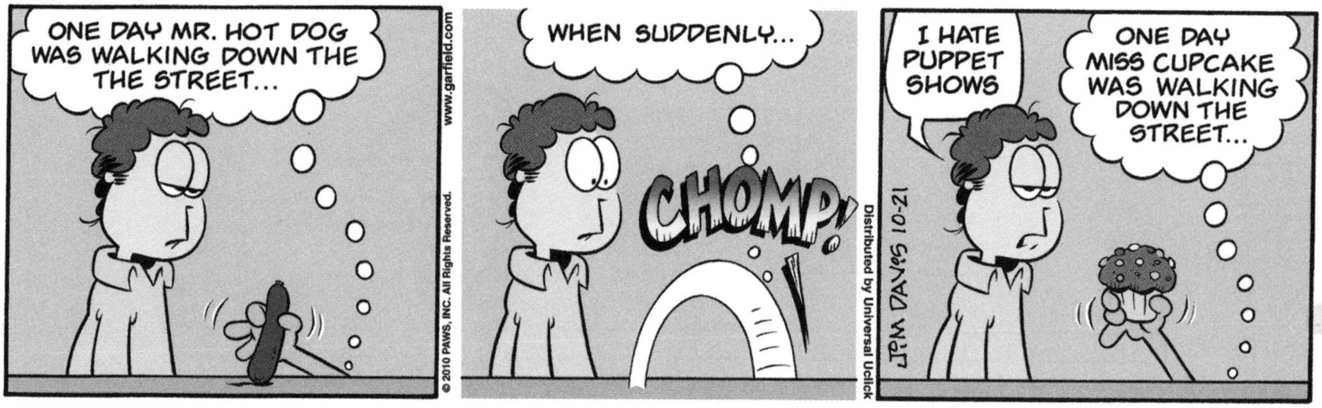
ONE DAY MR. HOT DOG WAS WALKING DOWN THE THE STREET...
WHEN SUDDENLY...
CHOMP!
I HATE PUPPET SHOWS
ONE DAY MISS CUPCAKE WAS WALKING DOWN THE STREET...
JIM DAVIS 10-21
www.garfield.com
© 2010 PAWS, INC. All Rights Reserved.
Distributed by Universal Uclick

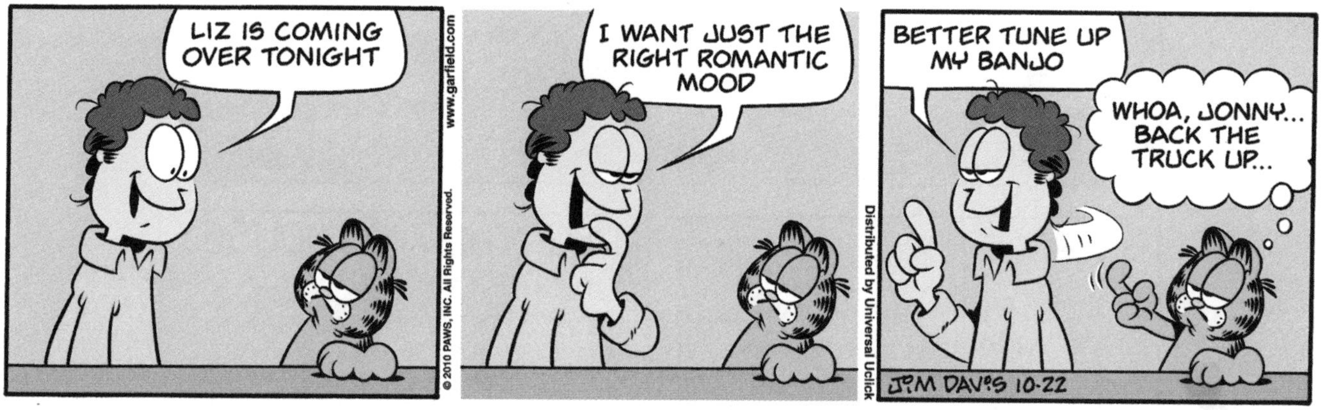
LIZ IS COMING OVER TONIGHT
I WANT JUST THE RIGHT ROMANTIC MOOD
BETTER TUNE UP MY BANJO
WHOA, JONNY... BACK THE TRUCK UP...
JIM DAVIS 10-22
www.garfield.com
© 2010 PAWS, INC. All Rights Reserved.
Distributed by Universal Uclick

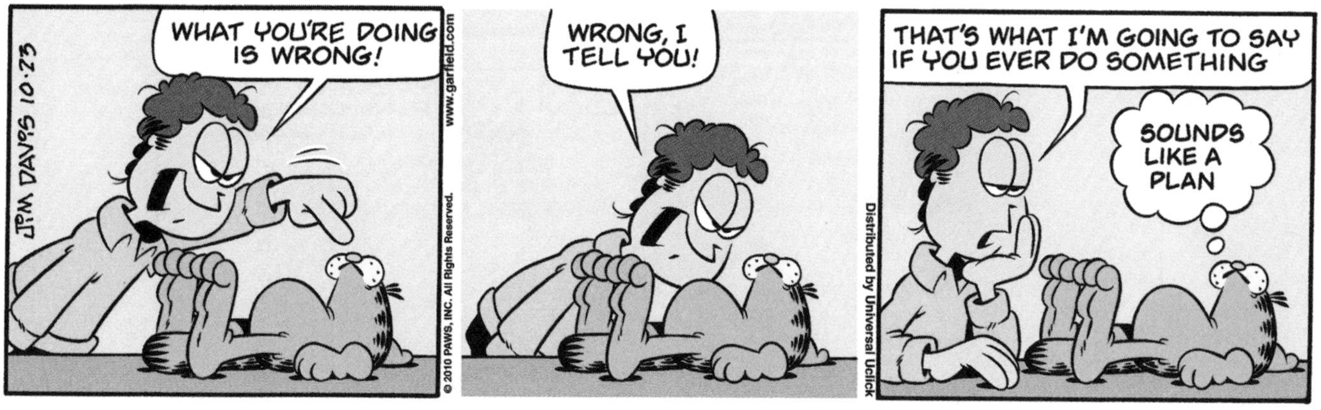
WHAT YOU'RE DOING IS WRONG!
WRONG, I TELL YOU!
THAT'S WHAT I'M GOING TO SAY IF YOU EVER DO SOMETHING
SOUNDS LIKE A PLAN
JIM DAVIS 10-23
www.garfield.com
© 2010 PAWS, INC. All Rights Reserved.
Distributed by Universal Uclick

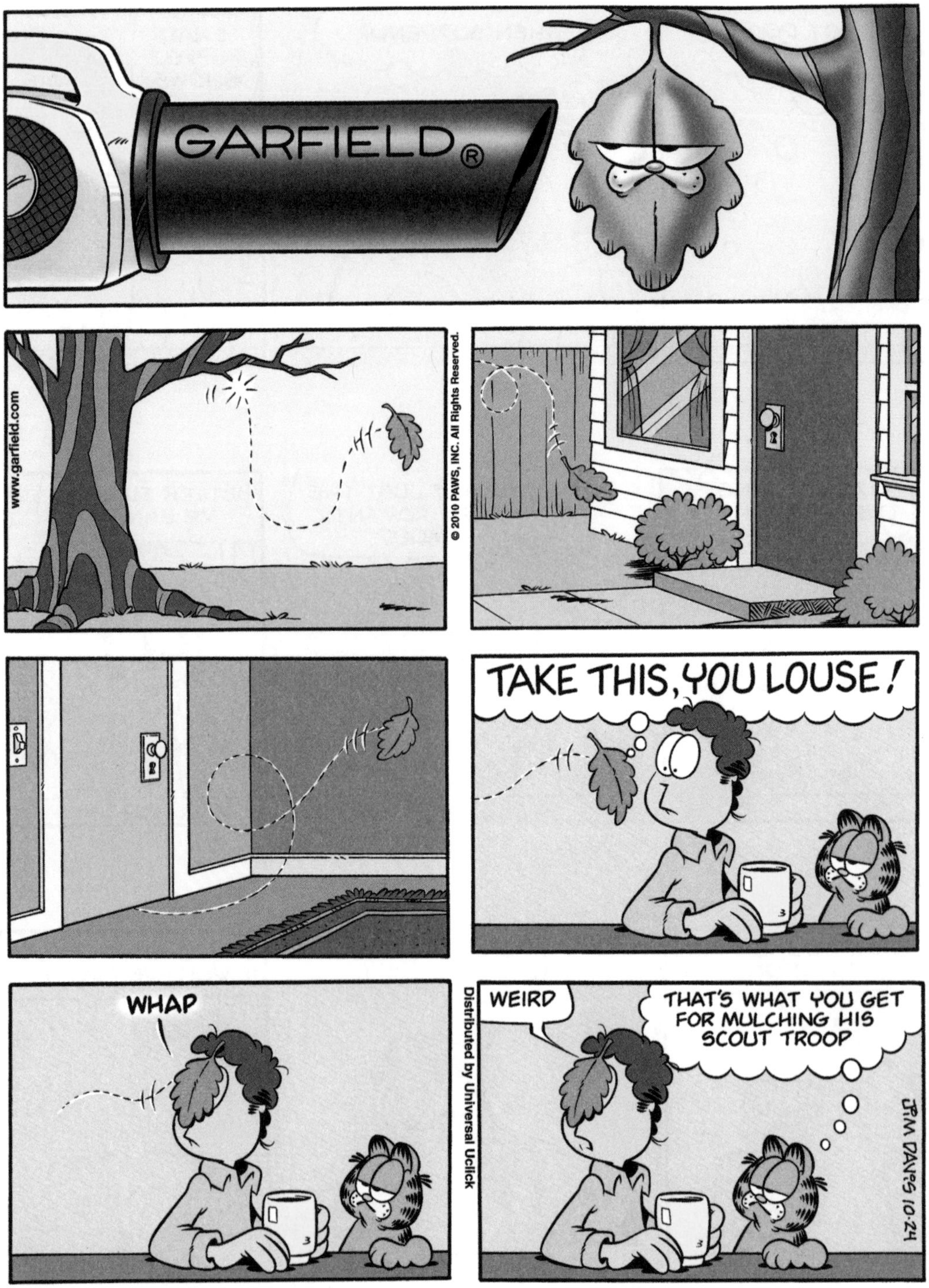
GARFIELD®
www.garfield.com
© 2010 PAWS, INC. All Rights Reserved.
TAKE THIS, YOU LOUSE!
WHAP
Distributed by Universal Uclick
WEIRD
THAT'S WHAT YOU GET FOR MULCHING HIS SCOUT TROOP
JIM DAVIS 10-24

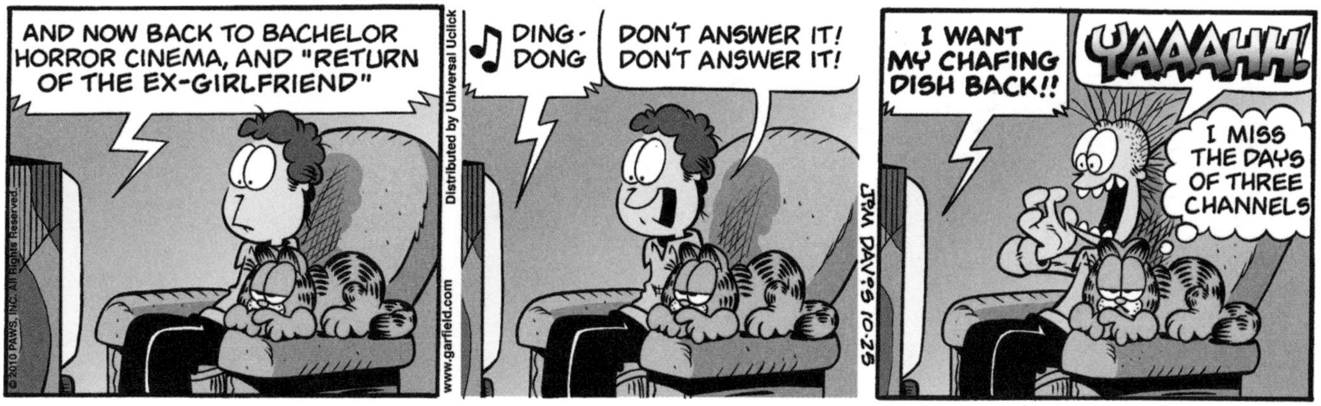
AND NOW BACK TO BACHELOR HORROR CINEMA, AND "RETURN OF THE EX-GIRLFRIEND"
DING-DONG
DON'T ANSWER IT! DON'T ANSWER IT!
I WANT MY CHAFING DISH BACK!!
YAAAHH!
I MISS THE DAYS OF THREE CHANNELS
JPM DAVIS 10-25
© 2010 PAWS, INC. All Rights Reserved.
Distributed by Universal Uclick
www.garfield.com

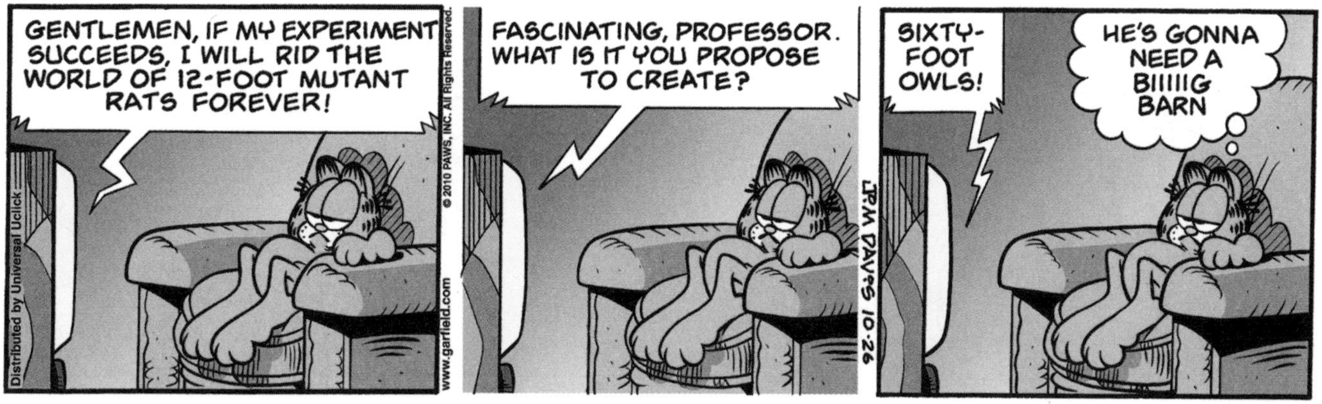
GENTLEMEN, IF MY EXPERIMENT SUCCEEDS, I WILL RID THE WORLD OF 12-FOOT MUTANT RATS FOREVER!
FASCINATING, PROFESSOR. WHAT IS IT YOU PROPOSE TO CREATE?
SIXTY-FOOT OWLS!
HE'S GONNA NEED A BIIIIIG BARN
JPM DAVIS 10-26
Distributed by Universal Uclick
www.garfield.com
© 2010 PAWS, INC. All Rights Reserved.

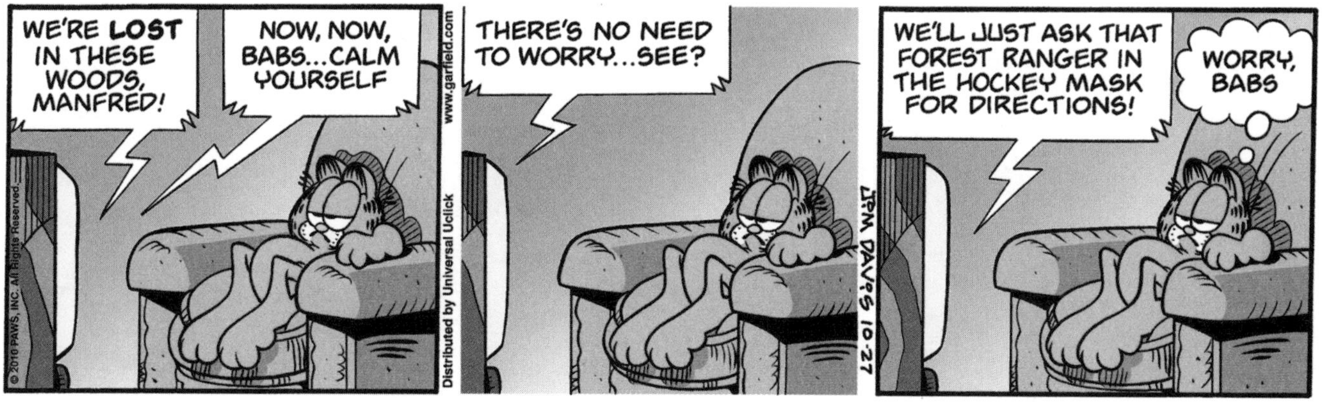
WE'RE **LOST** IN THESE WOODS, MANFRED!
NOW, NOW, BABS...CALM YOURSELF
THERE'S NO NEED TO WORRY...SEE?
WE'LL JUST ASK THAT FOREST RANGER IN THE HOCKEY MASK FOR DIRECTIONS!
WORRY, BABS
JPM DAVIS 10-27
© 2010 PAWS, INC. All Rights Reserved.
Distributed by Universal Uclick
www.garfield.com

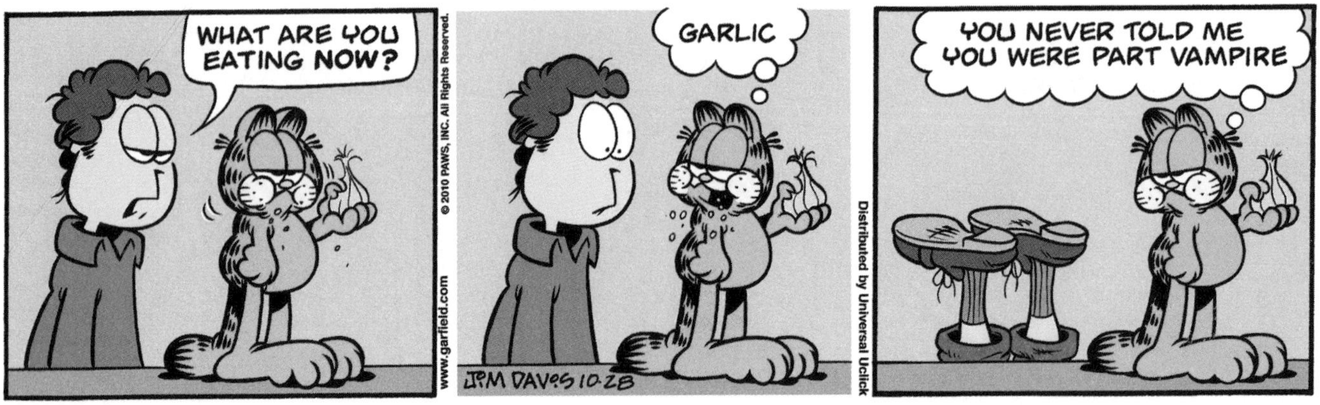
WHAT ARE YOU EATING NOW?
GARLIC
YOU NEVER TOLD ME YOU WERE PART VAMPIRE
© 2010 PAWS, INC. All Rights Reserved.
www.garfield.com
Distributed by Universal Uclick
JIM DAVIS 10-28

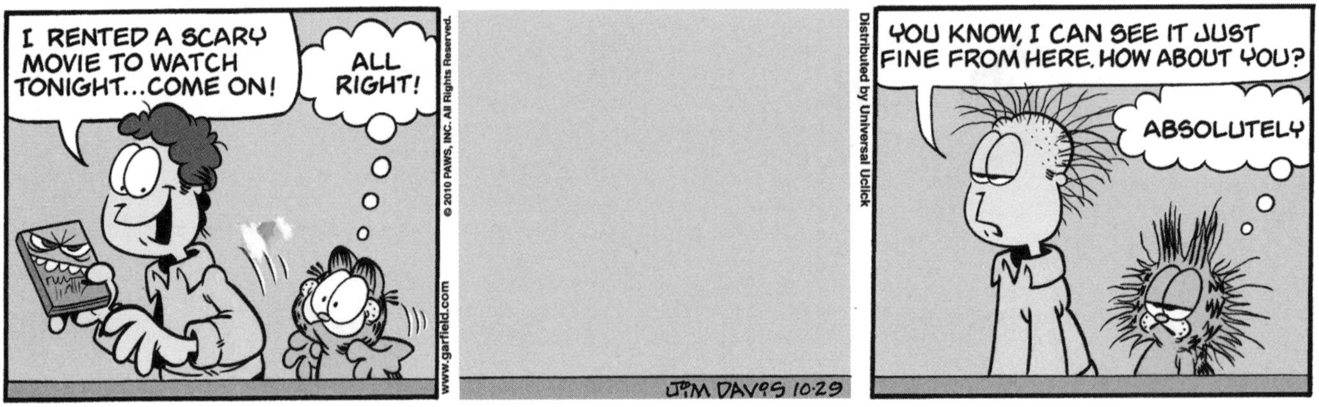
I RENTED A SCARY MOVIE TO WATCH TONIGHT...COME ON!
ALL RIGHT!
YOU KNOW, I CAN SEE IT JUST FINE FROM HERE. HOW ABOUT YOU?
ABSOLUTELY
© 2010 PAWS, INC. All Rights Reserved.
www.garfield.com
Distributed by Universal Uclick
JIM DAVIS 10-29

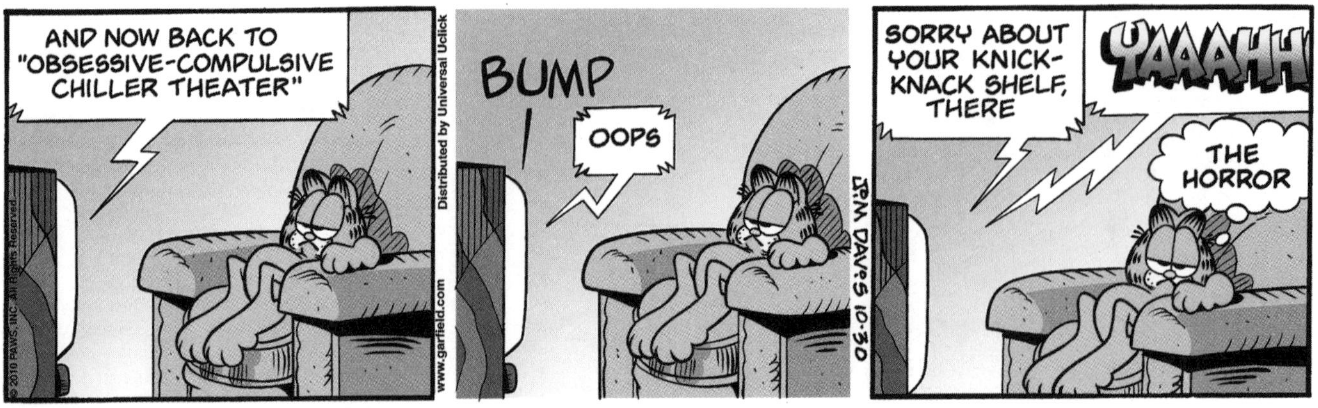
AND NOW BACK TO "OBSESSIVE-COMPULSIVE CHILLER THEATER"
BUMP
OOPS
SORRY ABOUT YOUR KNICK-KNACK SHELF, THERE
YAAAHH
THE HORROR
© 2010 PAWS, INC. All Rights Reserved.
www.garfield.com
Distributed by Universal Uclick
JIM DAVIS 10-30

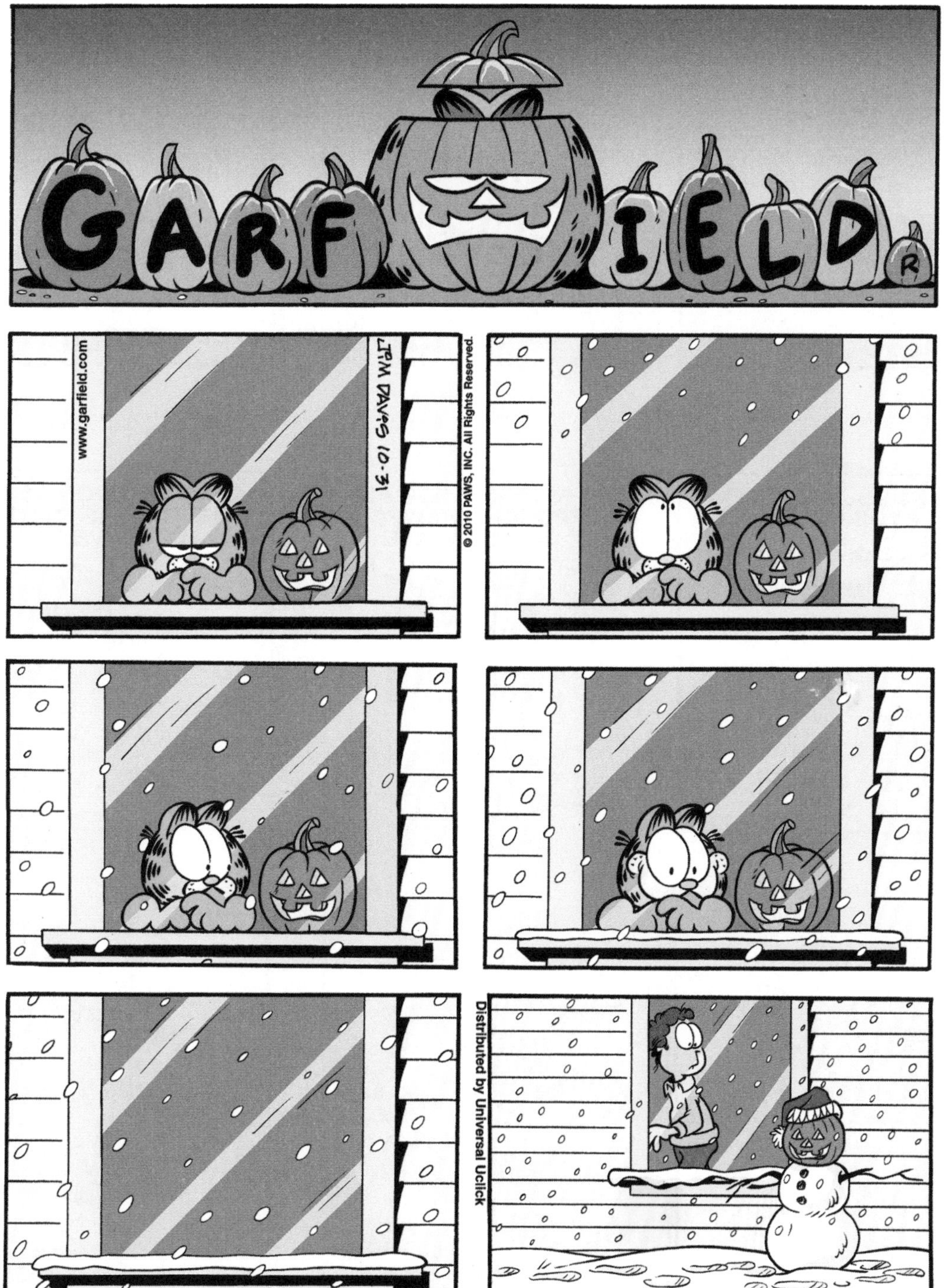
GARFIELD
www.garfield.com
JIM DAVIS 10-31
© 2010 PAWS, INC. All Rights Reserved.
Distributed by Universal Uclick

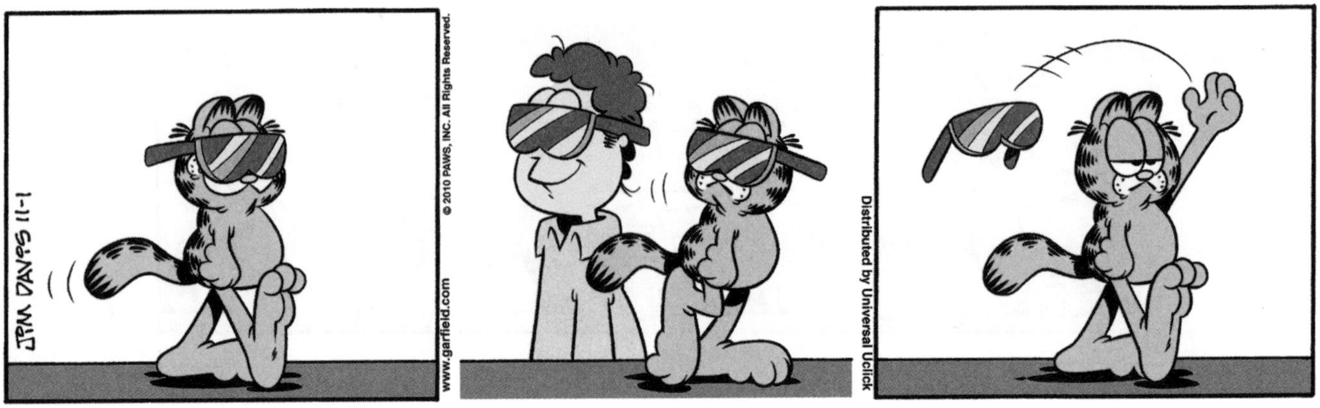
JIM DAVIS 11-1
© 2010 PAWS, INC. All Rights Reserved.
www.garfield.com
Distributed by Universal Uclick

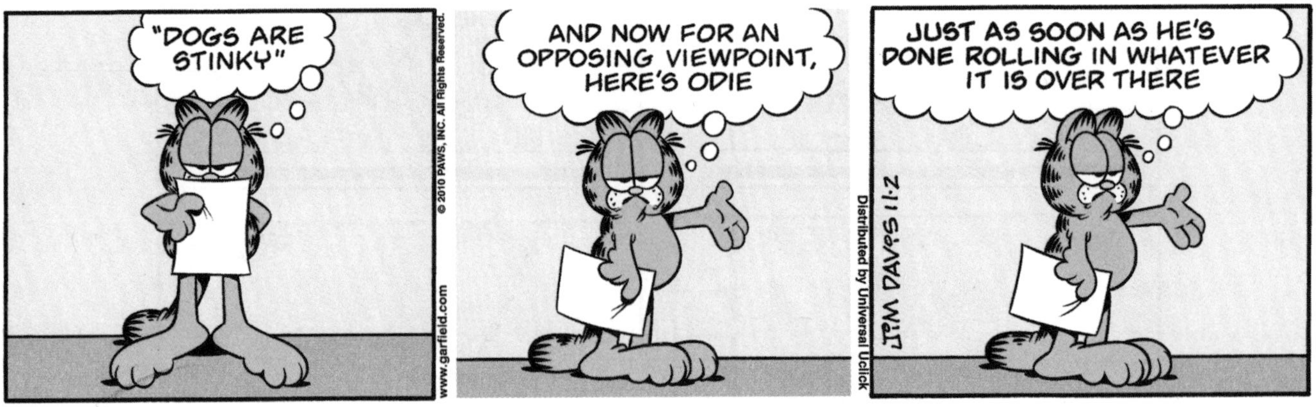
"DOGS ARE STINKY"
AND NOW FOR AN OPPOSING VIEWPOINT, HERE'S ODIE
JUST AS SOON AS HE'S DONE ROLLING IN WHATEVER IT IS OVER THERE
© 2010 PAWS, INC. All Rights Reserved.
www.garfield.com
Distributed by Universal Uclick
JIM DAVIS 11-2

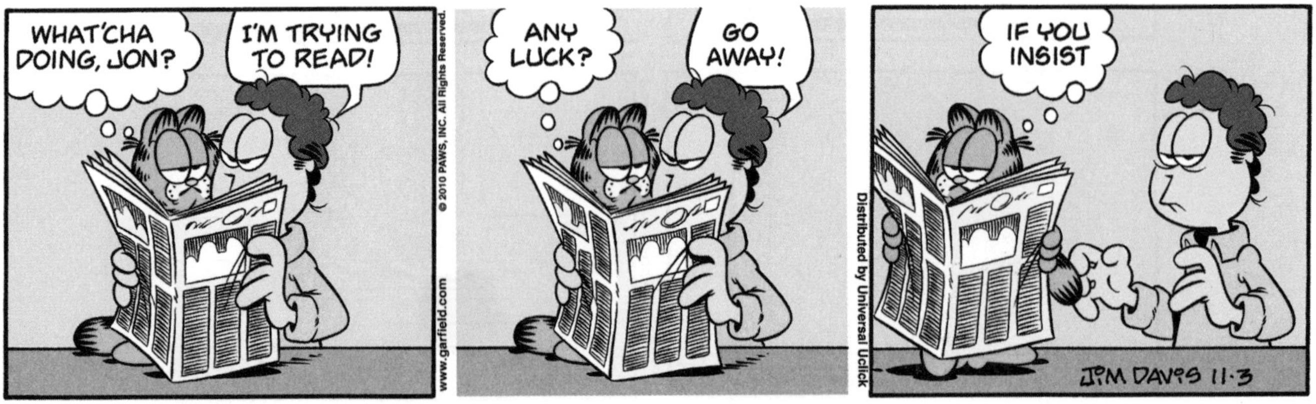
WHAT'CHA DOING, JON?
I'M TRYING TO READ!
ANY LUCK?
GO AWAY!
IF YOU INSIST
JIM DAVIS 11-3
© 2010 PAWS, INC. All Rights Reserved.
www.garfield.com
Distributed by Universal Uclick

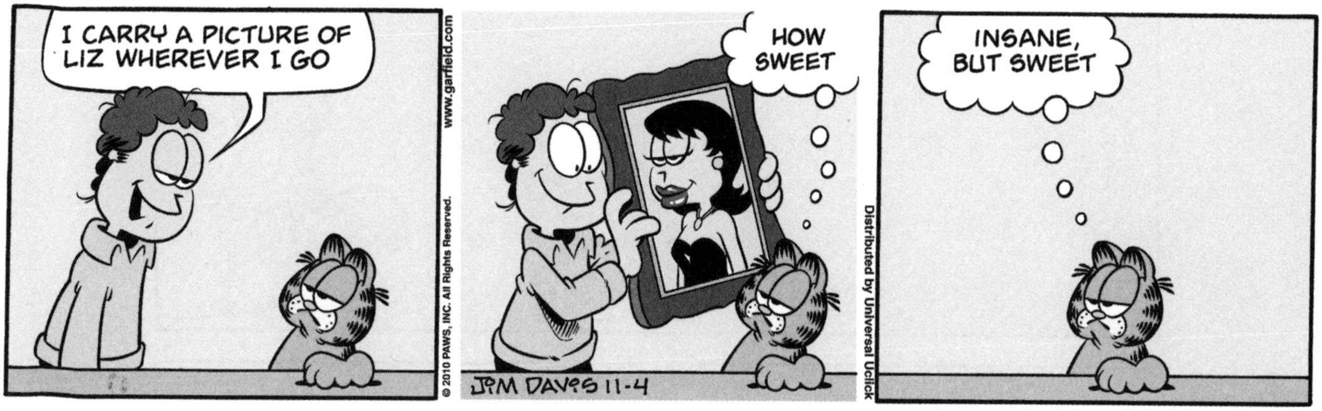
I CARRY A PICTURE OF LIZ WHEREVER I GO
HOW SWEET
INSANE, BUT SWEET
JIM DAVIS 11-4
www.garfield.com
© 2010 PAWS, INC. All Rights Reserved.
Distributed by Universal Uclick

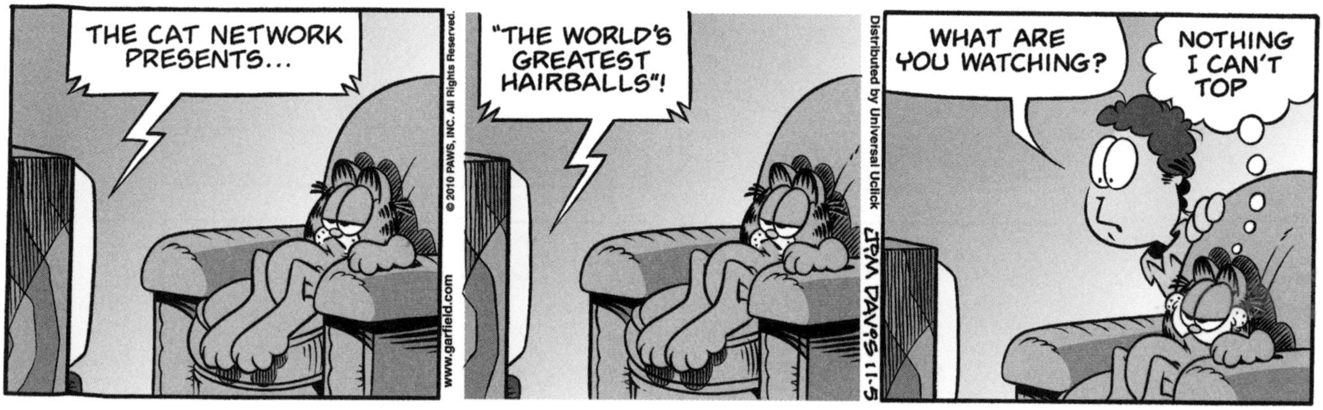
THE CAT NETWORK PRESENTS...
"THE WORLD'S GREATEST HAIRBALLS"!
WHAT ARE YOU WATCHING?
NOTHING I CAN'T TOP
JIM DAVIS 11-5
www.garfield.com
© 2010 PAWS, INC. All Rights Reserved.
Distributed by Universal Uclick

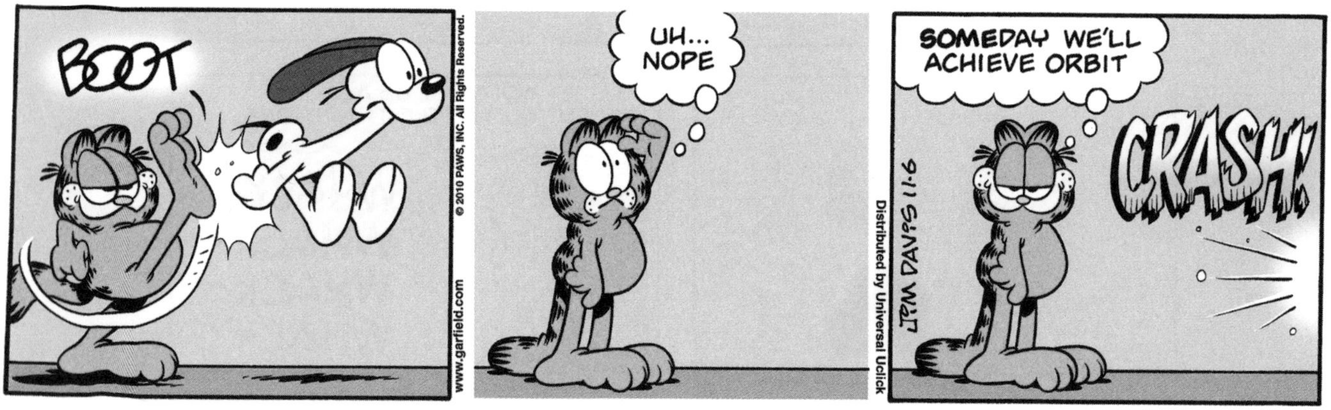
BOOT
UH... NOPE
SOMEDAY WE'LL ACHIEVE ORBIT
CRASH!
JIM DAVIS 11-6
www.garfield.com
© 2010 PAWS, INC. All Rights Reserved.
Distributed by Universal Uclick

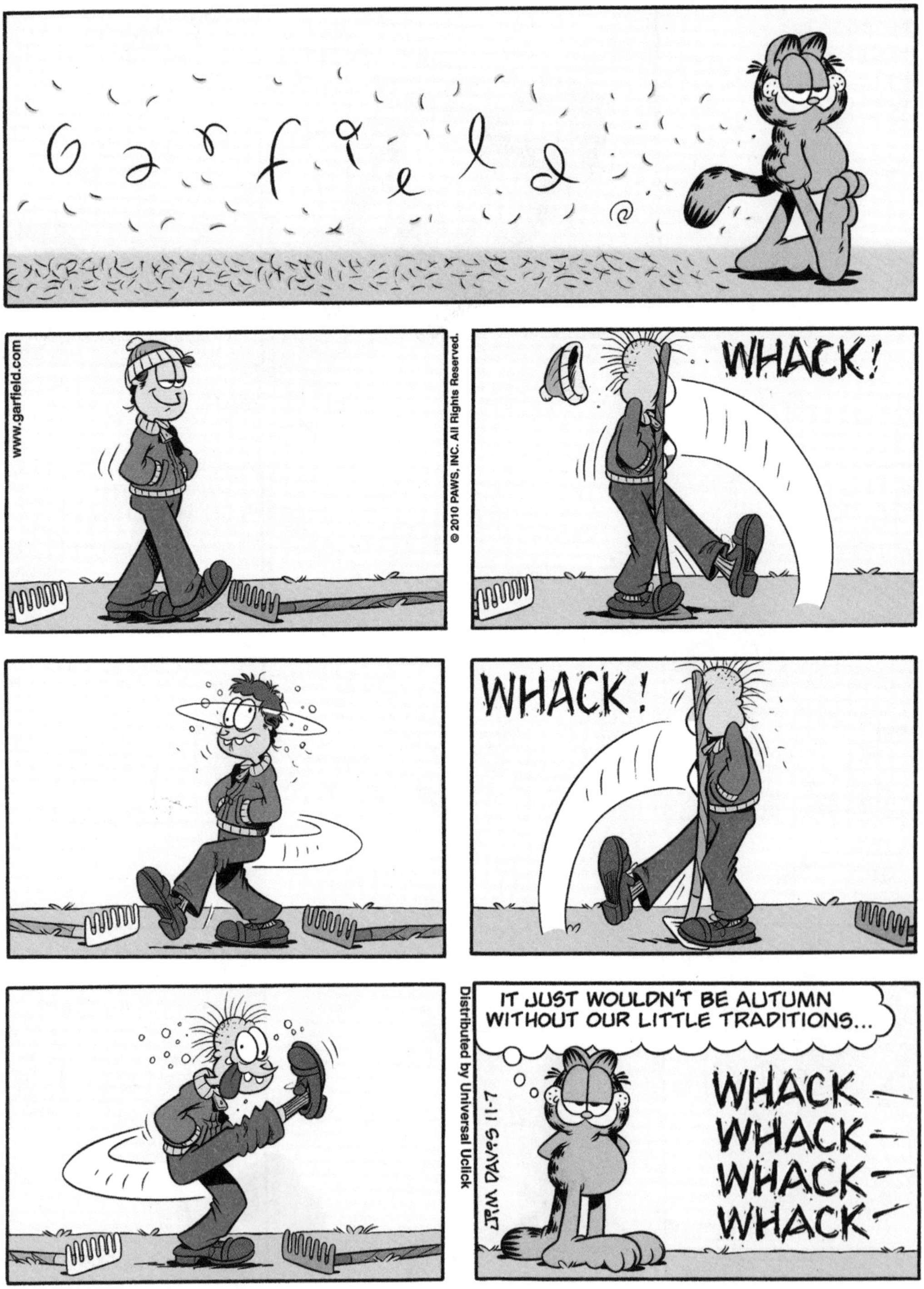
garfield
www.garfield.com
© 2010 PAWS, INC. All Rights Reserved.
WHACK!
WHACK!
Distributed by Universal Uclick
IT JUST WOULDN'T BE AUTUMN WITHOUT OUR LITTLE TRADITIONS...
WHACK-
WHACK-
WHACK-
WHACK-
JIM DAVIS 11-7

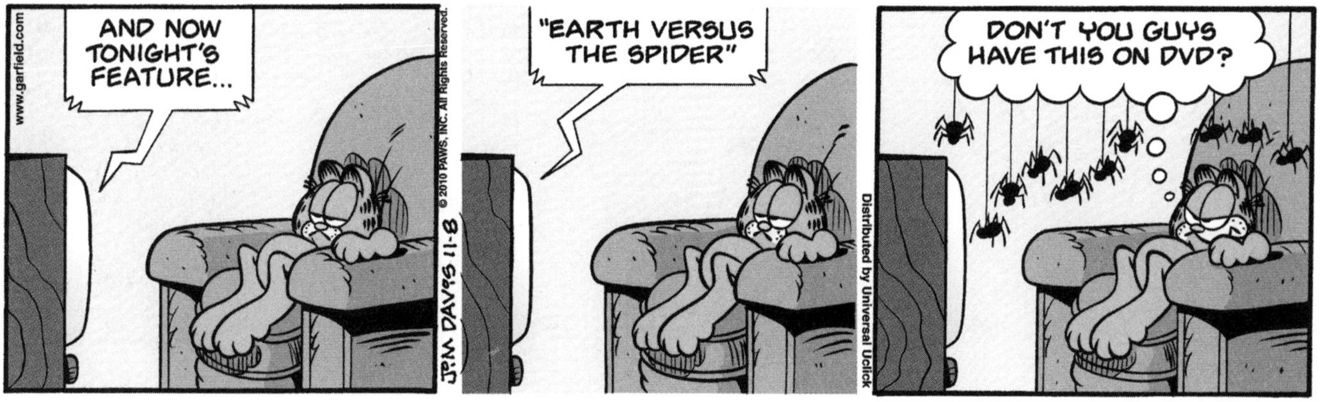
www.garfield.com
AND NOW TONIGHT'S FEATURE...
© 2010 PAWS, INC. All Rights Reserved.
JIM DAVIS 11-8
"EARTH VERSUS THE SPIDER"
Distributed by Universal Uclick
DON'T YOU GUYS HAVE THIS ON DVD?

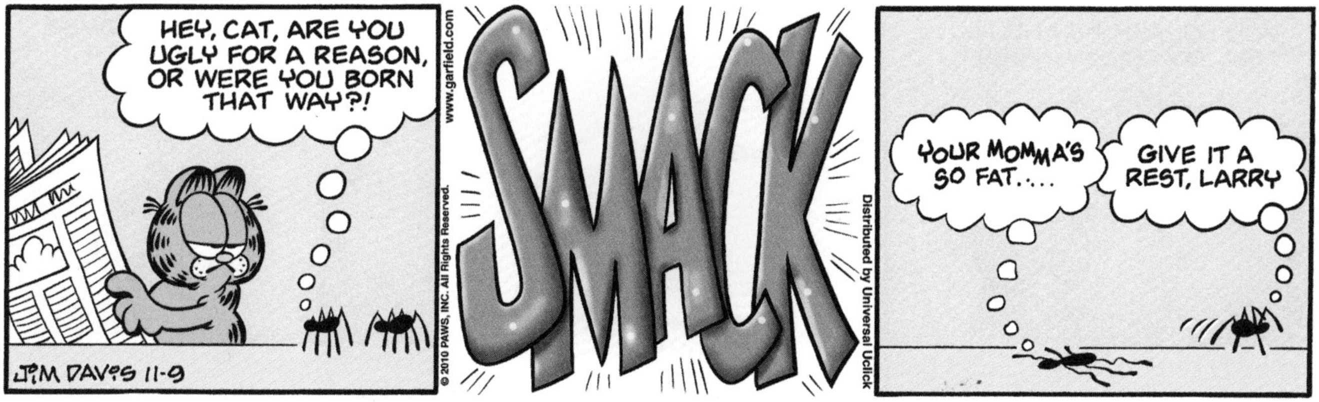
HEY, CAT, ARE YOU UGLY FOR A REASON, OR WERE YOU BORN THAT WAY?!
JIM DAVIS 11-9
www.garfield.com
© 2010 PAWS, INC. All Rights Reserved.
SMACK
Distributed by Universal Uclick
YOUR MOMMA'S SO FAT.....
GIVE IT A REST, LARRY

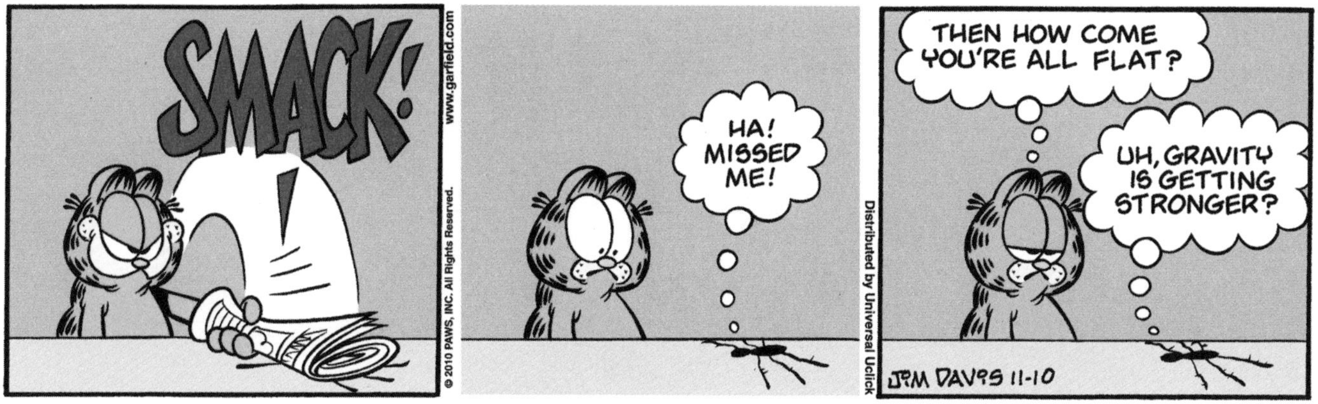
SMACK!
www.garfield.com
© 2010 PAWS, INC. All Rights Reserved.
HA! MISSED ME!
Distributed by Universal Uclick
THEN HOW COME YOU'RE ALL FLAT?
UH, GRAVITY IS GETTING STRONGER?
JIM DAVIS 11-10

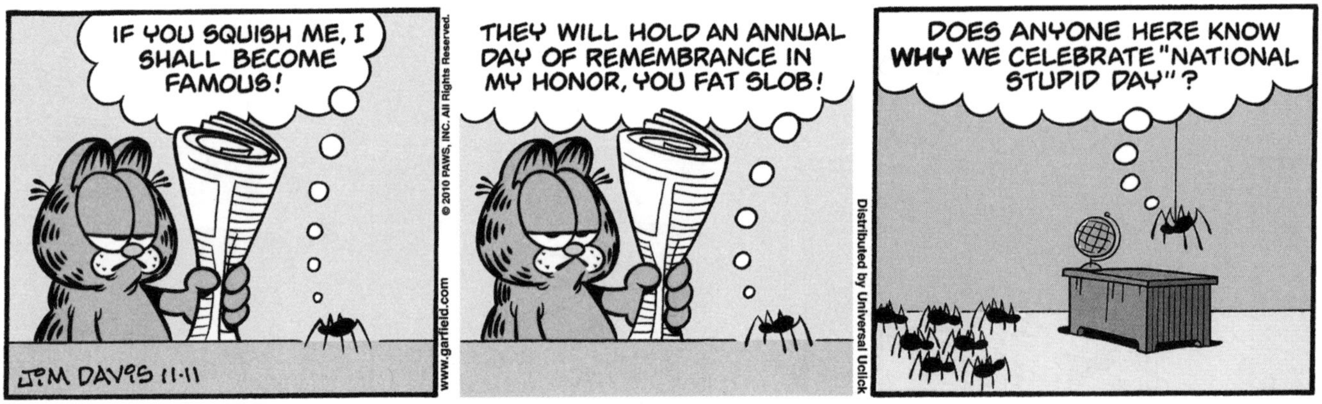
IF YOU SQUISH ME, I SHALL BECOME FAMOUS!
JIM DAVIS 11-11
© 2010 PAWS, INC. All Rights Reserved.
www.garfield.com
THEY WILL HOLD AN ANNUAL DAY OF REMEMBRANCE IN MY HONOR, YOU FAT SLOB!
Distributed by Universal Uclick
DOES ANYONE HERE KNOW WHY WE CELEBRATE "NATIONAL STUPID DAY"?

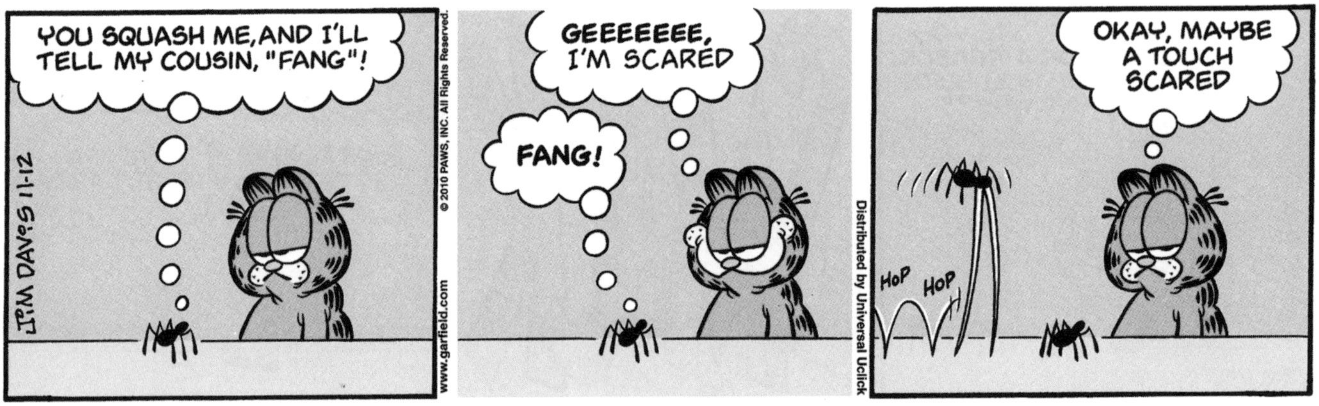
YOU SQUASH ME, AND I'LL TELL MY COUSIN, "FANG"!
JIM DAVIS 11-12
© 2010 PAWS, INC. All Rights Reserved.
www.garfield.com
GEEEEEEE, I'M SCARED
FANG!
Distributed by Universal Uclick
HOP
HOP
OKAY, MAYBE A TOUCH SCARED

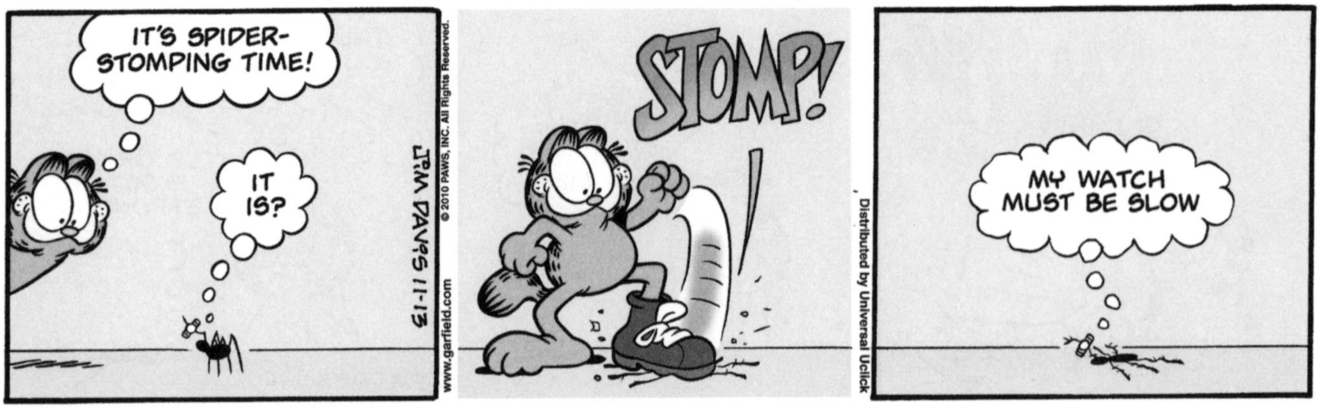
IT'S SPIDER-STOMPING TIME!
IT IS?
JIM DAVIS 11-13
© 2010 PAWS, INC. All Rights Reserved.
www.garfield.com
STOMP!
Distributed by Universal Uclick
MY WATCH MUST BE SLOW

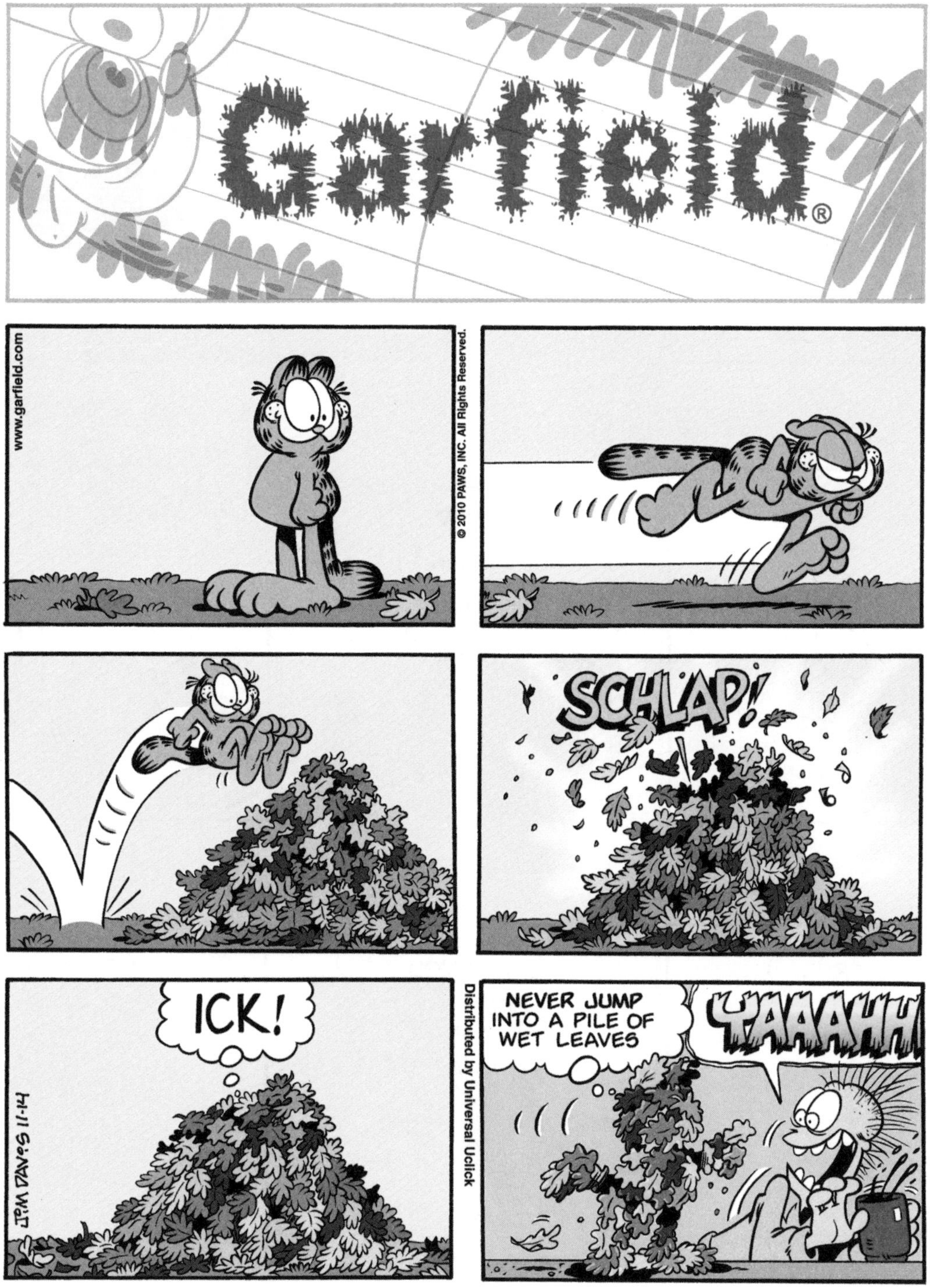
Garfield®
www.garfield.com
© 2010 PAWS, INC. All Rights Reserved.
SCHLAP!
ICK!
JIM DAVIS 11-14
Distributed by Universal Uclick
NEVER JUMP INTO A PILE OF WET LEAVES
YAAAHH

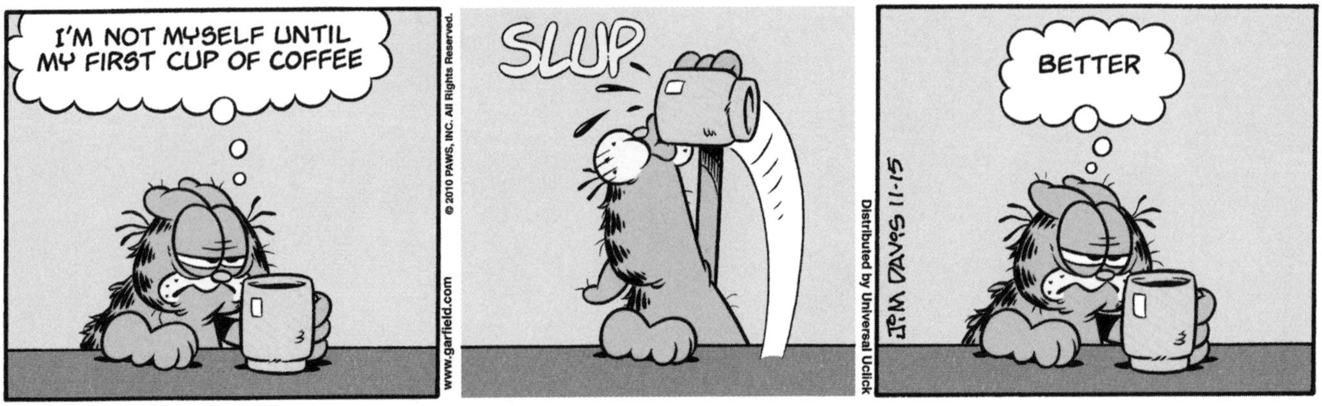
I'M NOT MYSELF UNTIL MY FIRST CUP OF COFFEE
SLUP
BETTER
JIM DAVIS 11-15
www.garfield.com
© 2010 PAWS, INC. All Rights Reserved.
Distributed by Universal Uclick

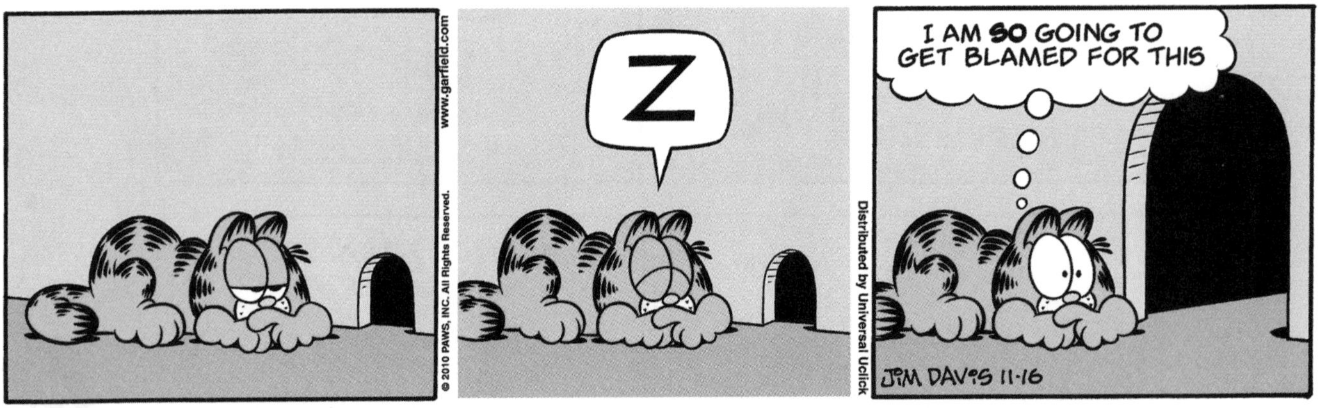
Z
I AM **SO** GOING TO GET BLAMED FOR THIS
JIM DAVIS 11-16
www.garfield.com
© 2010 PAWS, INC. All Rights Reserved.
Distributed by Universal Uclick

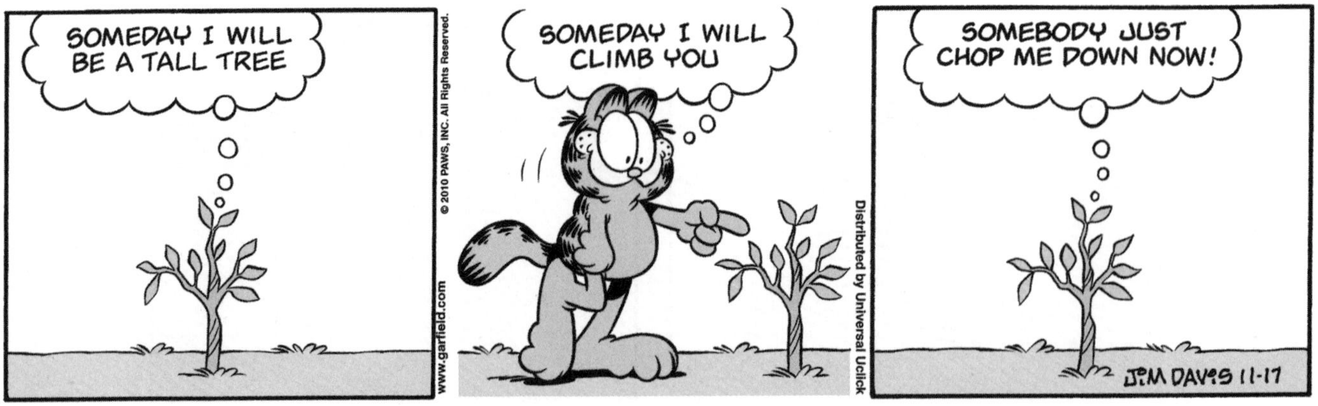
SOMEDAY I WILL BE A TALL TREE
SOMEDAY I WILL CLIMB YOU
SOMEBODY JUST CHOP ME DOWN NOW!
JIM DAVIS 11-17
www.garfield.com
© 2010 PAWS, INC. All Rights Reserved.
Distributed by Universal Uclick

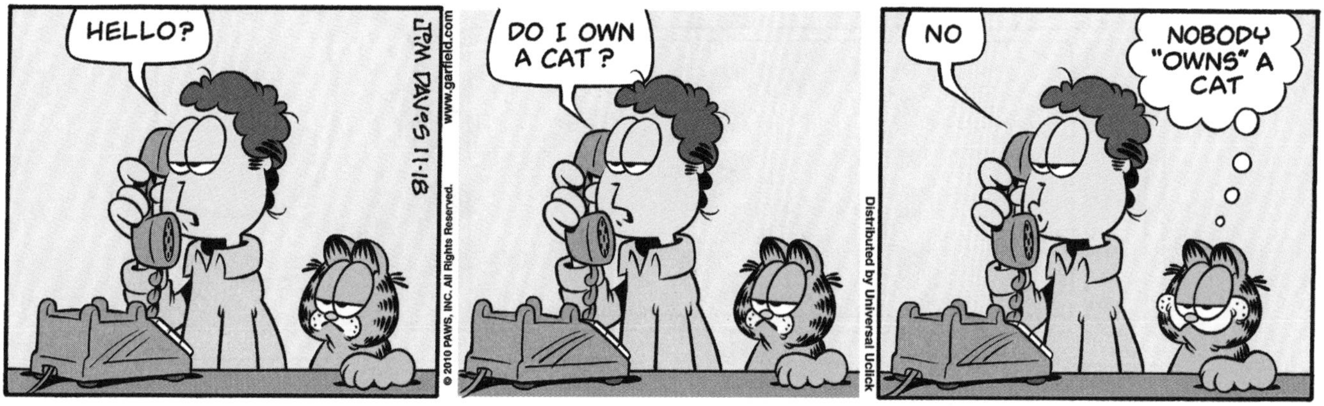
HELLO?
JIM DAVIS 11-18
DO I OWN A CAT?
NO
NOBODY "OWNS" A CAT
www.garfield.com
© 2010 PAWS, INC. All Rights Reserved.
Distributed by Universal Uclick

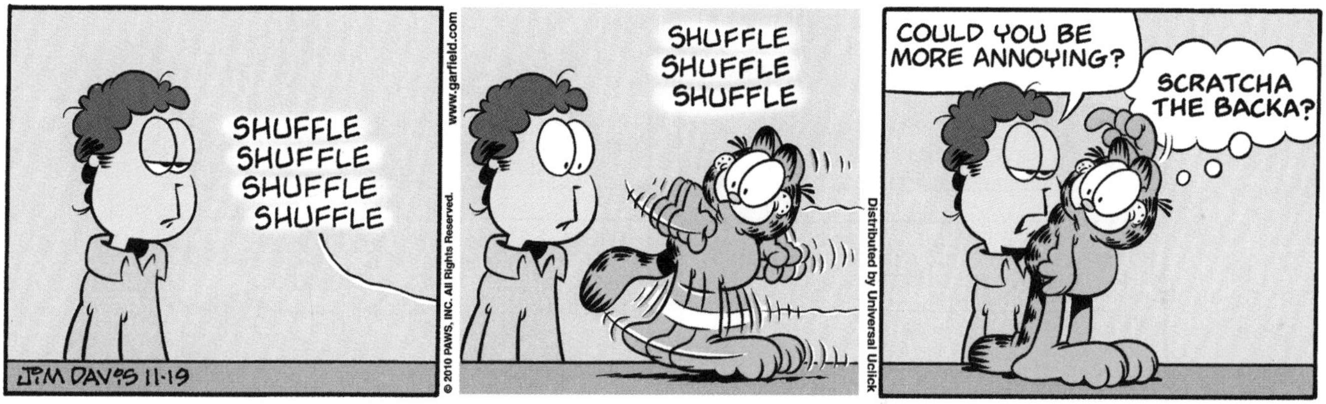
SHUFFLE SHUFFLE SHUFFLE SHUFFLE
JIM DAVIS 11-19
SHUFFLE SHUFFLE SHUFFLE
COULD YOU BE MORE ANNOYING?
SCRATCHA THE BACKA?
www.garfield.com
© 2010 PAWS, INC. All Rights Reserved.
Distributed by Universal Uclick

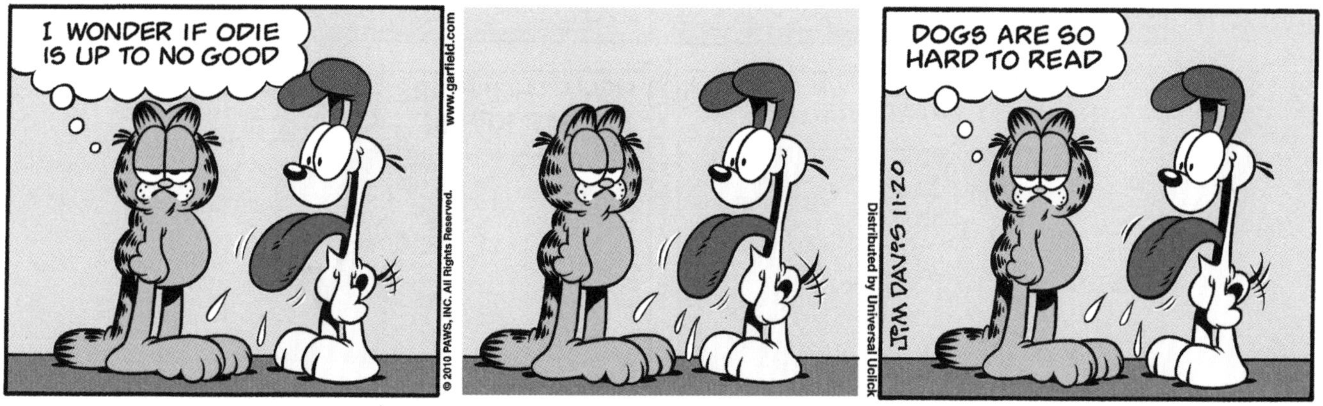
I WONDER IF ODIE IS UP TO NO GOOD
DOGS ARE SO HARD TO READ
JIM DAVIS 11-20
www.garfield.com
© 2010 PAWS, INC. All Rights Reserved.
Distributed by Universal Uclick

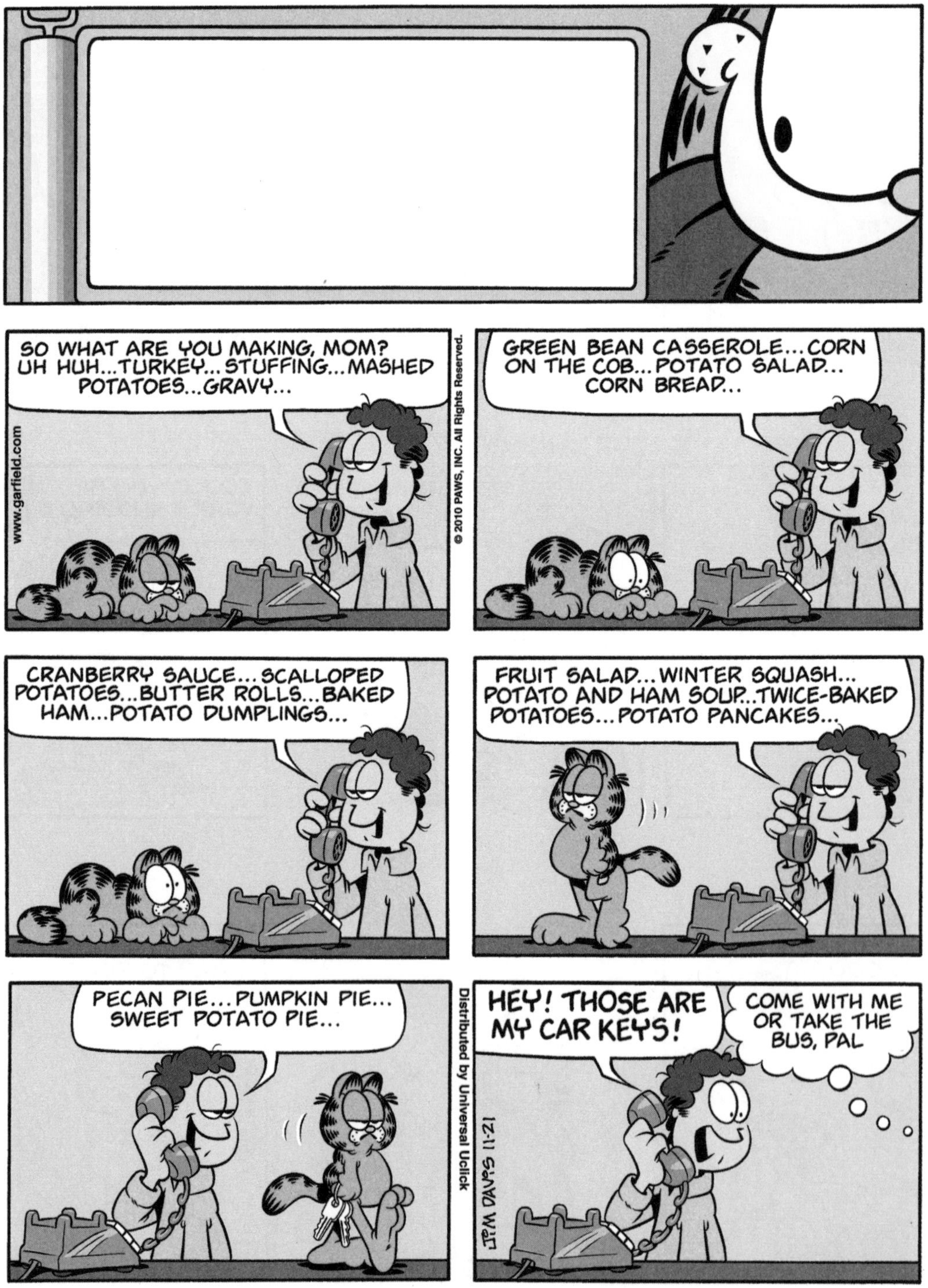
SO WHAT ARE YOU MAKING, MOM? UH HUH...TURKEY...STUFFING...MASHED POTATOES...GRAVY...
GREEN BEAN CASSEROLE...CORN ON THE COB...POTATO SALAD... CORN BREAD...
CRANBERRY SAUCE...SCALLOPED POTATOES...BUTTER ROLLS...BAKED HAM...POTATO DUMPLINGS...
FRUIT SALAD...WINTER SQUASH... POTATO AND HAM SOUP...TWICE-BAKED POTATOES...POTATO PANCAKES...
PECAN PIE...PUMPKIN PIE... SWEET POTATO PIE...
HEY! THOSE ARE MY CAR KEYS!
COME WITH ME OR TAKE THE BUS, PAL
www.garfield.com
© 2010 PAWS, INC. All Rights Reserved.
Distributed by Universal Uclick

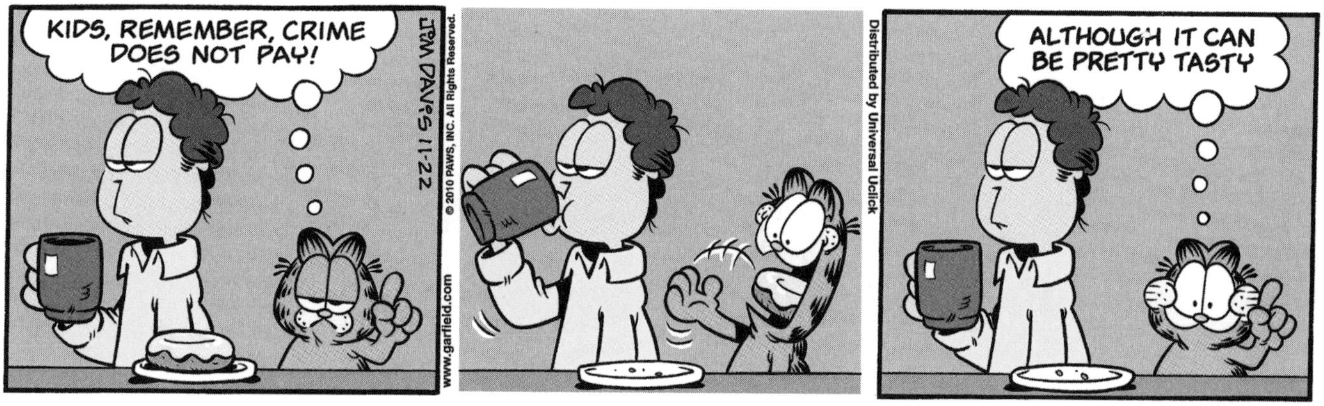
KIDS, REMEMBER, CRIME DOES NOT PAY!
JIM DAVIS 11-22
© 2010 PAWS, INC. All Rights Reserved.
www.garfield.com
Distributed by Universal Uclick
ALTHOUGH IT CAN BE PRETTY TASTY

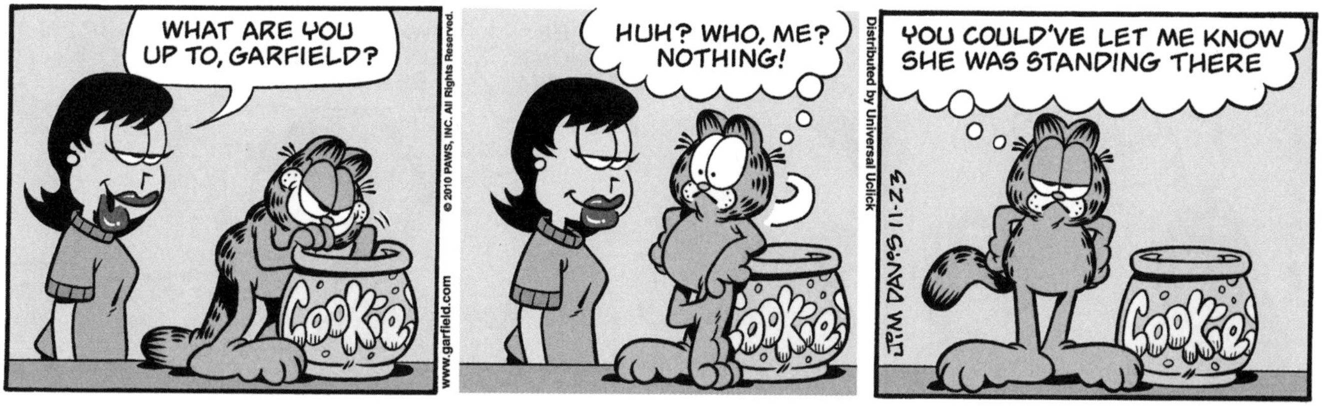
WHAT ARE YOU UP TO, GARFIELD?
© 2010 PAWS, INC. All Rights Reserved.
www.garfield.com
HUH? WHO, ME? NOTHING!
Distributed by Universal Uclick
YOU COULD'VE LET ME KNOW SHE WAS STANDING THERE
JIM DAVIS 11-23

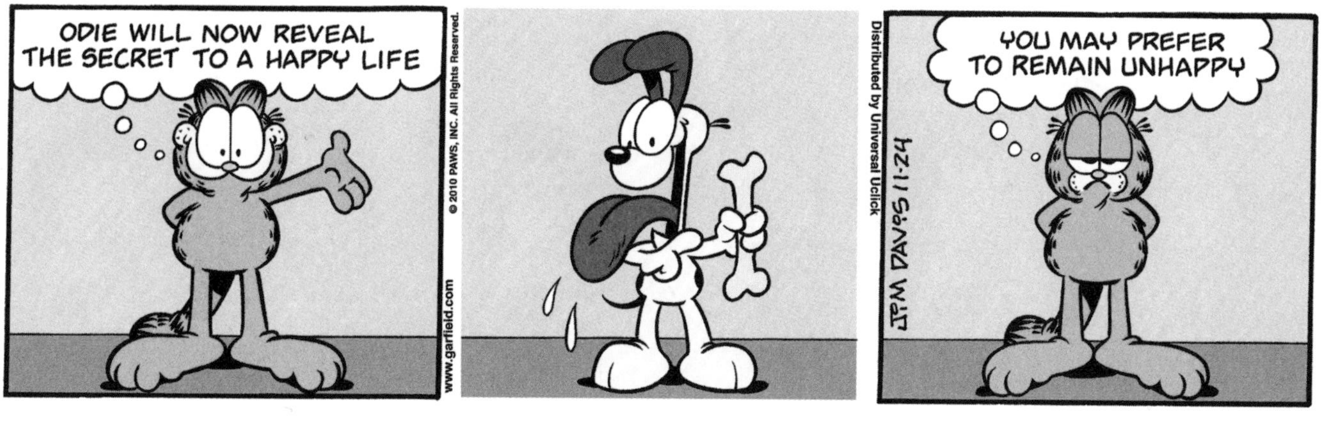
ODIE WILL NOW REVEAL THE SECRET TO A HAPPY LIFE
© 2010 PAWS, INC. All Rights Reserved.
www.garfield.com
Distributed by Universal Uclick
JIM DAVIS 11-24
YOU MAY PREFER TO REMAIN UNHAPPY

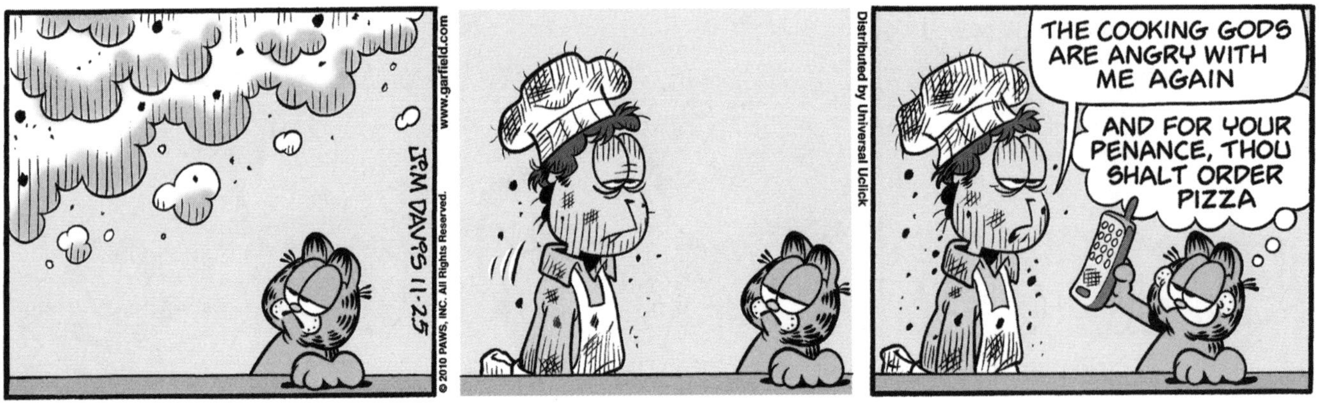
JPM DAVPS 11-25
© 2010 PAWS, INC. All Rights Reserved. www.garfield.com
Distributed by Universal Uclick
THE COOKING GODS ARE ANGRY WITH ME AGAIN
AND FOR YOUR PENANCE, THOU SHALT ORDER PIZZA

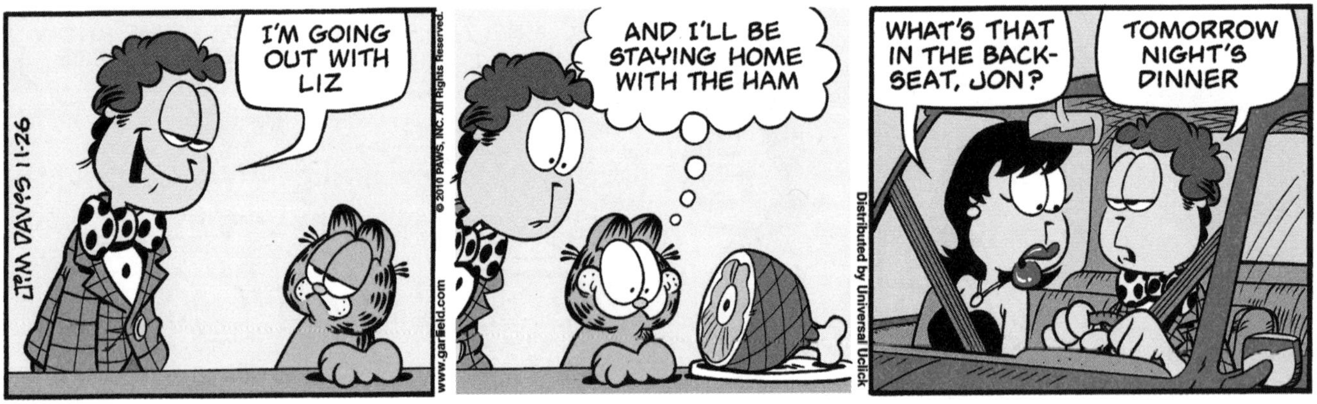
I'M GOING OUT WITH LIZ
JPM DAVPS 11-26
© 2010 PAWS, INC. All Rights Reserved. www.garfield.com
AND I'LL BE STAYING HOME WITH THE HAM
Distributed by Universal Uclick
WHAT'S THAT IN THE BACK-SEAT, JON?
TOMORROW NIGHT'S DINNER

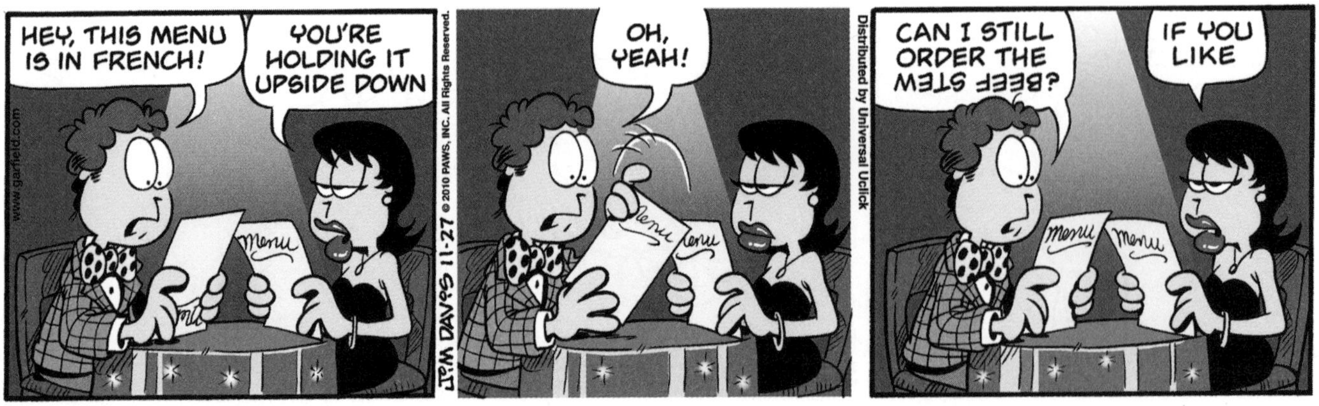
HEY, THIS MENU IS IN FRENCH!
YOU'RE HOLDING IT UPSIDE DOWN
www.garfield.com
JPM DAVPS 11-27 © 2010 PAWS, INC. All Rights Reserved.
OH, YEAH!
Distributed by Universal Uclick
CAN I STILL ORDER THE BEEF STEW?
IF YOU LIKE

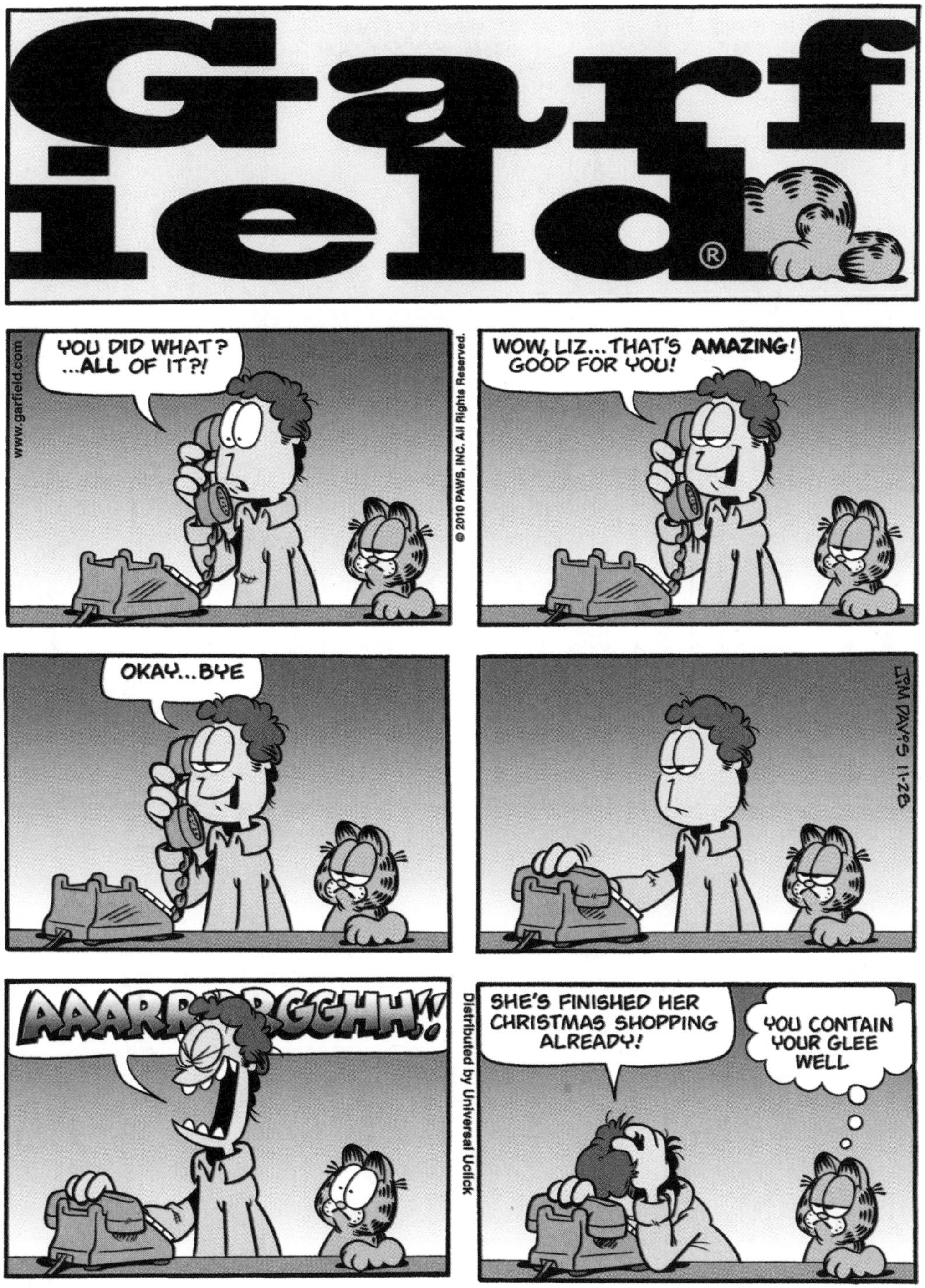
Garfield®
YOU DID WHAT? ...ALL OF IT?!
www.garfield.com
© 2010 PAWS, INC. All Rights Reserved.
WOW, LIZ... THAT'S AMAZING! GOOD FOR YOU!
OKAY... BYE
JIM DAVIS 11-28
AAARR GGHH!!
Distributed by Universal Uclick
SHE'S FINISHED HER CHRISTMAS SHOPPING ALREADY!
YOU CONTAIN YOUR GLEE WELL

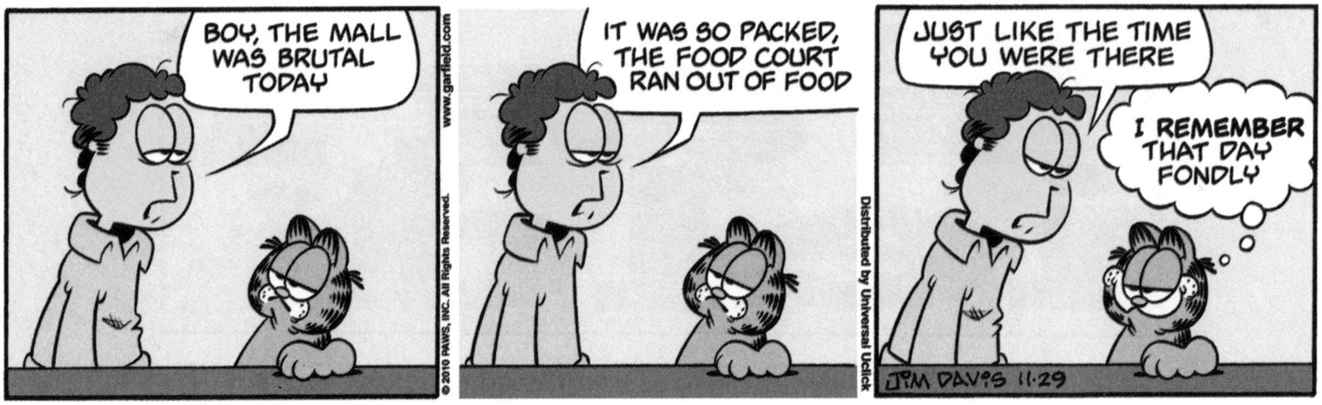
BOY, THE MALL WAS BRUTAL TODAY
IT WAS SO PACKED, THE FOOD COURT RAN OUT OF FOOD
JUST LIKE THE TIME YOU WERE THERE
I REMEMBER THAT DAY FONDLY
JIM DAVIS 11·29
© 2010 PAWS, INC. All Rights Reserved. www.garfield.com
Distributed by Universal Uclick

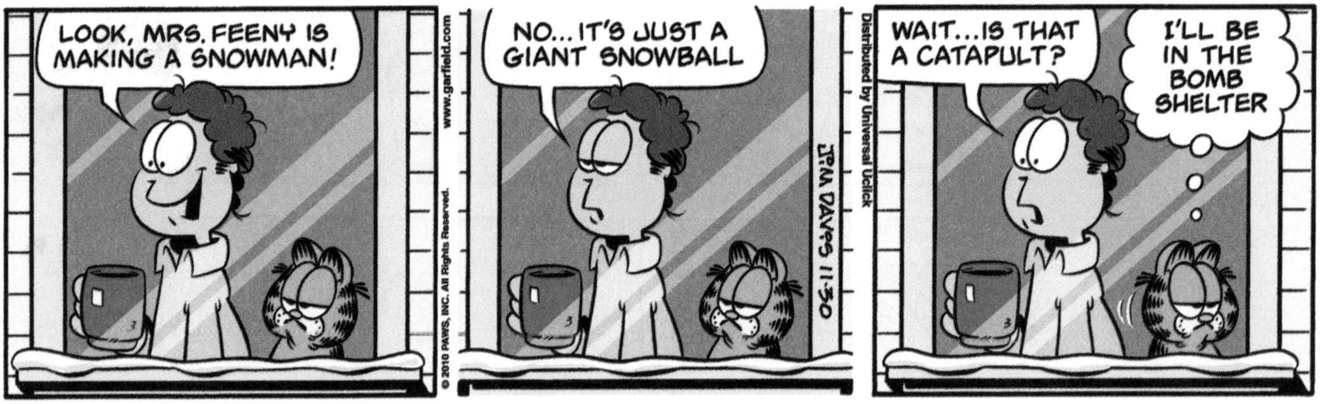
LOOK, MRS. FEENY IS MAKING A SNOWMAN!
NO... IT'S JUST A GIANT SNOWBALL
WAIT... IS THAT A CATAPULT?
I'LL BE IN THE BOMB SHELTER
JIM DAVIS 11·30
© 2010 PAWS, INC. All Rights Reserved. www.garfield.com
Distributed by Universal Uclick

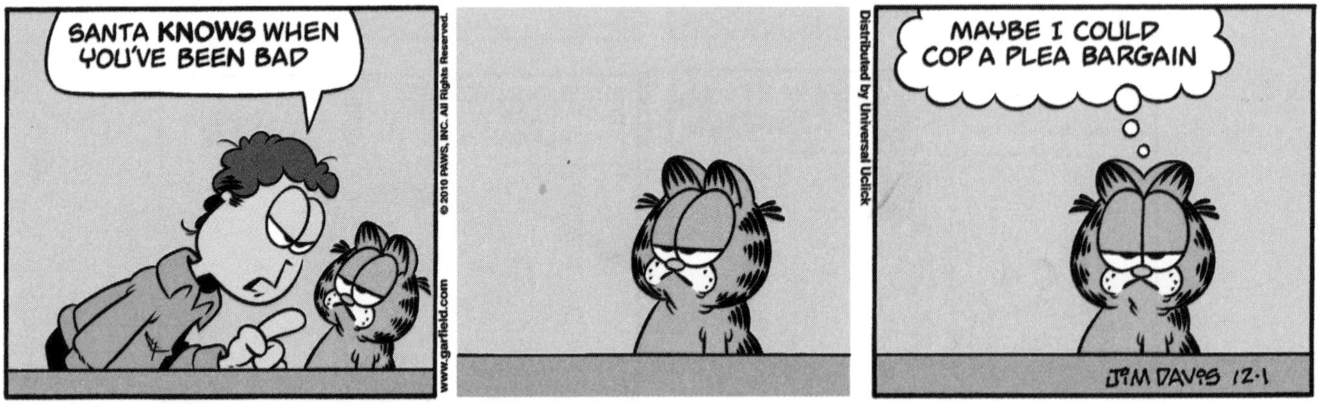
SANTA **KNOWS** WHEN YOU'VE BEEN BAD
MAYBE I COULD COP A PLEA BARGAIN
JIM DAVIS 12·1
© 2010 PAWS, INC. All Rights Reserved. www.garfield.com
Distributed by Universal Uclick

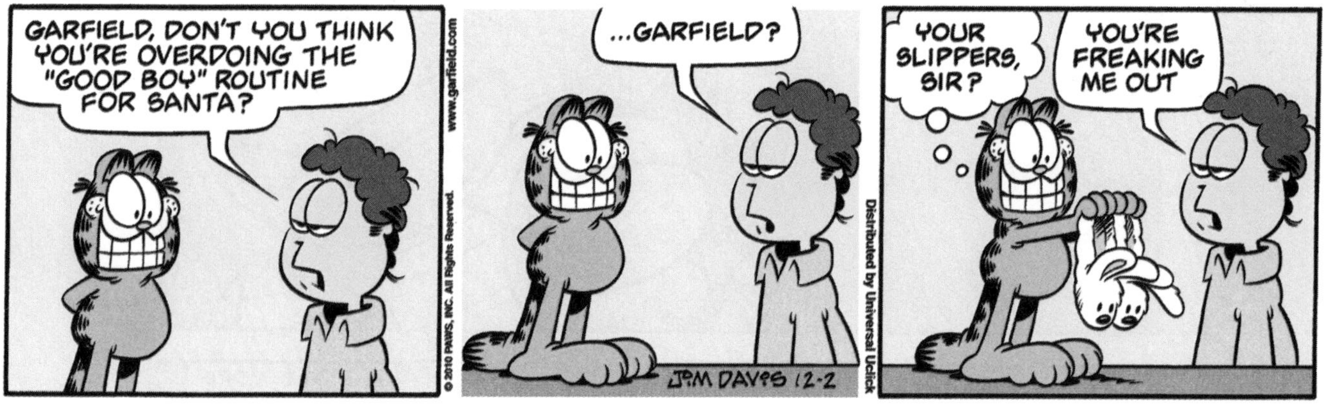
GARFIELD, DON'T YOU THINK YOU'RE OVERDOING THE "GOOD BOY" ROUTINE FOR SANTA?
© 2010 PAWS, INC. All Rights Reserved.
www.garfield.com
...GARFIELD?
JIM DAVIS 12-2
Distributed by Universal Uclick
YOUR SLIPPERS, SIR?
YOU'RE FREAKING ME OUT

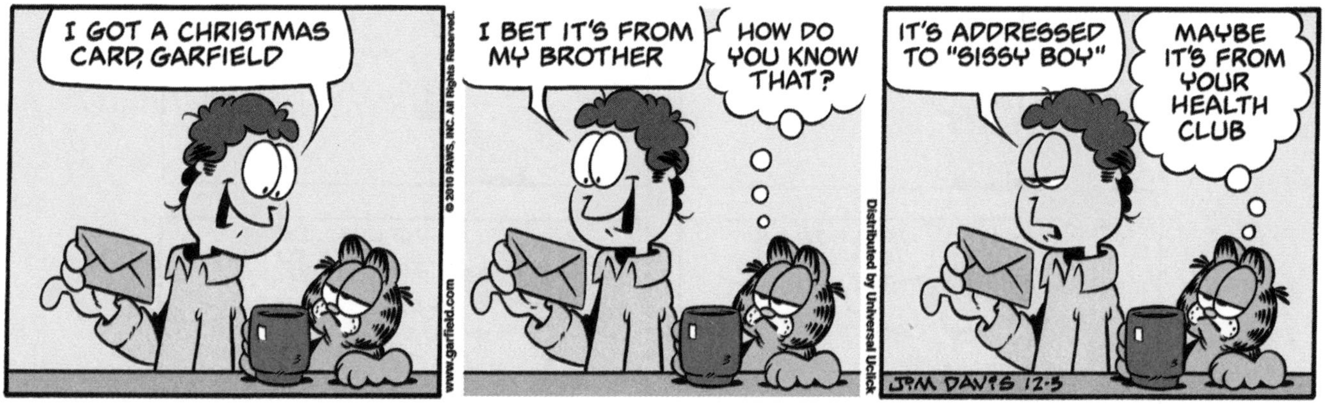
I GOT A CHRISTMAS CARD, GARFIELD
www.garfield.com
© 2010 PAWS, INC. All Rights Reserved.
I BET IT'S FROM MY BROTHER
HOW DO YOU KNOW THAT?
Distributed by Universal Uclick
IT'S ADDRESSED TO "SISSY BOY"
MAYBE IT'S FROM YOUR HEALTH CLUB
JIM DAVIS 12-3

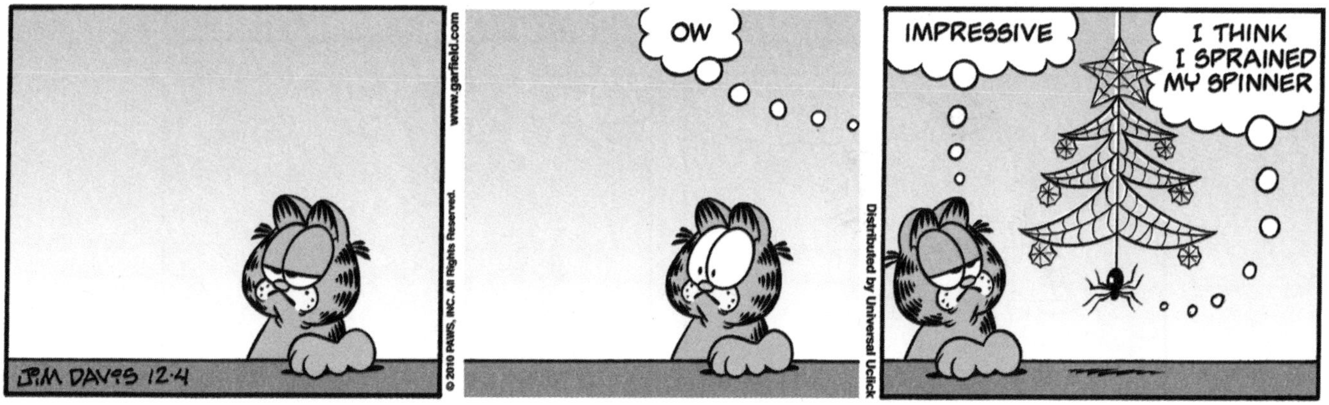
JIM DAVIS 12-4
www.garfield.com
© 2010 PAWS, INC. All Rights Reserved.
OW
Distributed by Universal Uclick
IMPRESSIVE
I THINK I SPRAINED MY SPINNER

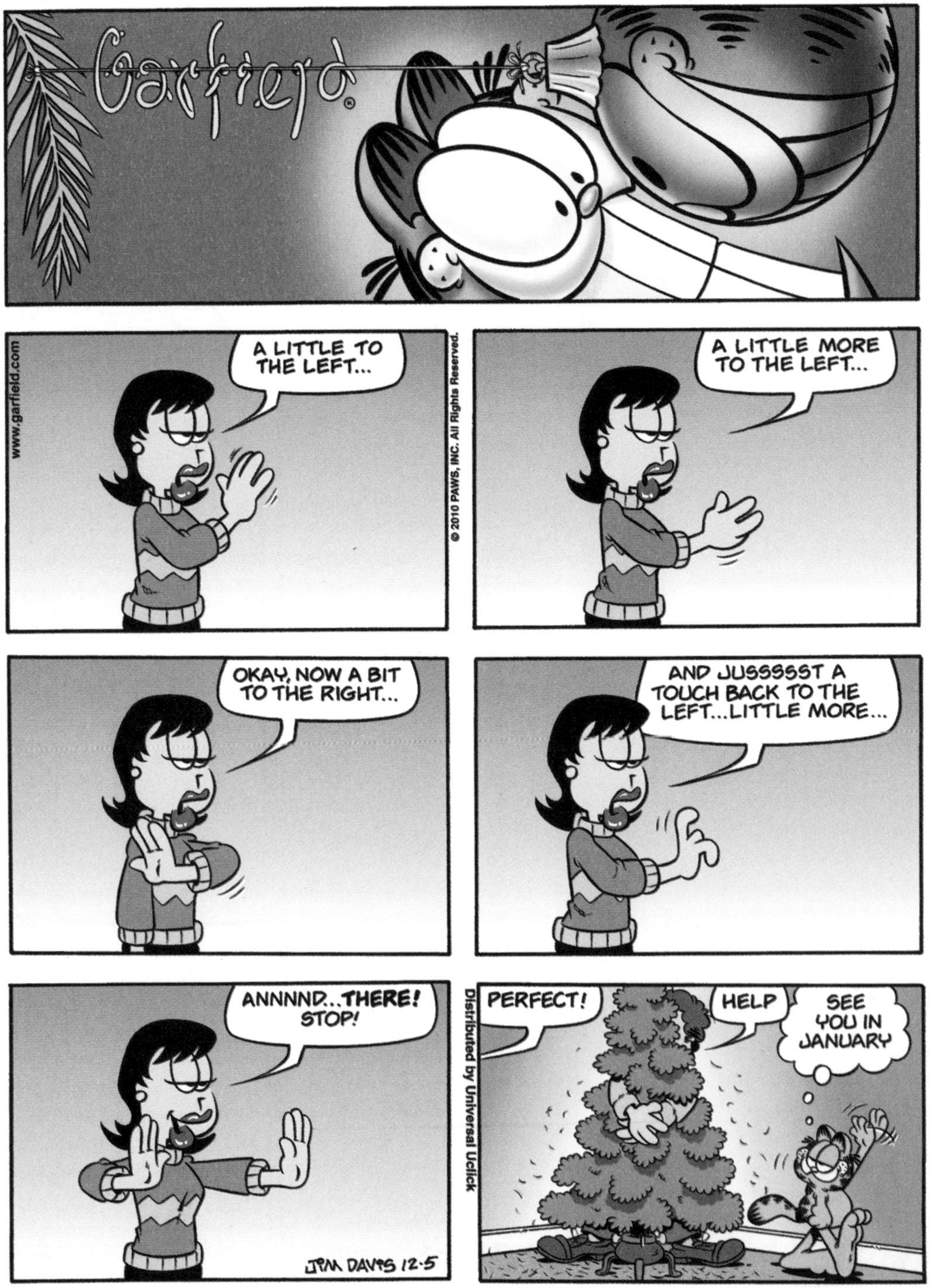
Garfield®
www.garfield.com
© 2010 PAWS, INC. All Rights Reserved.
A LITTLE TO THE LEFT...
A LITTLE MORE TO THE LEFT...
OKAY, NOW A BIT TO THE RIGHT...
AND JUSSSSST A TOUCH BACK TO THE LEFT...LITTLE MORE...
ANNNND...THERE! STOP!
JIM DAVIS 12-5
Distributed by Universal Uclick
PERFECT!
HELP
SEE YOU IN JANUARY

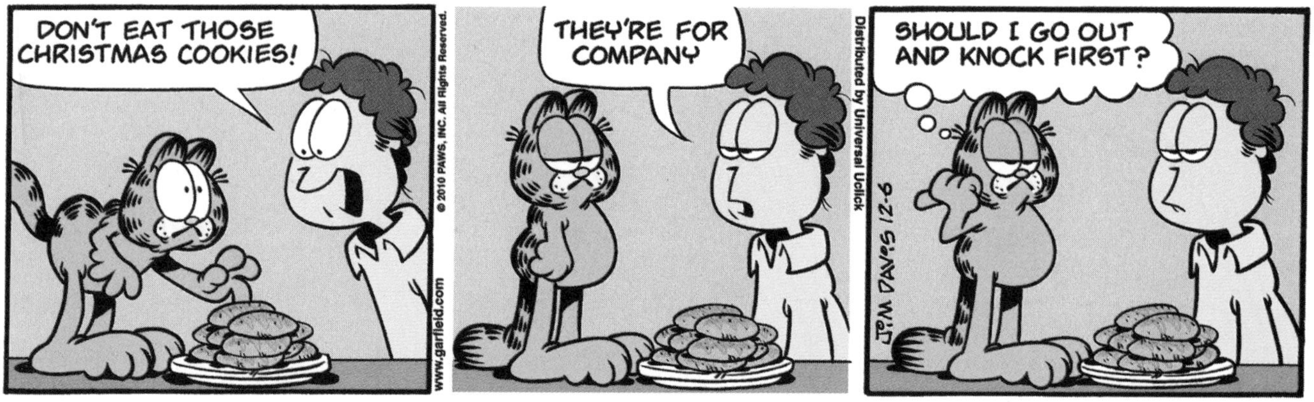
DON'T EAT THOSE CHRISTMAS COOKIES!
THEY'RE FOR COMPANY
SHOULD I GO OUT AND KNOCK FIRST?
© 2010 PAWS, INC. All Rights Reserved.
www.garfield.com
Distributed by Universal Uclick
JIM DAVIS 12-6

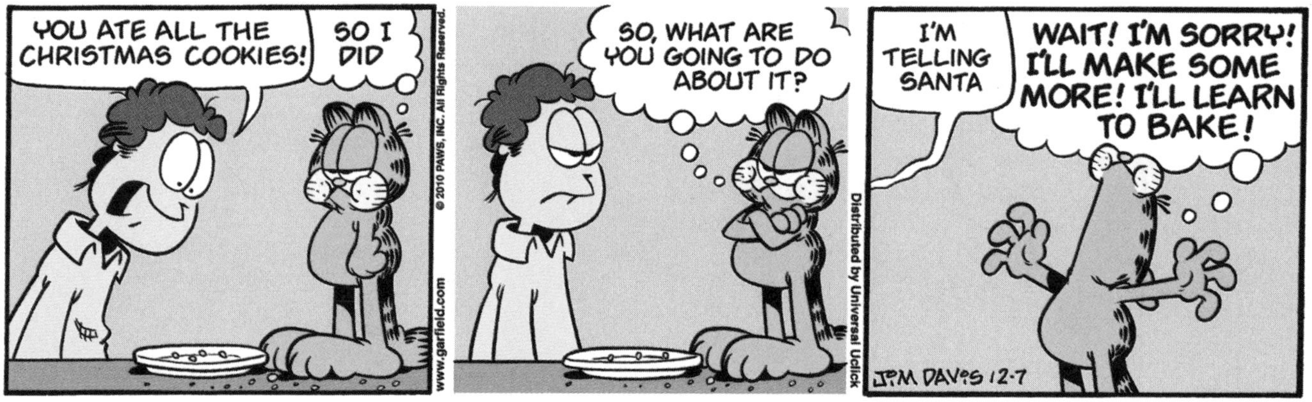
YOU ATE ALL THE CHRISTMAS COOKIES!
SO I DID
SO, WHAT ARE YOU GOING TO DO ABOUT IT?
I'M TELLING SANTA
WAIT! I'M SORRY! I'LL MAKE SOME MORE! I'LL LEARN TO BAKE!
© 2010 PAWS, INC. All Rights Reserved.
www.garfield.com
Distributed by Universal Uclick
JIM DAVIS 12-7

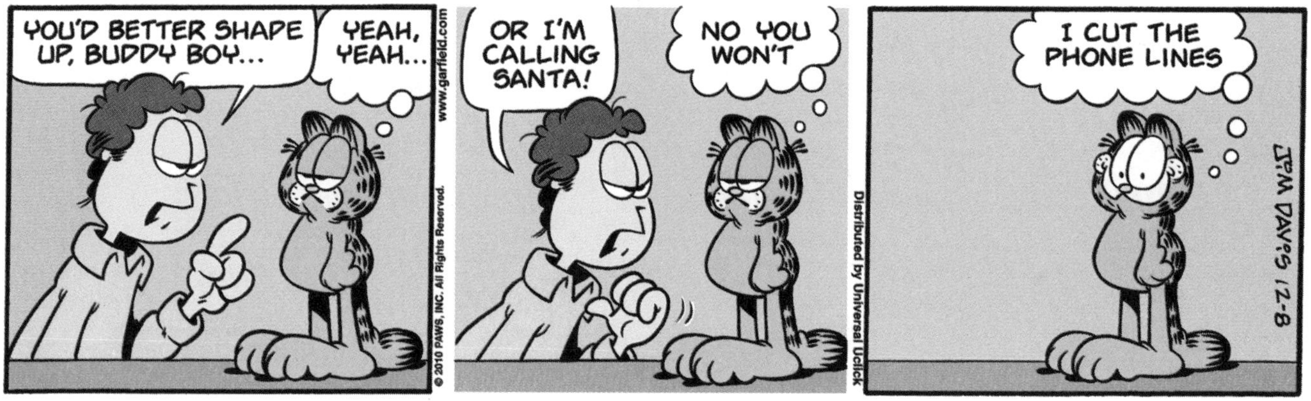
YOU'D BETTER SHAPE UP, BUDDY BOY...
YEAH, YEAH...
OR I'M CALLING SANTA!
NO YOU WON'T
I CUT THE PHONE LINES
www.garfield.com
© 2010 PAWS, INC. All Rights Reserved.
Distributed by Universal Uclick
JIM DAVIS 12-8

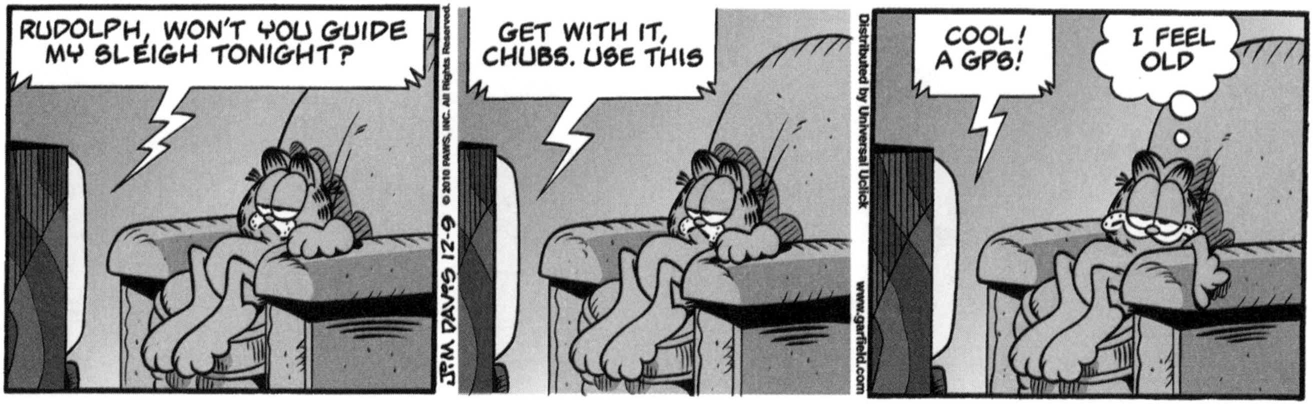
RUDOLPH, WON'T YOU GUIDE MY SLEIGH TONIGHT?
GET WITH IT, CHUBS. USE THIS
COOL! A GPS!
I FEEL OLD
JIM DAVIS 12-9
© 2010 PAWS, INC. All Rights Reserved.
Distributed by Universal Uclick
www.garfield.com

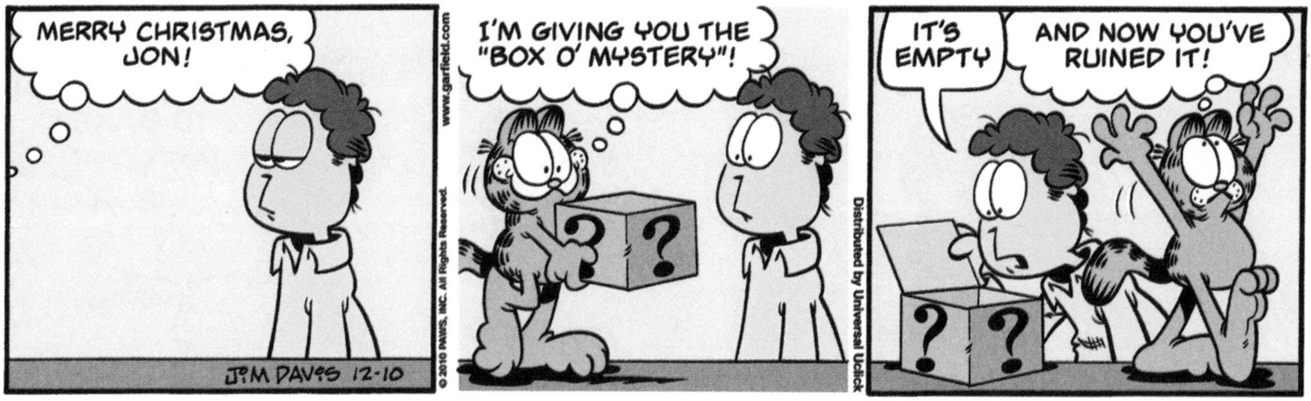
MERRY CHRISTMAS, JON!
I'M GIVING YOU THE "BOX O' MYSTERY"!
IT'S EMPTY
AND NOW YOU'VE RUINED IT!
JIM DAVIS 12-10
www.garfield.com
© 2010 PAWS, INC. All Rights Reserved.
Distributed by Universal Uclick

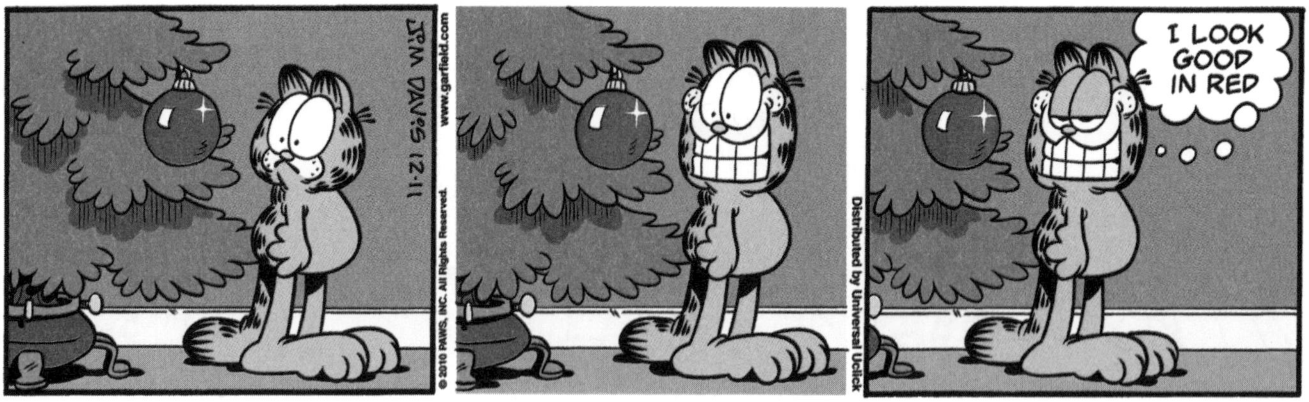
I LOOK GOOD IN RED
JIM DAVIS 12-11
www.garfield.com
© 2010 PAWS, INC. All Rights Reserved.
Distributed by Universal Uclick

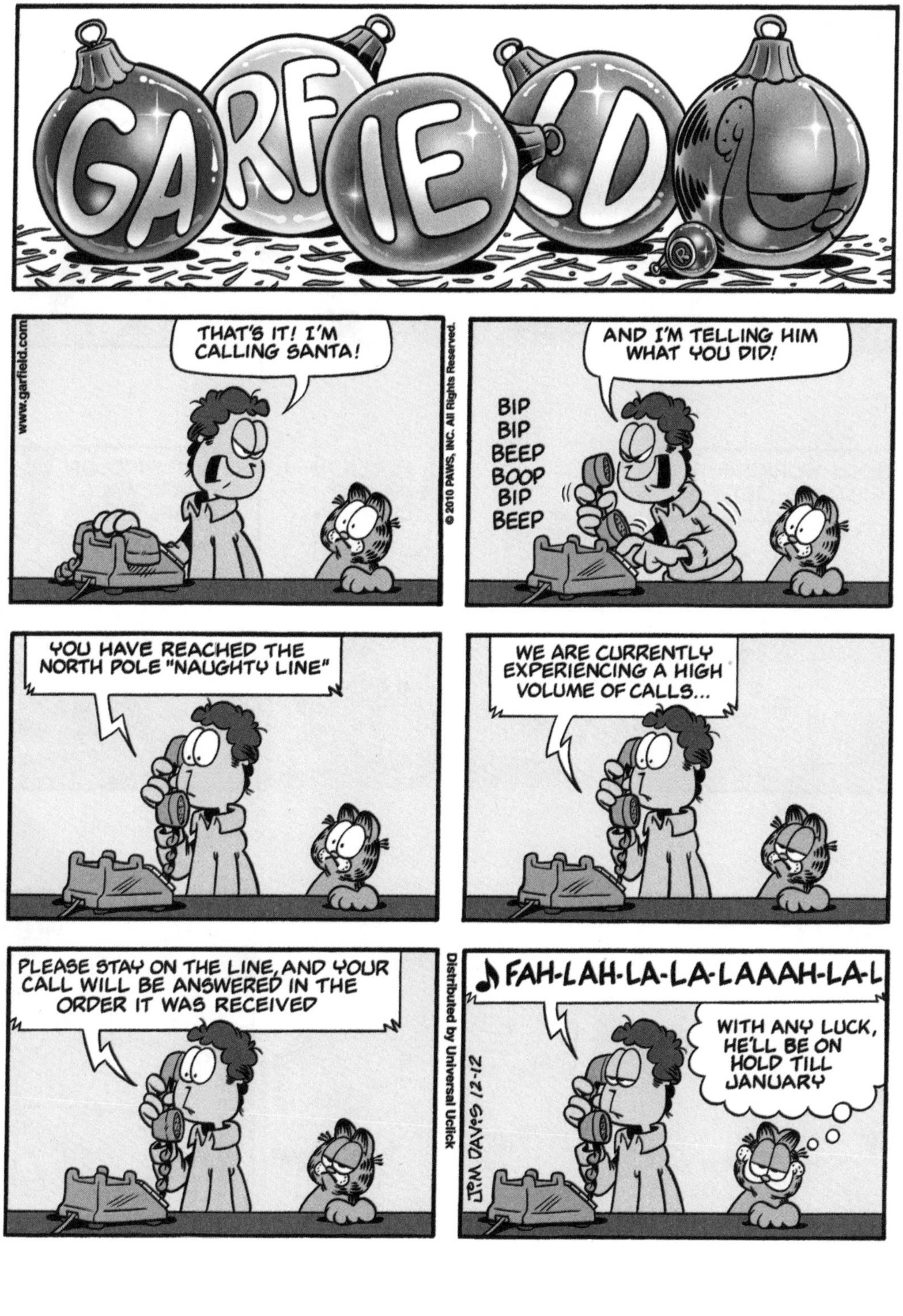
GARFIELD
www.garfield.com
© 2010 PAWS, INC. All Rights Reserved.
THAT'S IT! I'M CALLING SANTA!
AND I'M TELLING HIM WHAT YOU DID!
BIP BIP BEEP BOOP BIP BEEP
YOU HAVE REACHED THE NORTH POLE "NAUGHTY LINE"
WE ARE CURRENTLY EXPERIENCING A HIGH VOLUME OF CALLS...
PLEASE STAY ON THE LINE, AND YOUR CALL WILL BE ANSWERED IN THE ORDER IT WAS RECEIVED
Distributed by Universal Uclick
JIM DAVIS 12-12
FAH-LAH-LA-LA-LAAAH-LA-L
WITH ANY LUCK, HE'LL BE ON HOLD TILL JANUARY

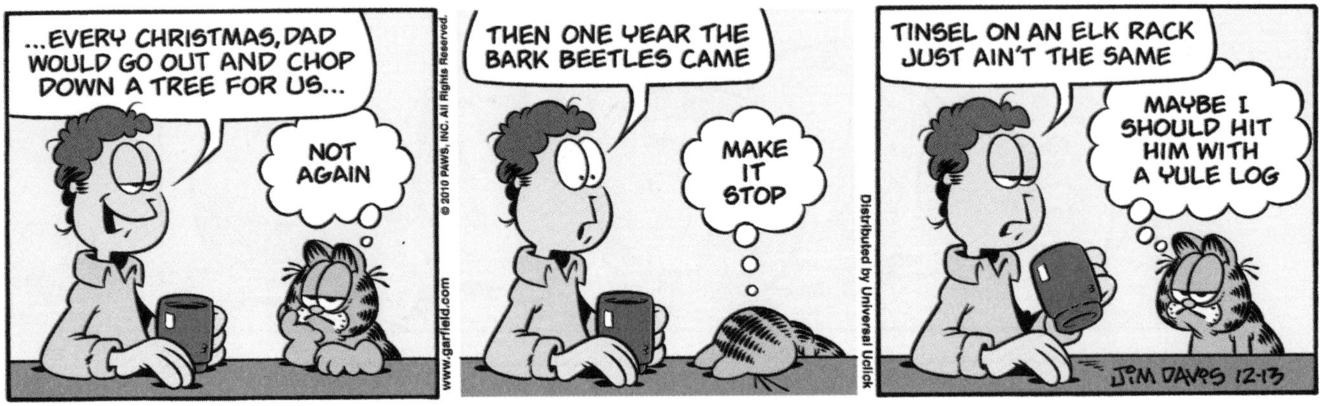
...EVERY CHRISTMAS, DAD WOULD GO OUT AND CHOP DOWN A TREE FOR US...
NOT AGAIN
THEN ONE YEAR THE BARK BEETLES CAME
MAKE IT STOP
TINSEL ON AN ELK RACK JUST AIN'T THE SAME
MAYBE I SHOULD HIT HIM WITH A YULE LOG
JIM DAVIS 12-13
© 2010 PAWS, INC. All Rights Reserved.
www.garfield.com
Distributed by Universal Uclick

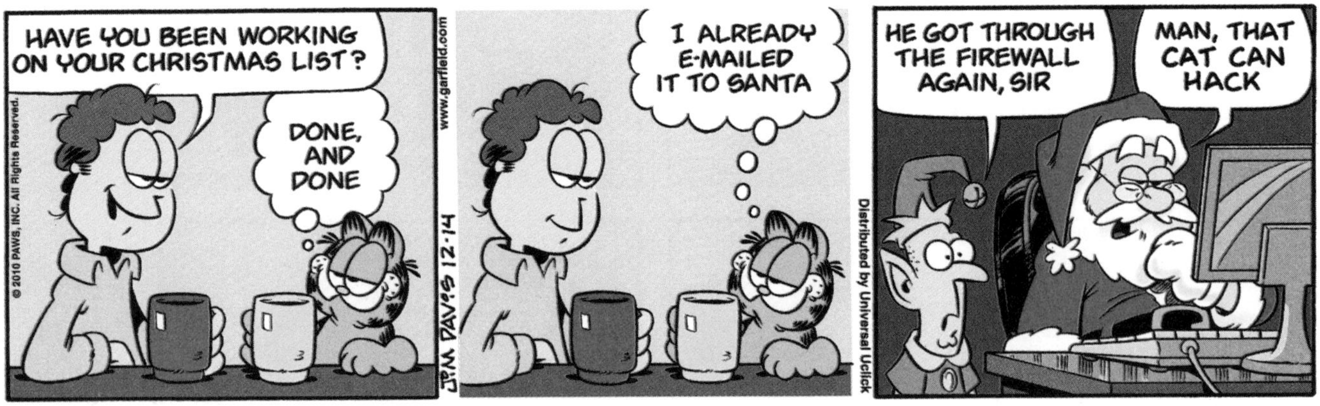
HAVE YOU BEEN WORKING ON YOUR CHRISTMAS LIST?
DONE, AND DONE
I ALREADY E-MAILED IT TO SANTA
HE GOT THROUGH THE FIREWALL AGAIN, SIR
MAN, THAT CAT CAN HACK
JIM DAVIS 12-14
© 2010 PAWS, INC. All Rights Reserved.
www.garfield.com
Distributed by Universal Uclick

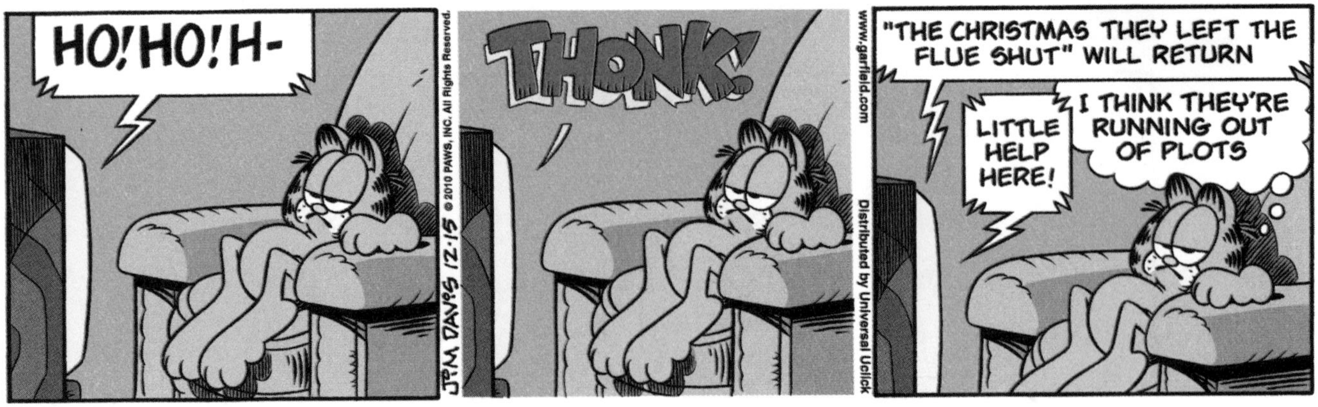
HO! HO! H-
THONK!
"THE CHRISTMAS THEY LEFT THE FLUE SHUT" WILL RETURN
LITTLE HELP HERE!
I THINK THEY'RE RUNNING OUT OF PLOTS
JIM DAVIS 12-15
© 2010 PAWS, INC. All Rights Reserved.
www.garfield.com
Distributed by Universal Uclick

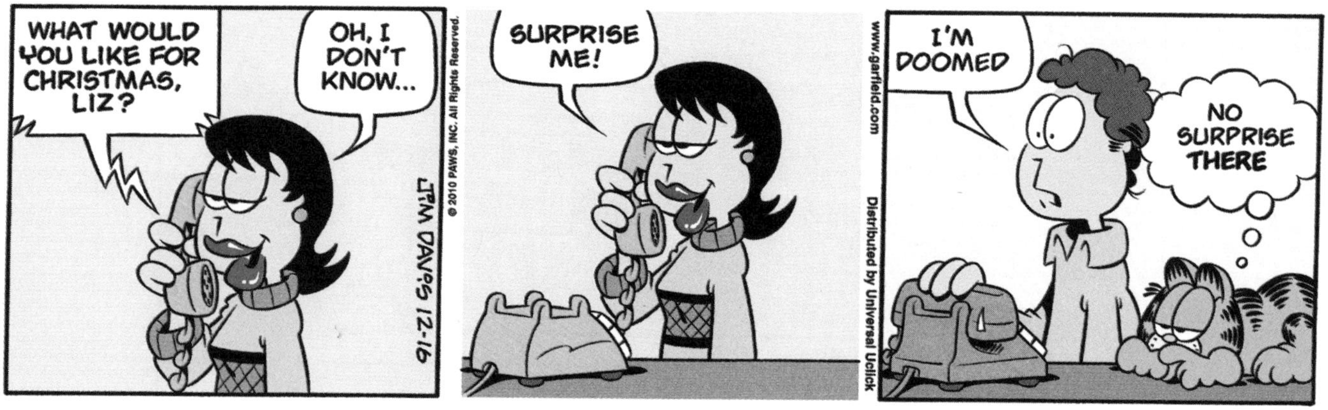
WHAT WOULD YOU LIKE FOR CHRISTMAS, LIZ?
OH, I DON'T KNOW...
JIM DAVIS 12-16
© 2010 PAWS, INC. All Rights Reserved.
SURPRISE ME!
www.garfield.com
Distributed by Universal Uclick
I'M DOOMED
NO SURPRISE THERE

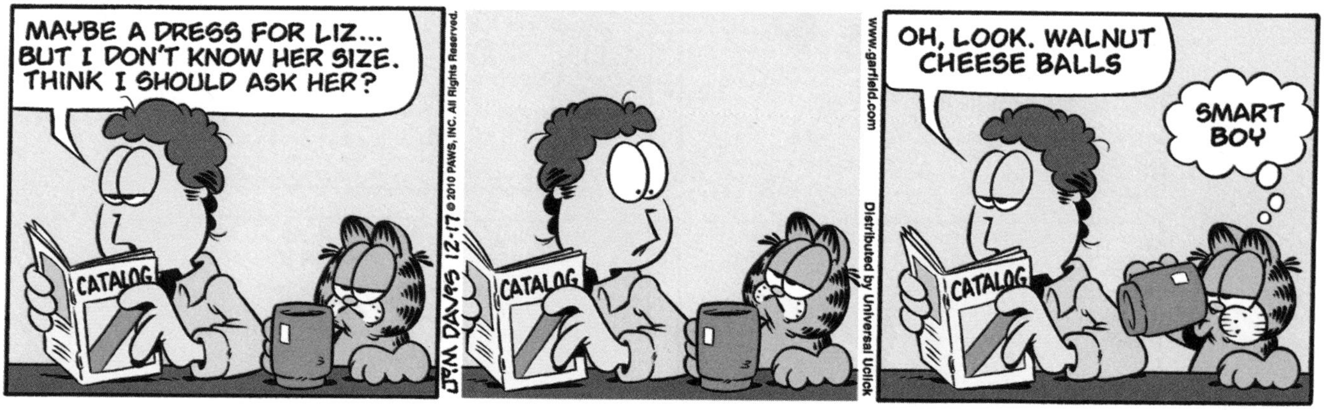
MAYBE A DRESS FOR LIZ... BUT I DON'T KNOW HER SIZE. THINK I SHOULD ASK HER?
CATALOG
JIM DAVIS 12-17 © 2010 PAWS, INC. All Rights Reserved.
CATALOG
www.garfield.com
Distributed by Universal Uclick
OH, LOOK. WALNUT CHEESE BALLS
SMART BOY
CATALOG

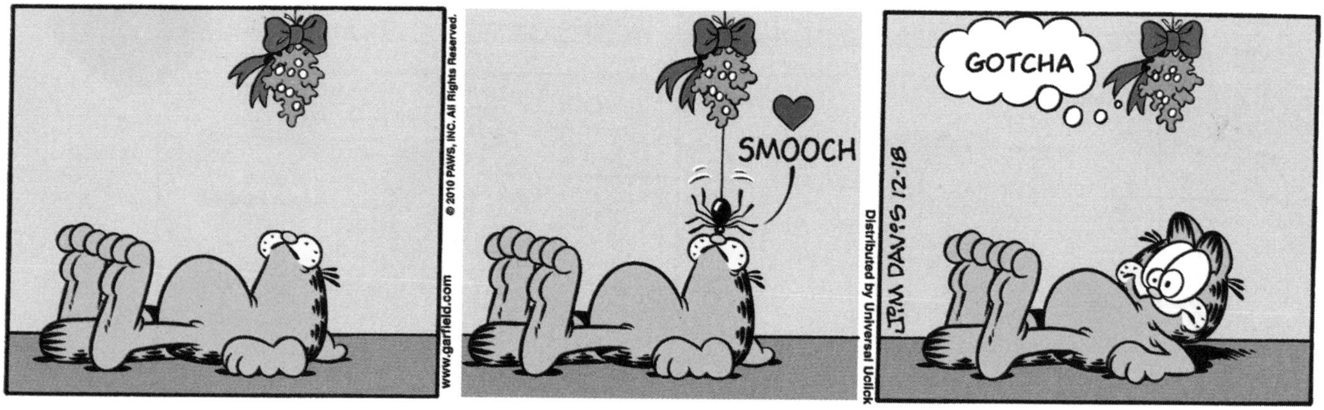
© 2010 PAWS, INC. All Rights Reserved.
www.garfield.com
SMOOCH
JIM DAVIS 12-18
Distributed by Universal Uclick
GOTCHA

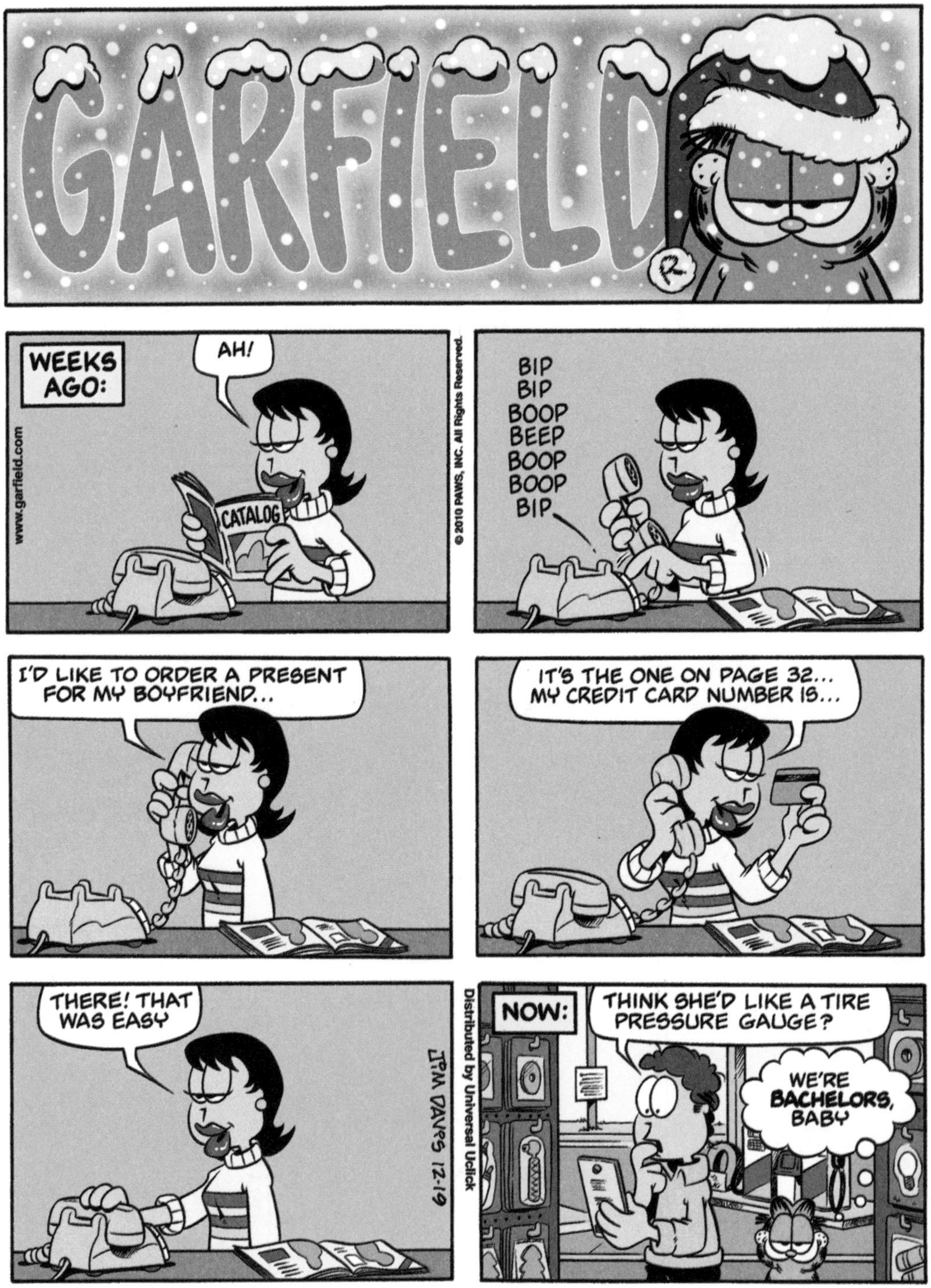
GARFIELD
WEEKS AGO:
AH!
CATALOG
www.garfield.com
© 2010 PAWS, INC. All Rights Reserved.
BIP BIP BOOP BEEP BOOP BOOP BIP
I'D LIKE TO ORDER A PRESENT FOR MY BOYFRIEND...
IT'S THE ONE ON PAGE 32... MY CREDIT CARD NUMBER IS...
THERE! THAT WAS EASY
JPM DAVIS 12-19
Distributed by Universal Uclick
NOW:
THINK SHE'D LIKE A TIRE PRESSURE GAUGE?
WE'RE **BACHELORS,** BABY

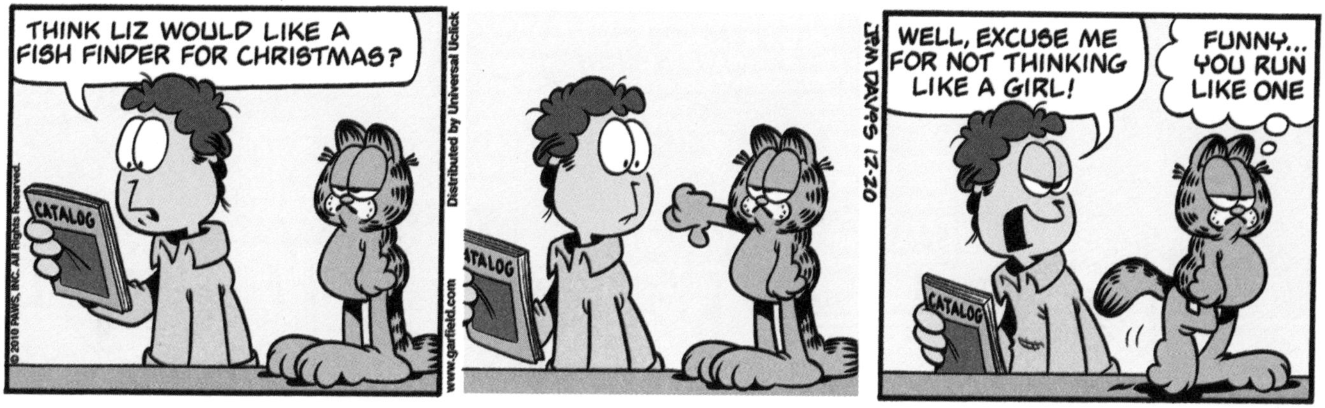
THINK LIZ WOULD LIKE A FISH FINDER FOR CHRISTMAS?
CATALOG
© 2010 PAWS, INC. All Rights Reserved.
Distributed by Universal Uclick
www.garfield.com
JIM DAVIS 12-20
WELL, EXCUSE ME FOR NOT THINKING LIKE A GIRL!
FUNNY... YOU RUN LIKE ONE

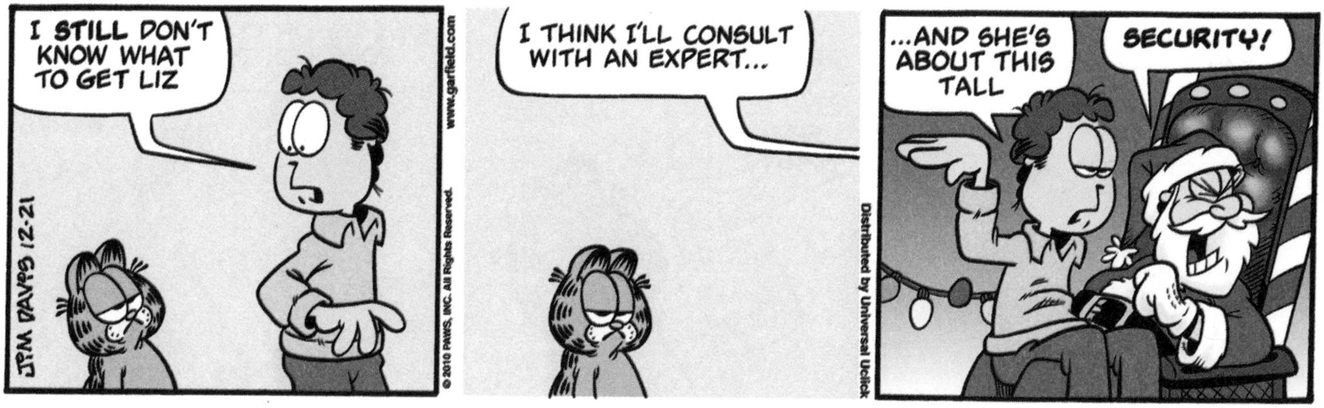
I STILL DON'T KNOW WHAT TO GET LIZ
JIM DAVIS 12-21
www.garfield.com
© 2010 PAWS, INC. All Rights Reserved.
I THINK I'LL CONSULT WITH AN EXPERT...
Distributed by Universal Uclick
...AND SHE'S ABOUT THIS TALL
SECURITY!

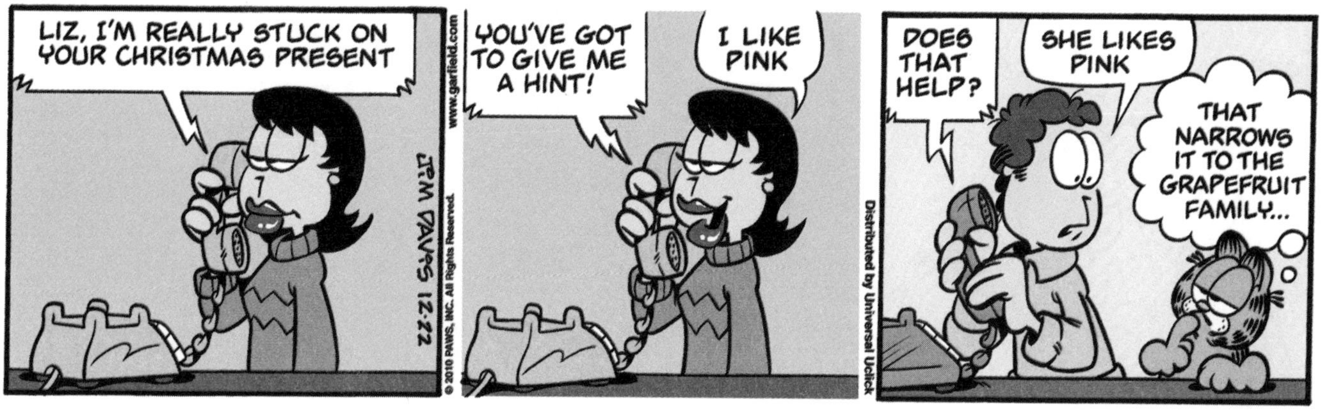
LIZ, I'M REALLY STUCK ON YOUR CHRISTMAS PRESENT
JIM DAVIS 12-22
www.garfield.com
© 2010 PAWS, INC. All Rights Reserved.
YOU'VE GOT TO GIVE ME A HINT!
I LIKE PINK
Distributed by Universal Uclick
DOES THAT HELP?
SHE LIKES PINK
THAT NARROWS IT TO THE GRAPEFRUIT FAMILY...

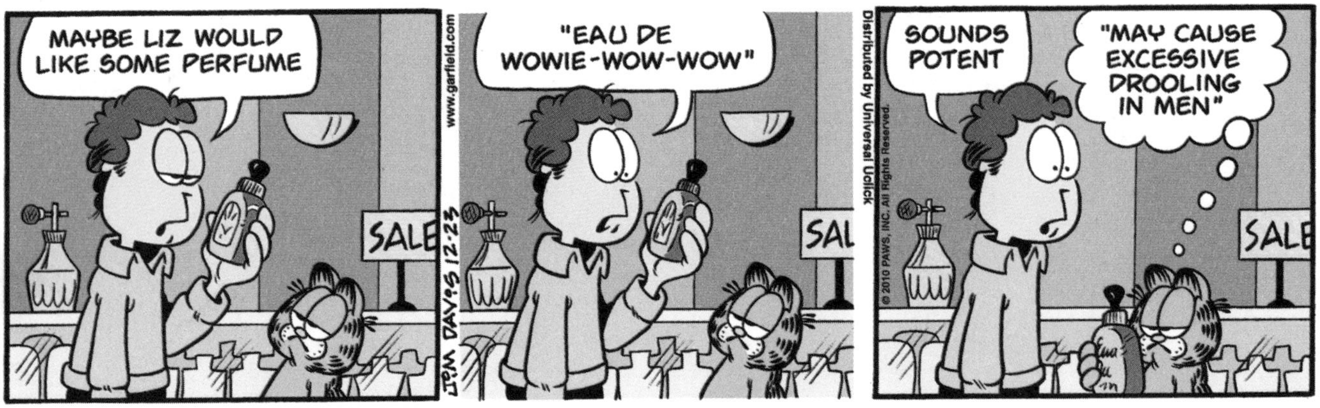
MAYBE LIZ WOULD LIKE SOME PERFUME
SALE
"EAU DE WOWIE-WOW-WOW"
SOUNDS POTENT
"MAY CAUSE EXCESSIVE DROOLING IN MEN"
JIM DAVIS 12-23
www.garfield.com
Distributed by Universal Uclick
© 2010 PAWS, INC. All Rights Reserved.

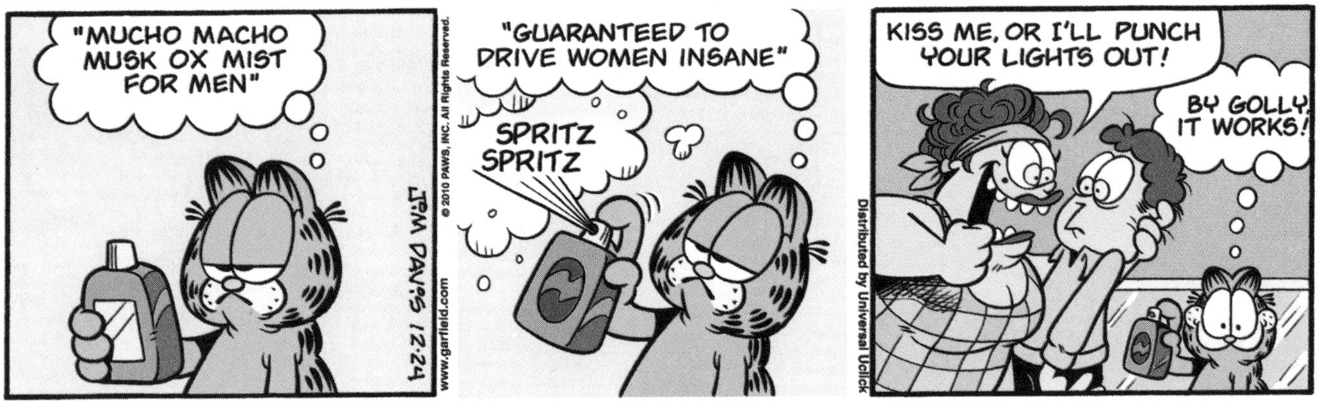
"MUCHO MACHO MUSK OX MIST FOR MEN"
"GUARANTEED TO DRIVE WOMEN INSANE"
SPRITZ SPRITZ
KISS ME, OR I'LL PUNCH YOUR LIGHTS OUT!
BY GOLLY, IT WORKS!
JIM DAVIS 12-24
www.garfield.com
© 2010 PAWS, INC. All Rights Reserved.
Distributed by Universal Uclick

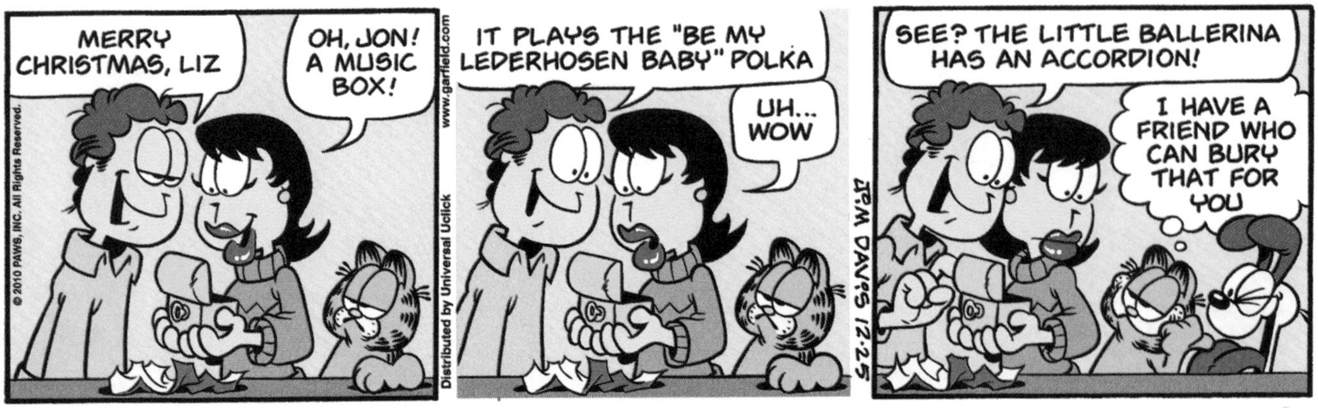
MERRY CHRISTMAS, LIZ
OH, JON! A MUSIC BOX!
IT PLAYS THE "BE MY LEDERHOSEN BABY" POLKA
UH... WOW
SEE? THE LITTLE BALLERINA HAS AN ACCORDION!
I HAVE A FRIEND WHO CAN BURY THAT FOR YOU
JIM DAVIS 12-25
© 2010 PAWS, INC. All Rights Reserved.
www.garfield.com
Distributed by Universal Uclick

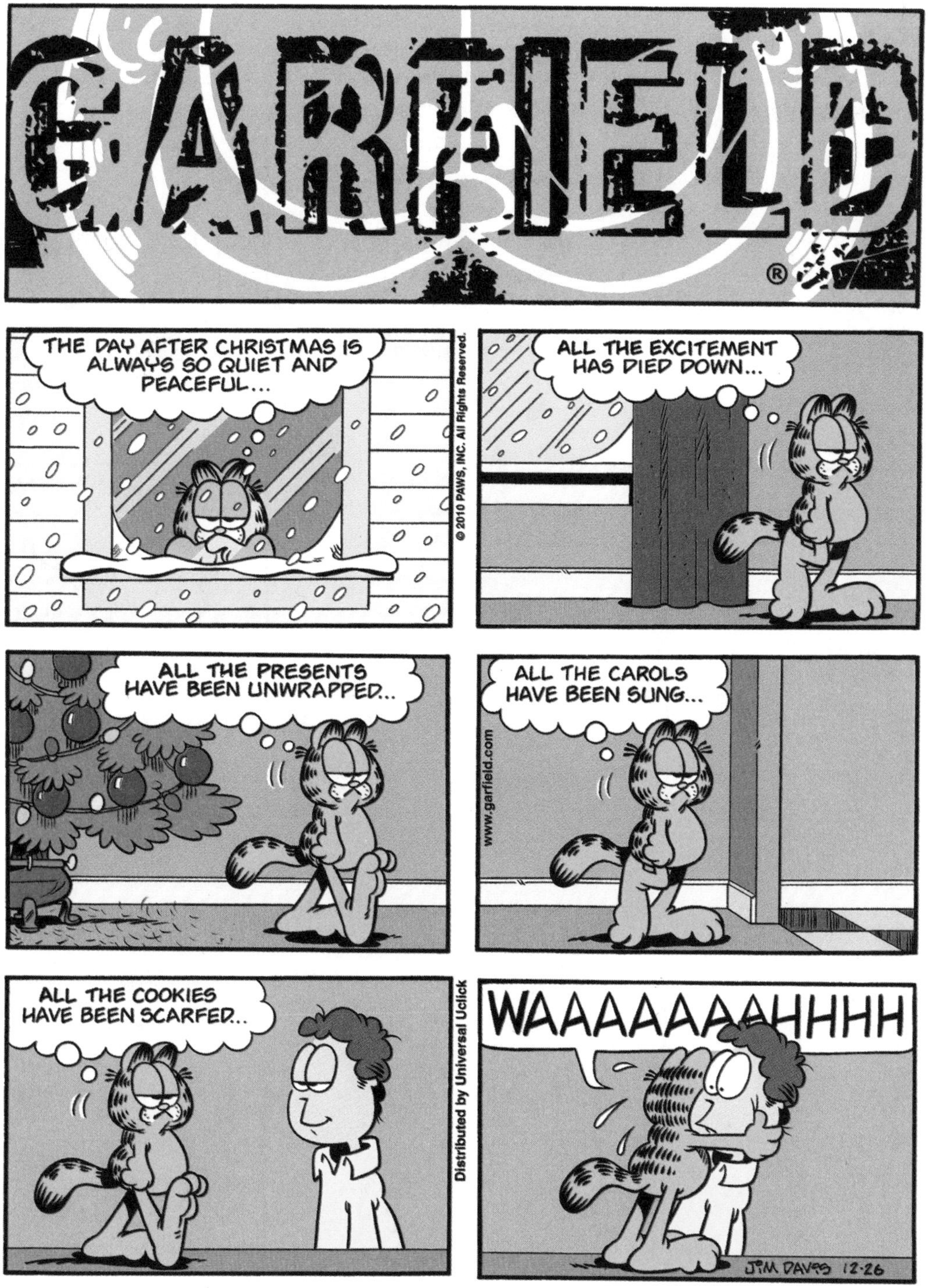
GARFIELD®
THE DAY AFTER CHRISTMAS IS ALWAYS SO QUIET AND PEACEFUL...
© 2010 PAWS, INC. All Rights Reserved.
ALL THE EXCITEMENT HAS DIED DOWN...
ALL THE PRESENTS HAVE BEEN UNWRAPPED...
www.garfield.com
ALL THE CAROLS HAVE BEEN SUNG...
ALL THE COOKIES HAVE BEEN SCARFED...
Distributed by Universal Uclick
WAAAAAAAHHHH
JIM DAVIS 12·26

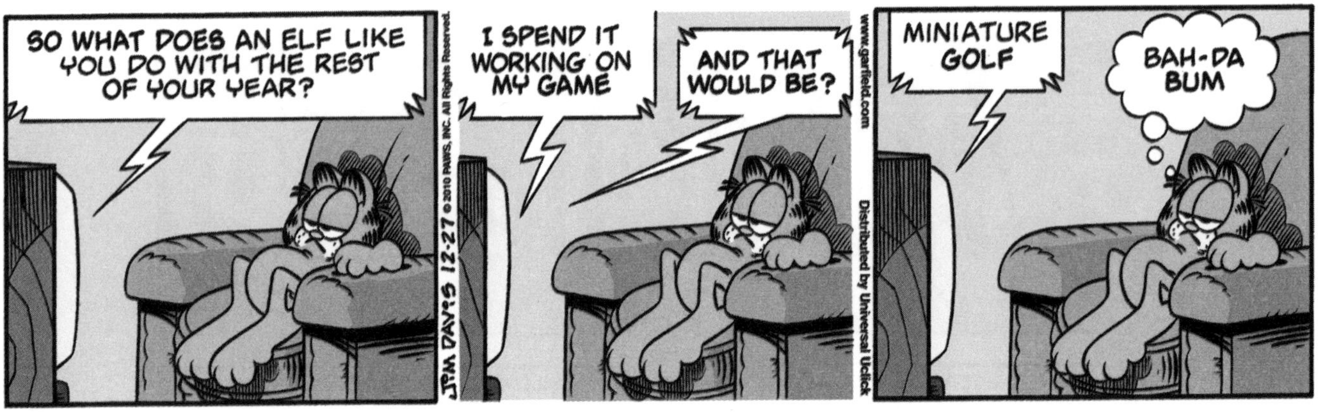
SO WHAT DOES AN ELF LIKE YOU DO WITH THE REST OF YOUR YEAR?
I SPEND IT WORKING ON MY GAME
AND THAT WOULD BE?
MINIATURE GOLF
BAH-DA BUM
JIM DAVIS 12-27
© 2010 PAWS, INC. All Rights Reserved.
www.garfield.com
Distributed by Universal Uclick

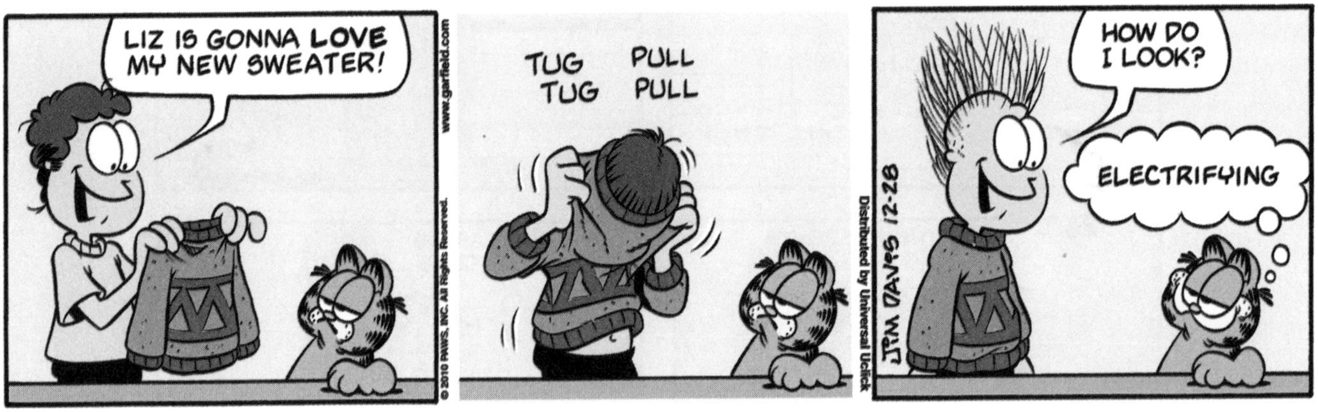
LIZ IS GONNA **LOVE** MY NEW SWEATER!
TUG TUG
PULL PULL
HOW DO I LOOK?
ELECTRIFYING
JIM DAVIS 12-28
© 2010 PAWS, INC. All Rights Reserved.
www.garfield.com
Distributed by Universal Uclick

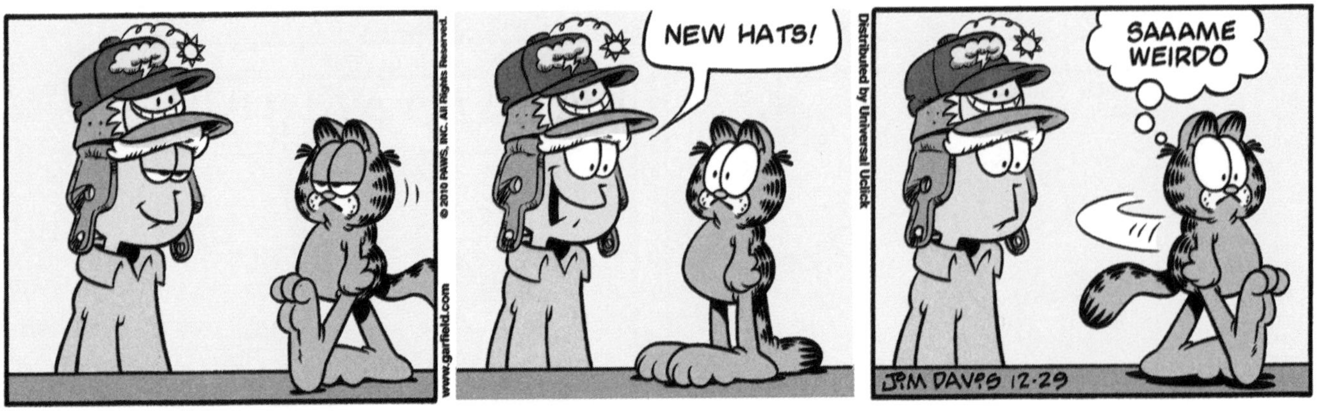
NEW HATS!
SAAAME WEIRDO
JIM DAVIS 12-29
© 2010 PAWS, INC. All Rights Reserved.
www.garfield.com
Distributed by Universal Uclick

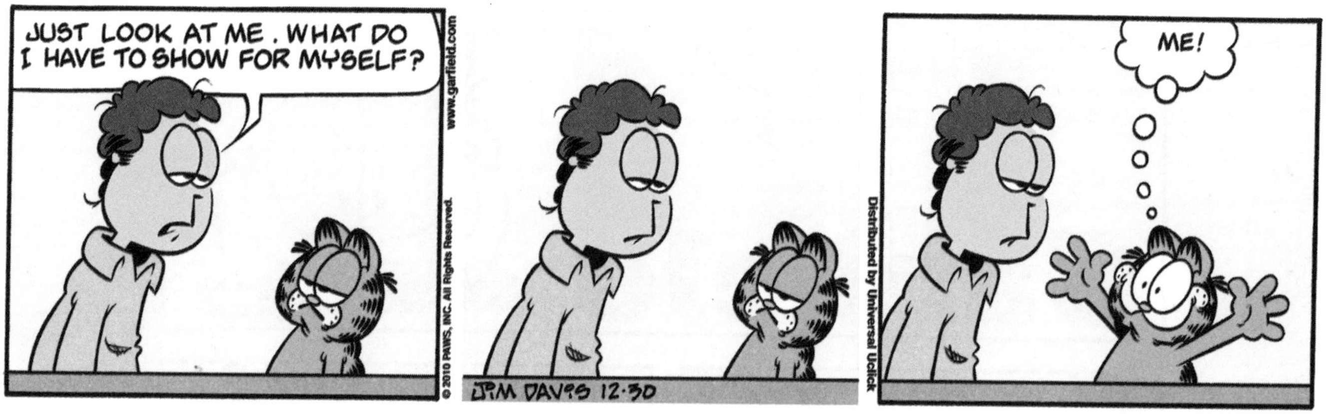
JUST LOOK AT ME. WHAT DO I HAVE TO SHOW FOR MYSELF?
ME!
© 2010 PAWS, INC. All Rights Reserved.
www.garfield.com
JIM DAVIS 12-30
Distributed by Universal Uclick

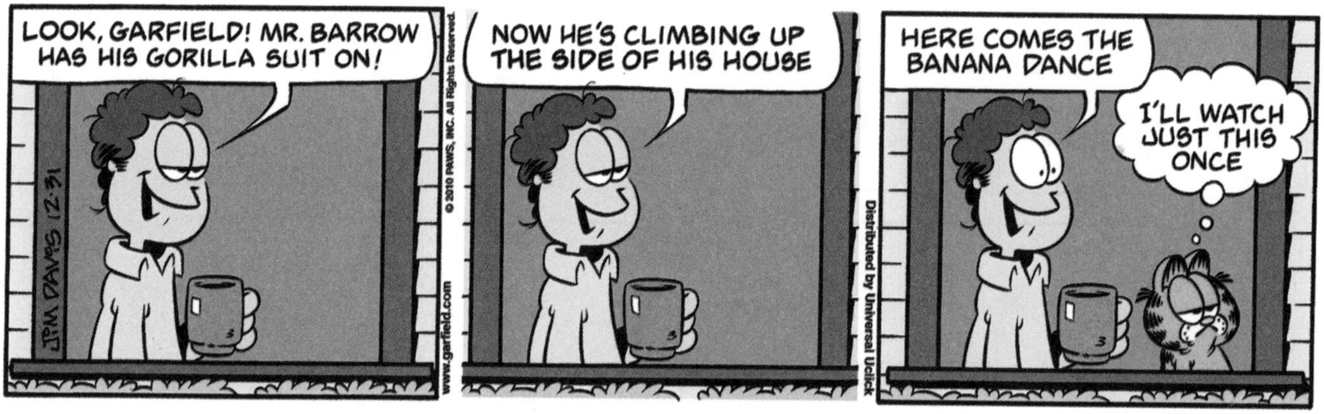
LOOK, GARFIELD! MR. BARROW HAS HIS GORILLA SUIT ON!
JIM DAVIS 12-31
© 2010 PAWS, INC. All Rights Reserved.
www.garfield.com
NOW HE'S CLIMBING UP THE SIDE OF HIS HOUSE
Distributed by Universal Uclick
HERE COMES THE BANANA DANCE
I'LL WATCH JUST THIS ONCE

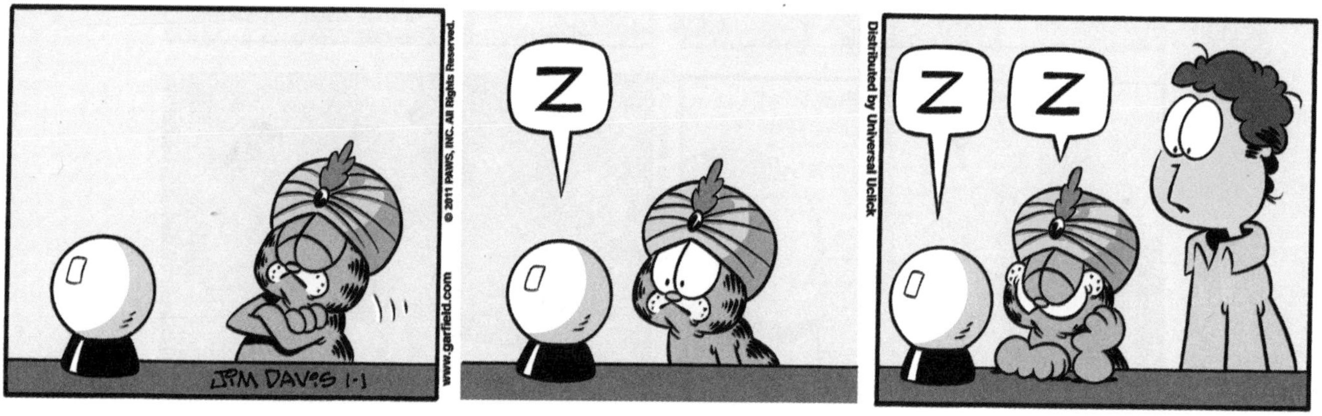
JIM DAVIS 1-1
© 2011 PAWS, INC. All Rights Reserved.
www.garfield.com
Z
Distributed by Universal Uclick
Z
Z

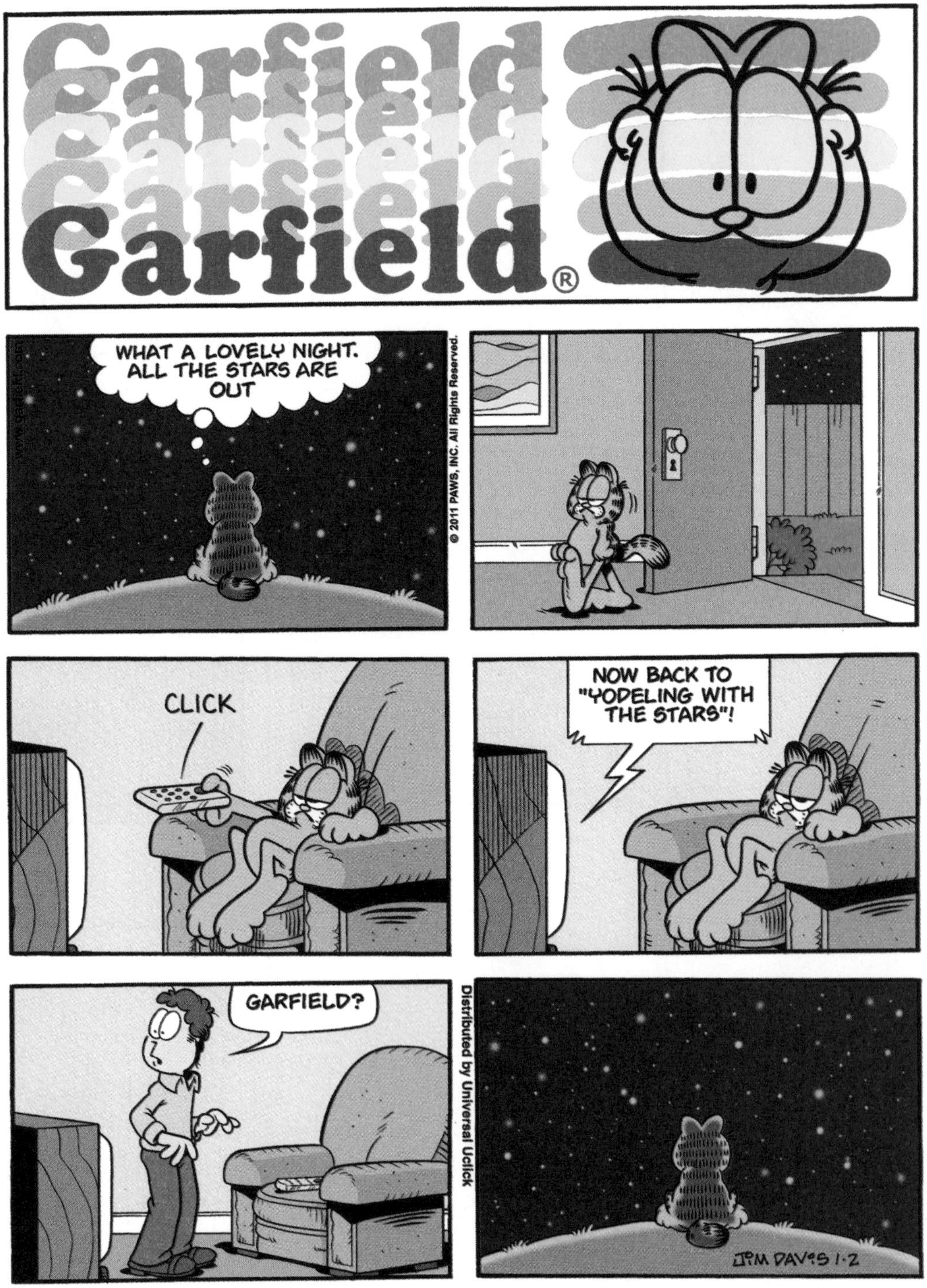
Garfield
WHAT A LOVELY NIGHT. ALL THE STARS ARE OUT
CLICK
NOW BACK TO "YODELING WITH THE STARS"!
GARFIELD?
© 2011 PAWS, INC. All Rights Reserved.
Distributed by Universal Uclick
JIM DAVIS 1-2

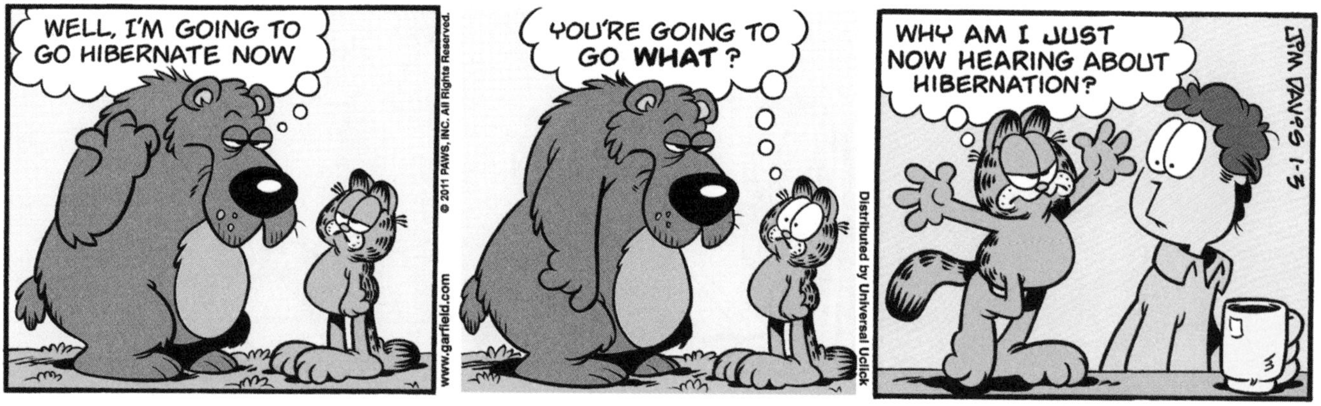
WELL, I'M GOING TO GO HIBERNATE NOW
www.garfield.com
© 2011 PAWS, INC. All Rights Reserved.
YOU'RE GOING TO GO **WHAT**?
Distributed by Universal Uclick
WHY AM I JUST NOW HEARING ABOUT HIBERNATION?

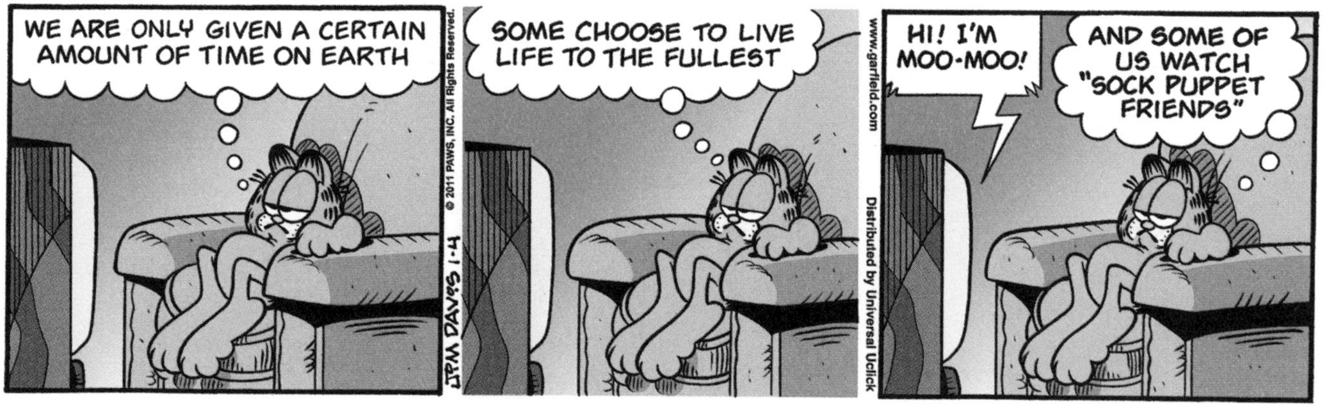
WE ARE ONLY GIVEN A CERTAIN AMOUNT OF TIME ON EARTH
© 2011 PAWS, INC. All Rights Reserved.
SOME CHOOSE TO LIVE LIFE TO THE FULLEST
www.garfield.com
Distributed by Universal Uclick
HI! I'M MOO-MOO!
AND SOME OF US WATCH "SOCK PUPPET FRIENDS"

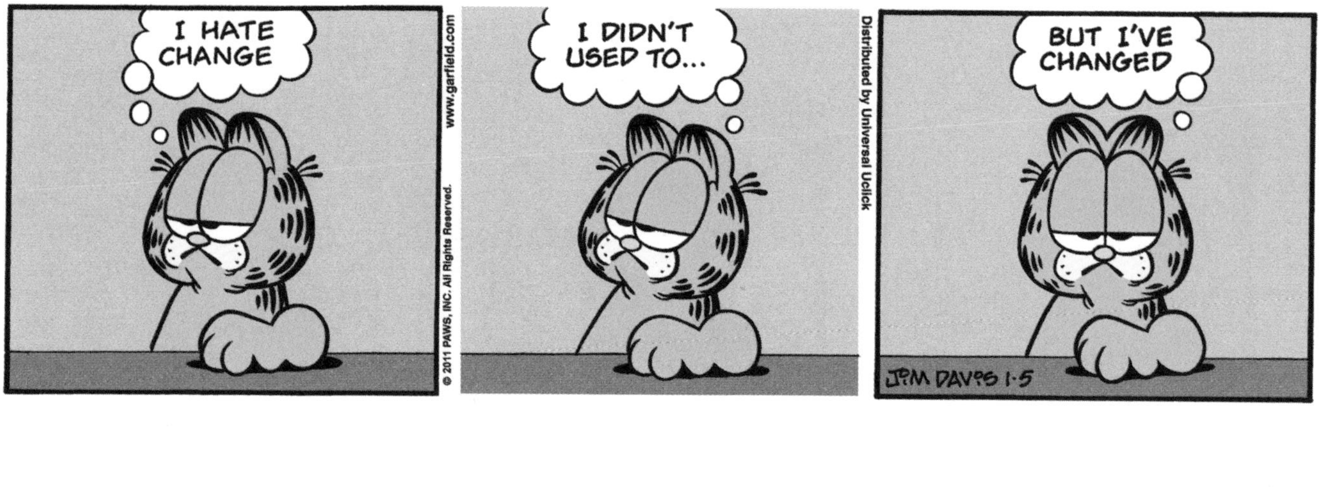
I HATE CHANGE
www.garfield.com
© 2011 PAWS, INC. All Rights Reserved.
I DIDN'T USED TO...
Distributed by Universal Uclick
BUT I'VE CHANGED

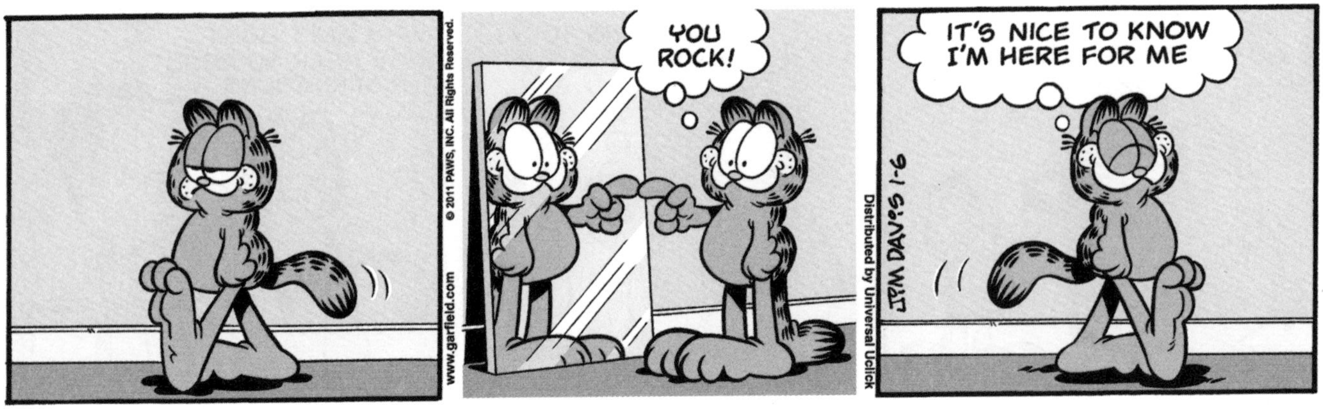
YOU ROCK!
IT'S NICE TO KNOW I'M HERE FOR ME
© 2011 PAWS, INC. All Rights Reserved.
www.garfield.com
Distributed by Universal Uclick

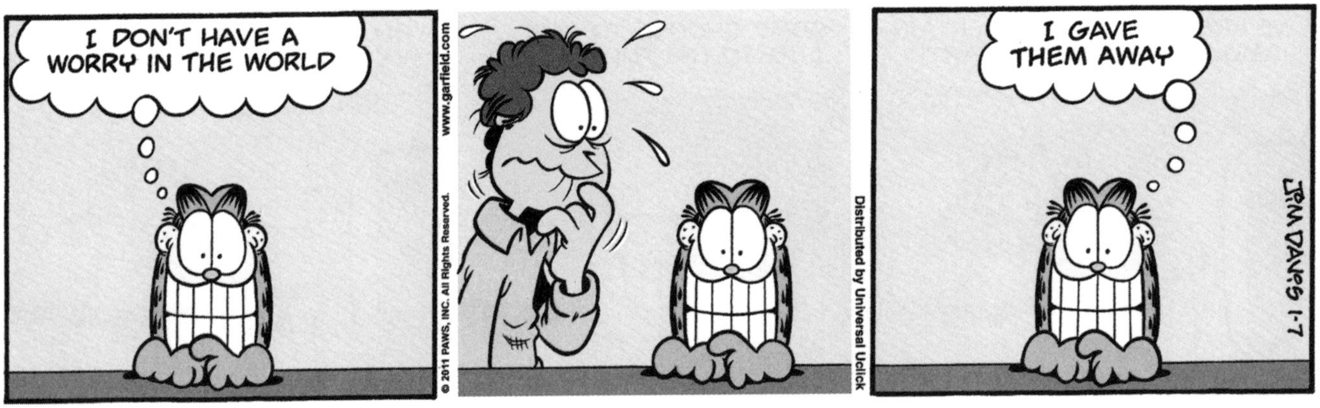
I DON'T HAVE A WORRY IN THE WORLD
I GAVE THEM AWAY
© 2011 PAWS, INC. All Rights Reserved.
www.garfield.com
Distributed by Universal Uclick

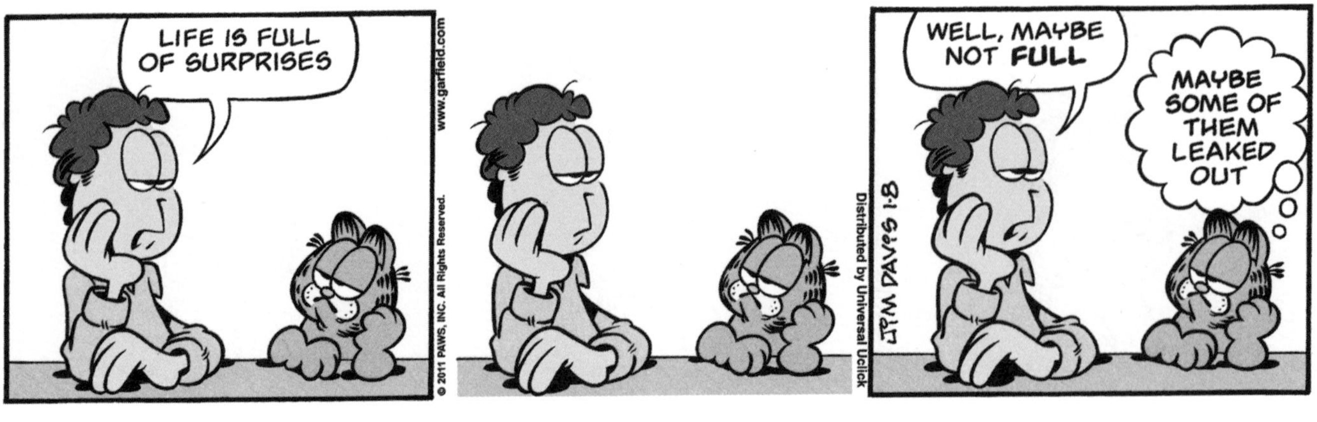
LIFE IS FULL OF SURPRISES
WELL, MAYBE NOT **FULL**
MAYBE SOME OF THEM LEAKED OUT
© 2011 PAWS, INC. All Rights Reserved.
www.garfield.com
Distributed by Universal Uclick

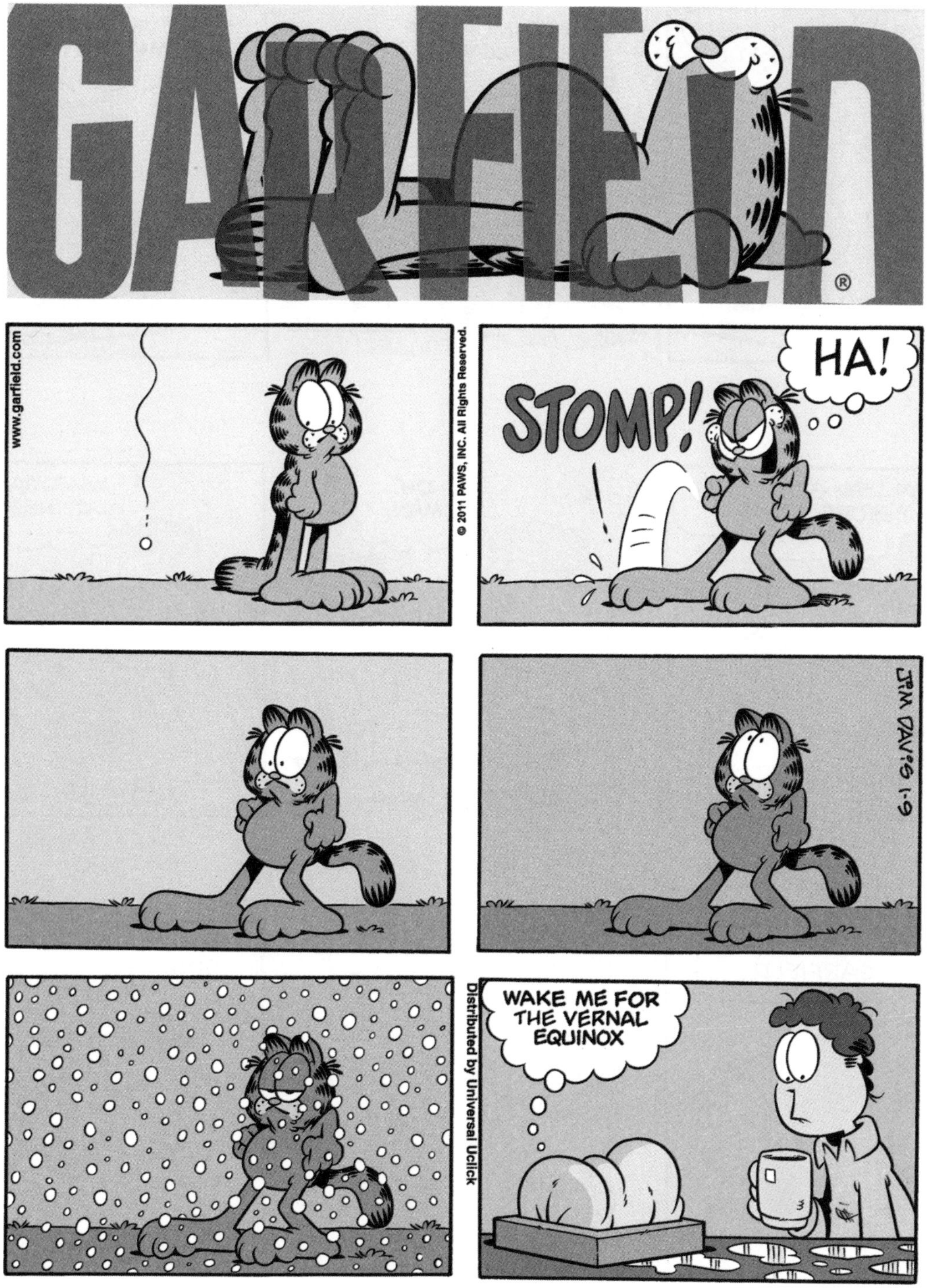
GARFIELD®
www.garfield.com
© 2011 PAWS, INC. All Rights Reserved.
STOMP!
HA!
JIM DAVIS 1-9
Distributed by Universal Uclick
WAKE ME FOR THE VERNAL EQUINOX

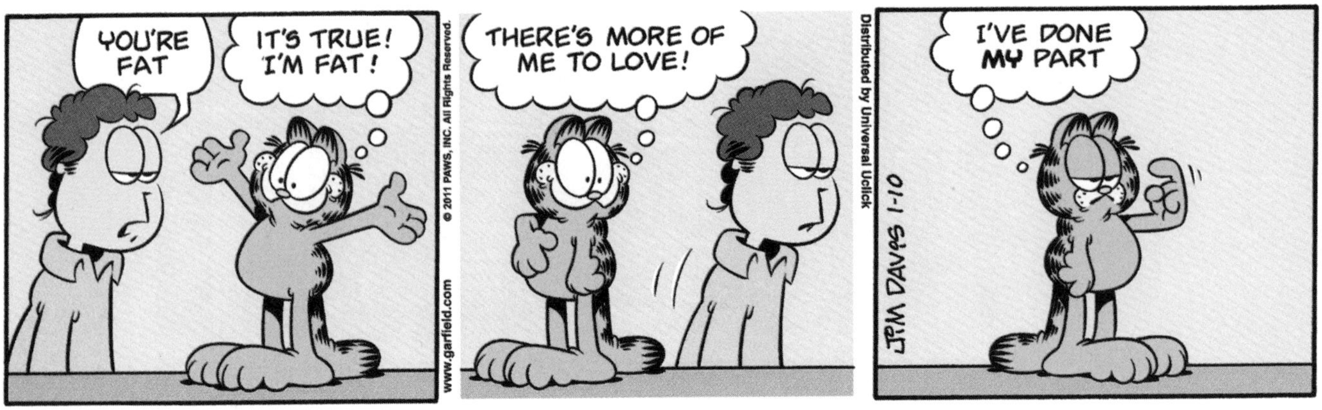
YOU'RE FAT
IT'S TRUE! I'M FAT!
THERE'S MORE OF ME TO LOVE!
I'VE DONE **MY** PART
© 2011 PAWS, INC. All Rights Reserved.
www.garfield.com
Distributed by Universal Uclick
JIM DAVIS 1-10

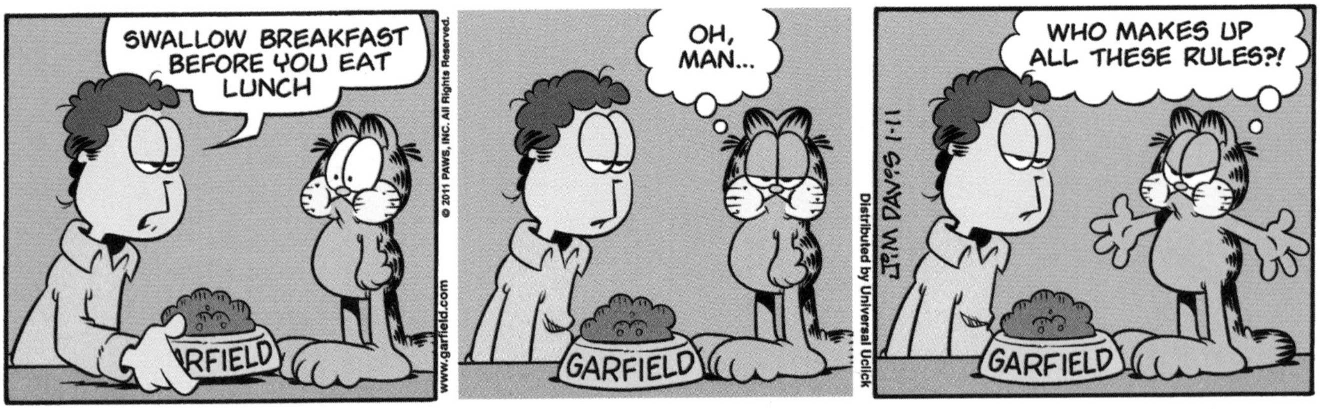
SWALLOW BREAKFAST BEFORE YOU EAT LUNCH
OH, MAN...
WHO MAKES UP ALL THESE RULES?!
GARFIELD
© 2011 PAWS, INC. All Rights Reserved.
www.garfield.com
Distributed by Universal Uclick
JIM DAVIS 1-11

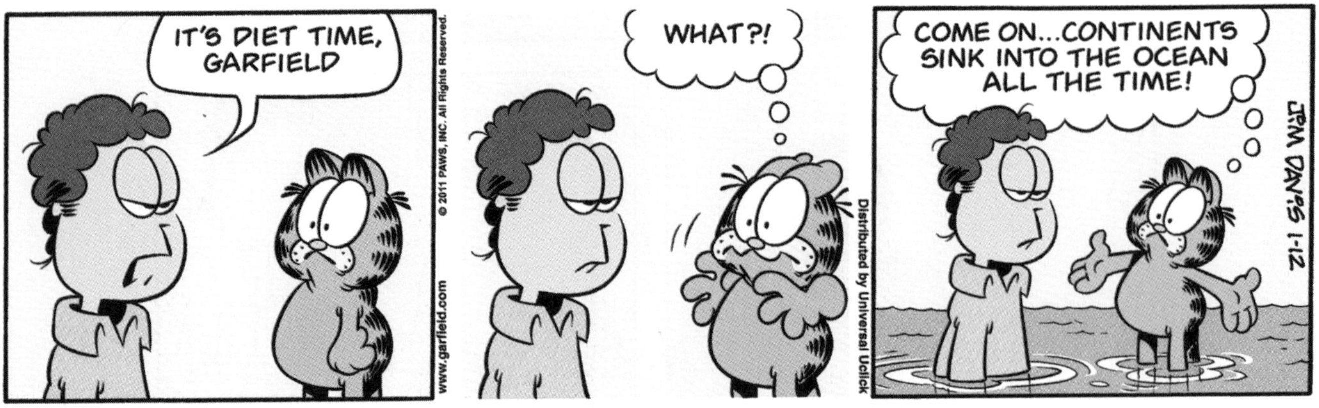
IT'S DIET TIME, GARFIELD
WHAT?!
COME ON...CONTINENTS SINK INTO THE OCEAN ALL THE TIME!
© 2011 PAWS, INC. All Rights Reserved.
www.garfield.com
Distributed by Universal Uclick
JIM DAVIS 1-12

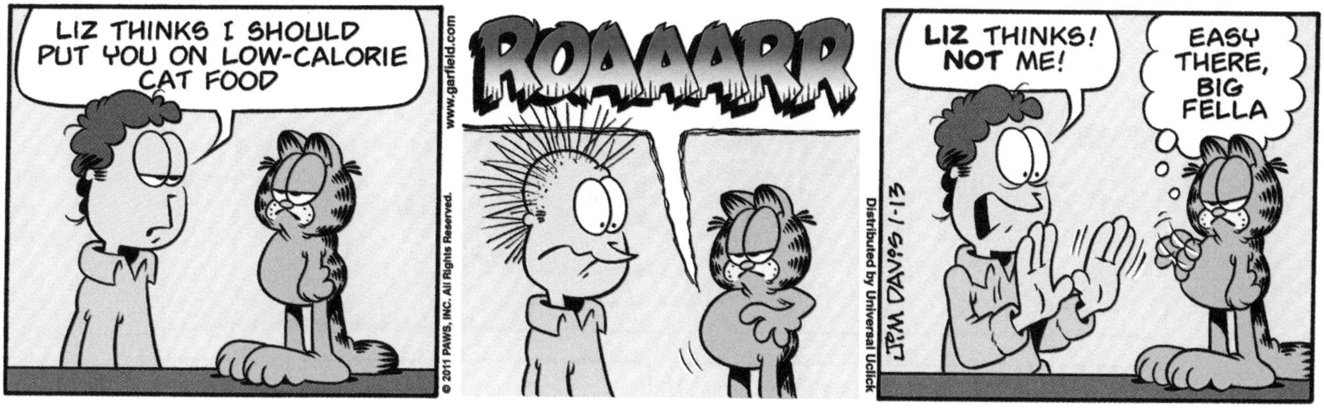
LIZ THINKS I SHOULD PUT YOU ON LOW-CALORIE CAT FOOD
ROAAARR
LIZ THINKS! NOT ME!
EASY THERE, BIG FELLA
© 2011 PAWS, INC. All Rights Reserved. www.garfield.com
Distributed by Universal Uclick
JIM DAVIS 1-13

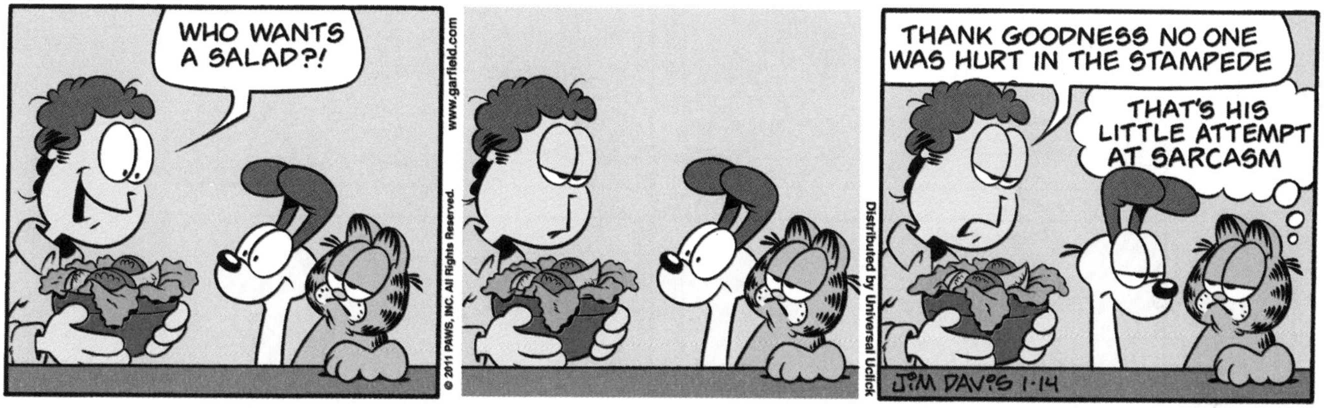
WHO WANTS A SALAD?!
THANK GOODNESS NO ONE WAS HURT IN THE STAMPEDE
THAT'S HIS LITTLE ATTEMPT AT SARCASM
© 2011 PAWS, INC. All Rights Reserved. www.garfield.com
Distributed by Universal Uclick
JIM DAVIS 1-14

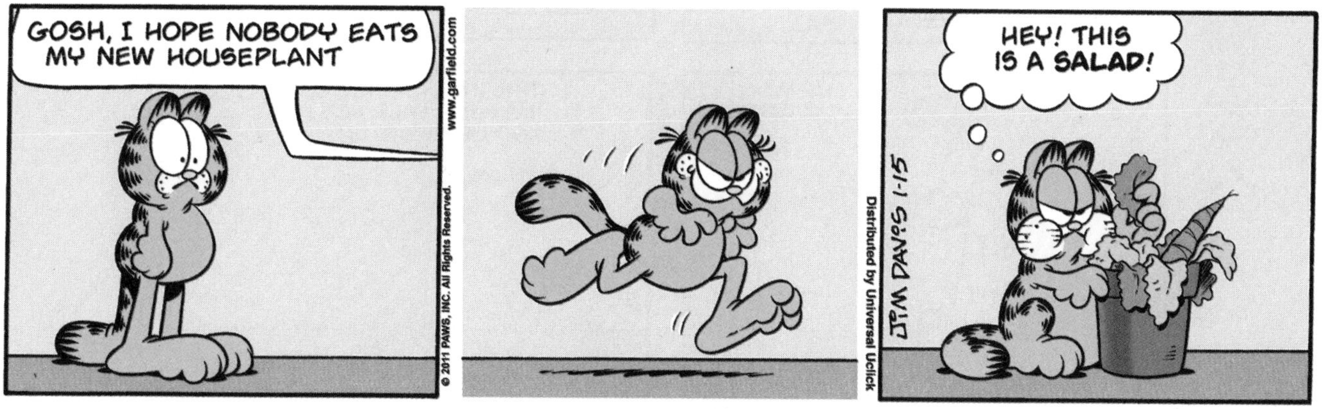
GOSH, I HOPE NOBODY EATS MY NEW HOUSEPLANT
HEY! THIS IS A SALAD!
© 2011 PAWS, INC. All Rights Reserved. www.garfield.com
Distributed by Universal Uclick
JIM DAVIS 1-15

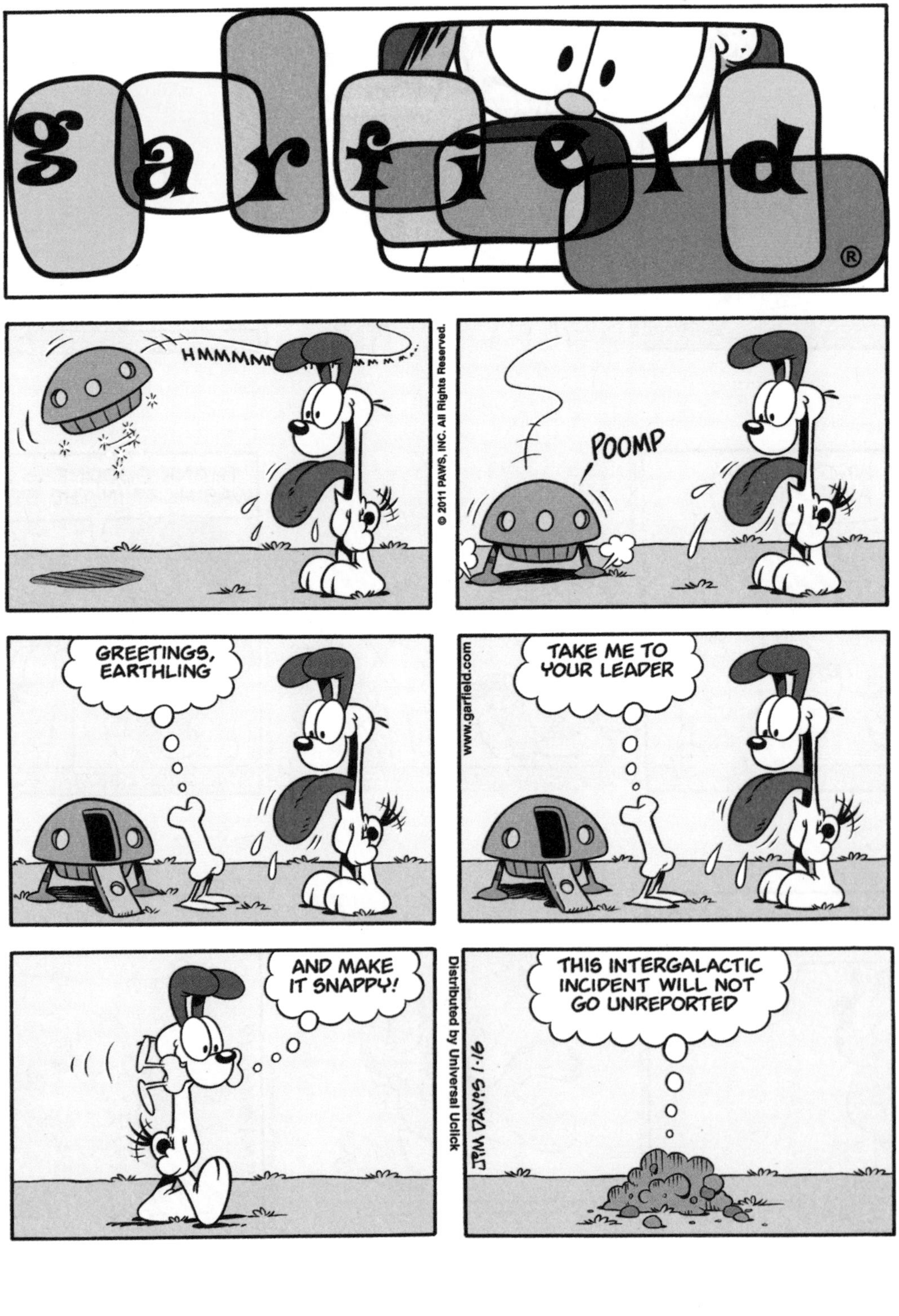
garfield
HMMMMM
© 2011 PAWS, INC. All Rights Reserved.
POOMP
GREETINGS, EARTHLING
www.garfield.com
TAKE ME TO YOUR LEADER
AND MAKE IT SNAPPY!
Distributed by Universal Uclick
JPM DAVOS 1-16
THIS INTERGALACTIC INCIDENT WILL NOT GO UNREPORTED

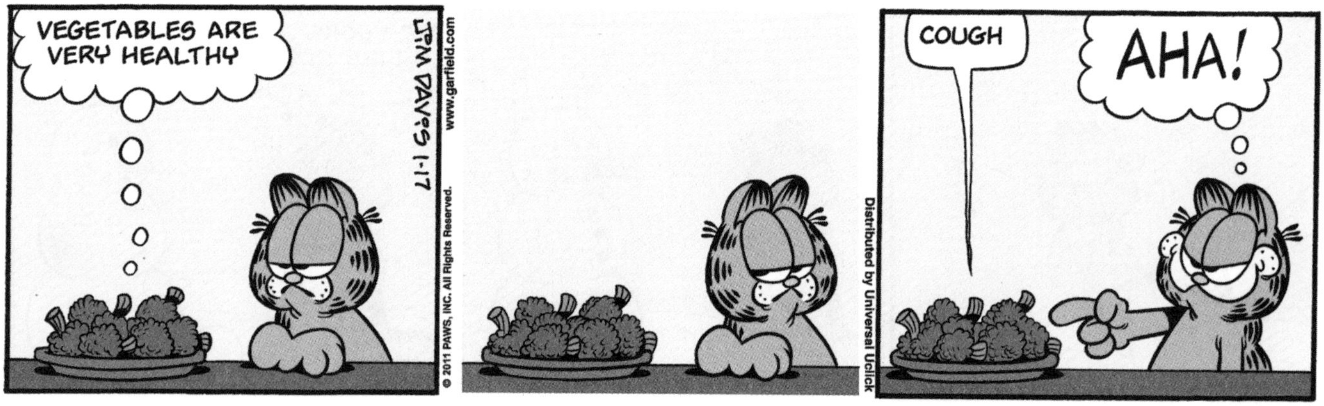
VEGETABLES ARE VERY HEALTHY
JIM DAVIS 1-17
www.garfield.com
© 2011 PAWS, INC. All Rights Reserved.
Distributed by Universal Uclick
COUGH
AHA!

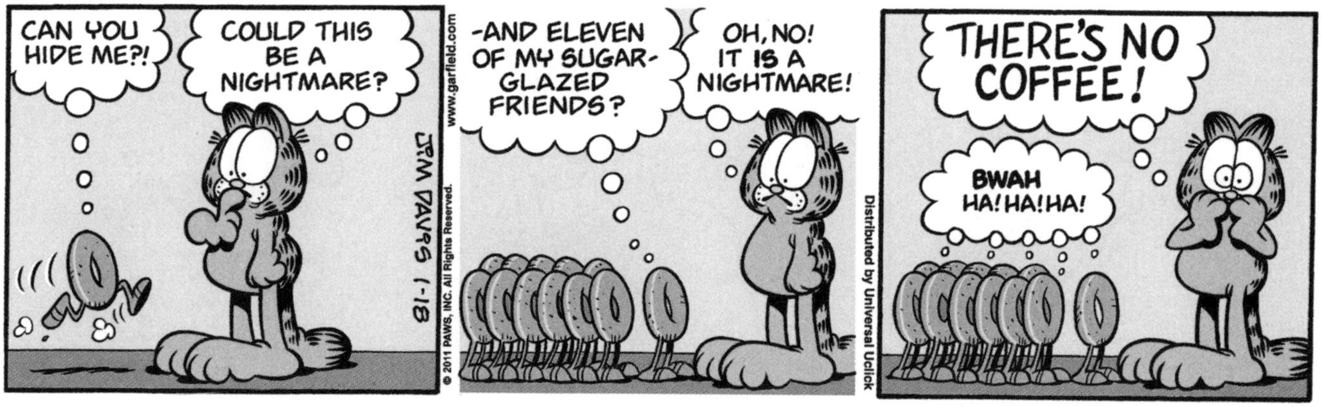
CAN YOU HIDE ME?!
COULD THIS BE A NIGHTMARE?
JIM DAVIS 1-18
www.garfield.com
© 2011 PAWS, INC. All Rights Reserved.
-AND ELEVEN OF MY SUGAR-GLAZED FRIENDS?
OH, NO! IT IS A NIGHTMARE!
Distributed by Universal Uclick
THERE'S NO COFFEE!
BWAH HA! HA! HA!

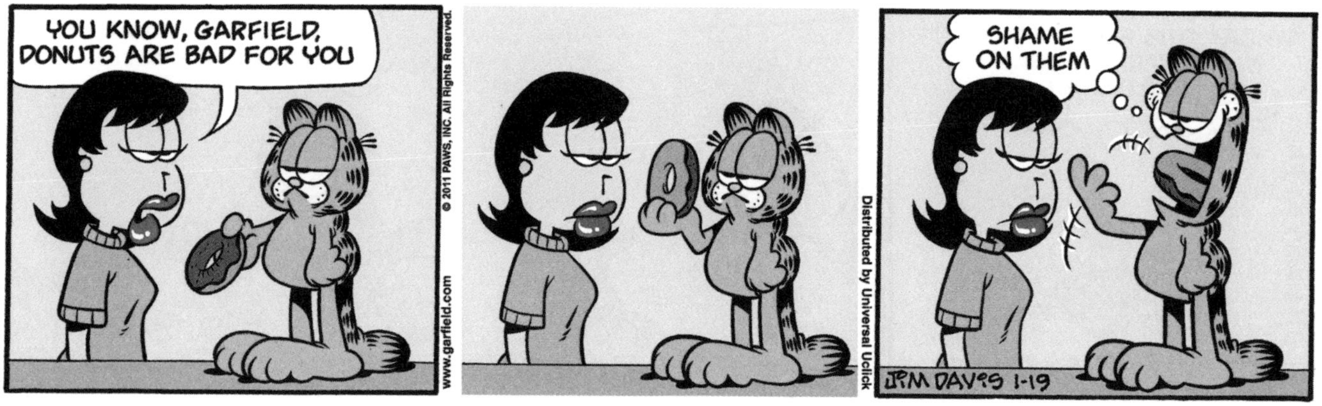
YOU KNOW, GARFIELD, DONUTS ARE BAD FOR YOU
www.garfield.com
© 2011 PAWS, INC. All Rights Reserved.
Distributed by Universal Uclick
SHAME ON THEM
JIM DAVIS 1-19

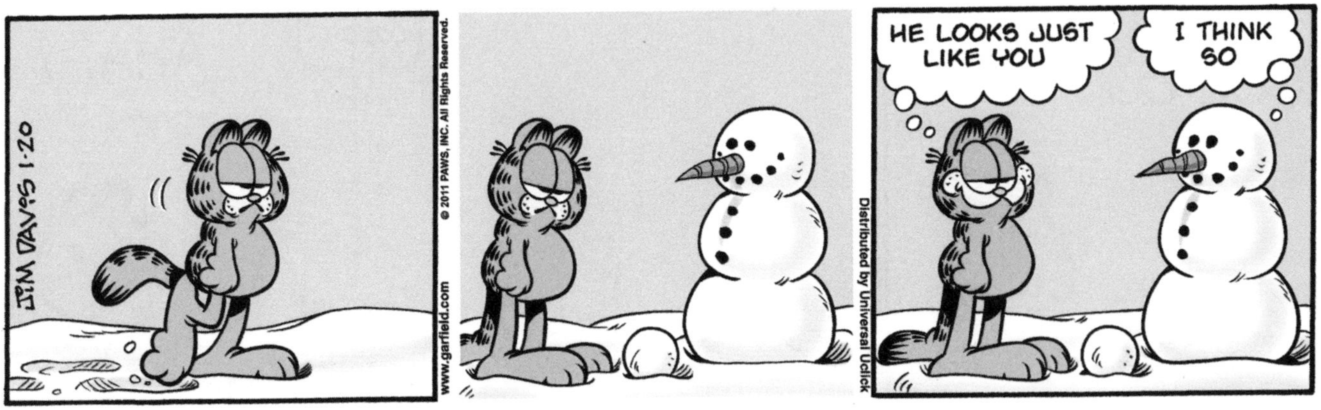
JIM DAVIS 1-20
© 2011 PAWS, INC. All Rights Reserved.
www.garfield.com
HE LOOKS JUST LIKE YOU
I THINK SO
Distributed by Universal Uclick

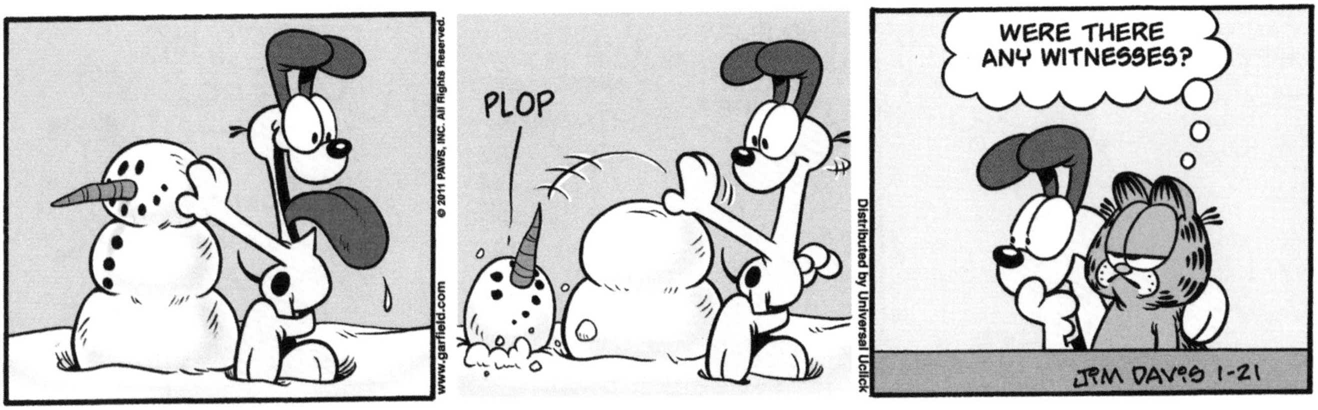
© 2011 PAWS, INC. All Rights Reserved.
www.garfield.com
PLOP
Distributed by Universal Uclick
WERE THERE ANY WITNESSES?
JIM DAVIS 1-21

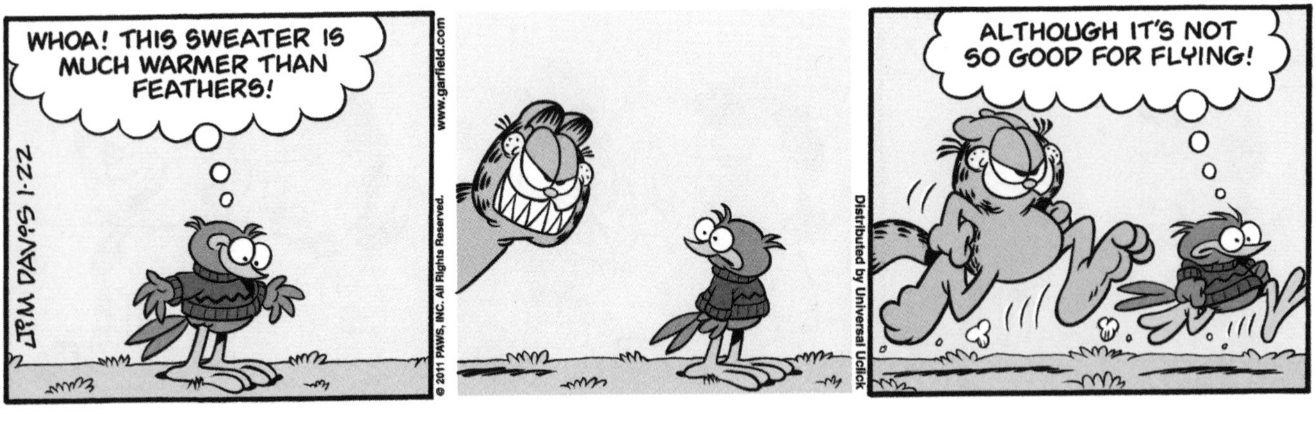
WHOA! THIS SWEATER IS MUCH WARMER THAN FEATHERS!
JIM DAVIS 1-22
www.garfield.com
© 2011 PAWS, INC. All Rights Reserved.
Distributed by Universal Uclick
ALTHOUGH IT'S NOT SO GOOD FOR FLYING!

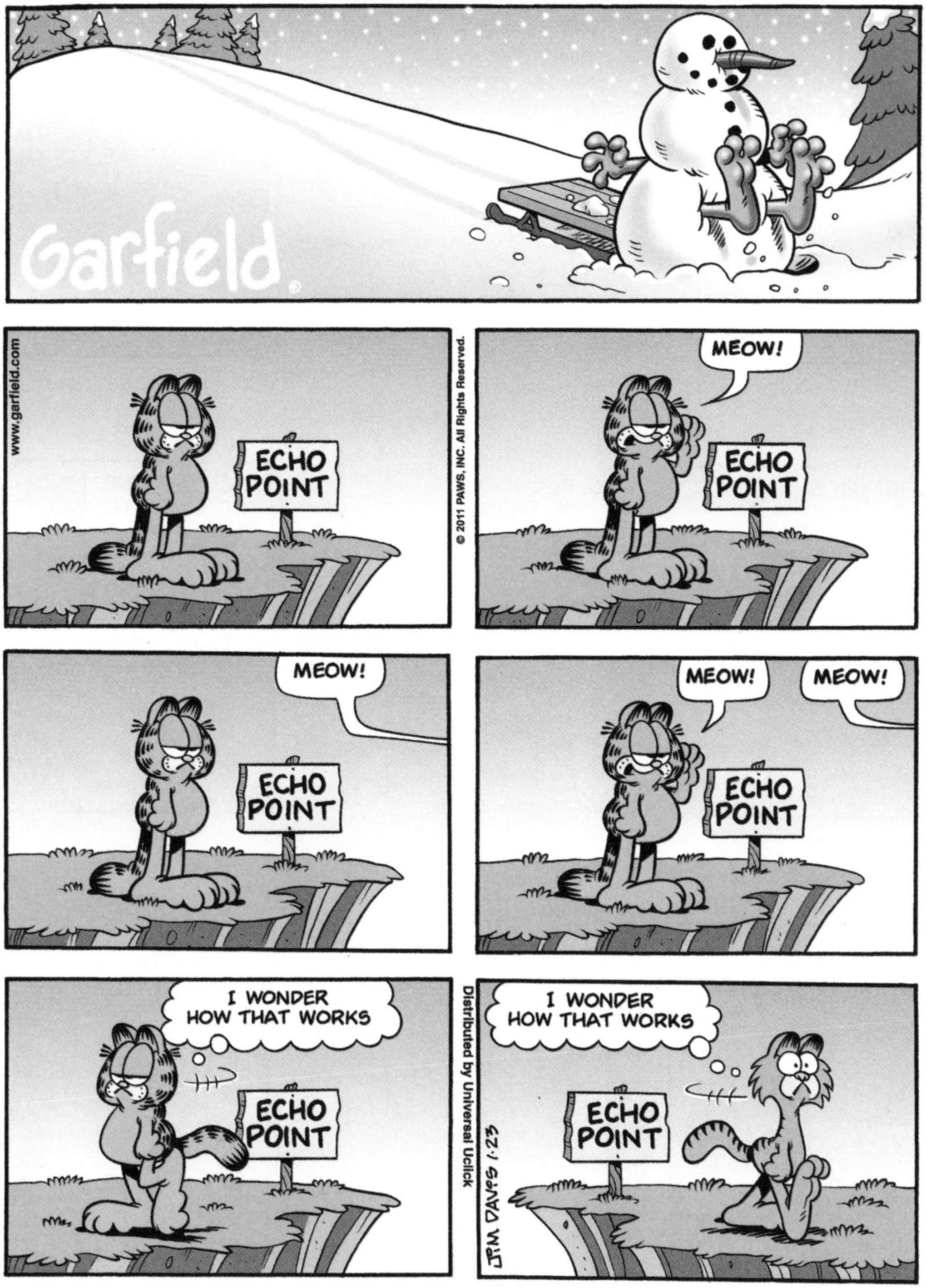
Garfield
www.garfield.com
© 2011 PAWS, INC. All Rights Reserved.
ECHO POINT
MEOW!
MEOW!
MEOW!
MEOW!
I WONDER HOW THAT WORKS
I WONDER HOW THAT WORKS
Distributed by Universal Uclick
JPM DAVIS 1-23

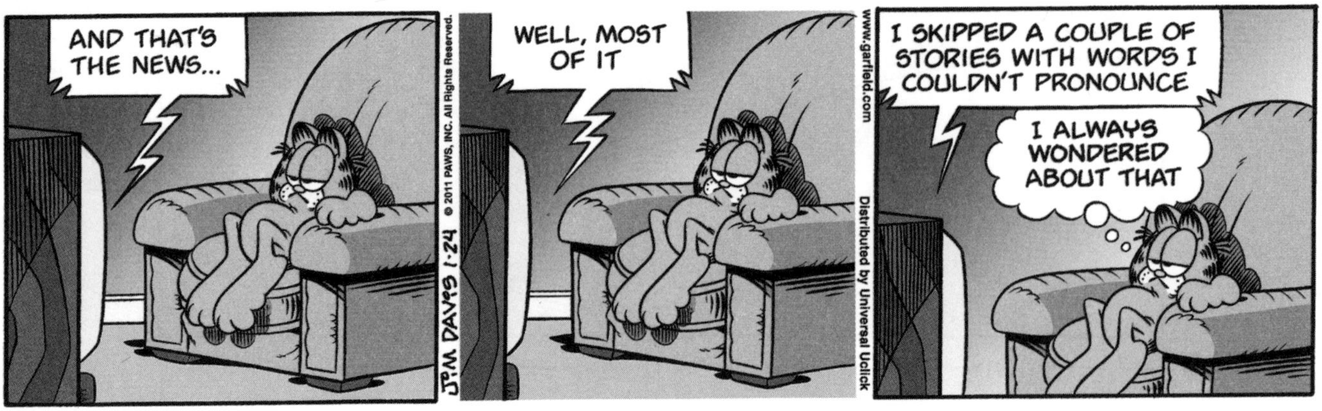
AND THAT'S THE NEWS...
JIM DAVIS 1·24
© 2011 PAWS, INC. All Rights Reserved.
WELL, MOST OF IT
www.garfield.com
Distributed by Universal Uclick
I SKIPPED A COUPLE OF STORIES WITH WORDS I COULDN'T PRONOUNCE
I ALWAYS WONDERED ABOUT THAT

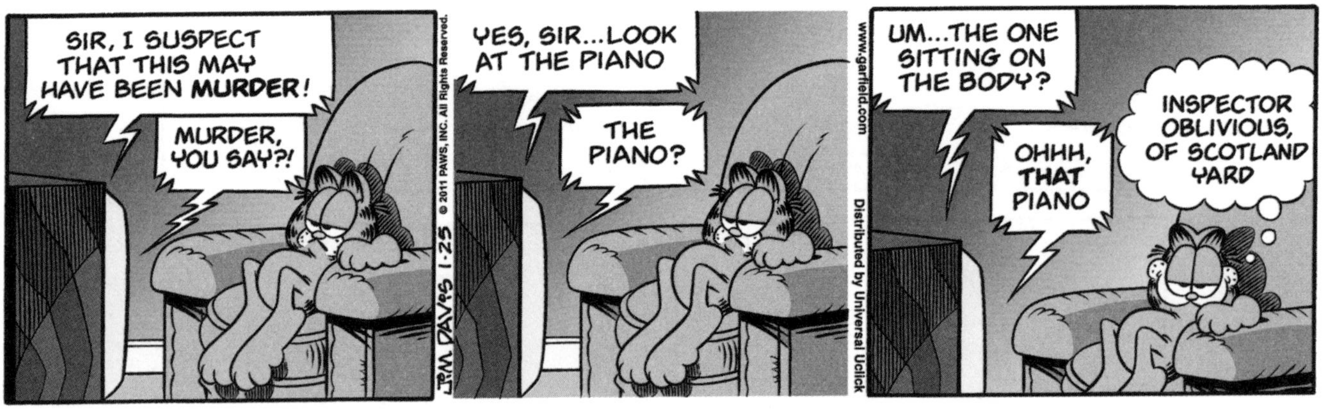
SIR, I SUSPECT THAT THIS MAY HAVE BEEN **MURDER**!
MURDER, YOU SAY?!
JIM DAVIS 1·25
© 2011 PAWS, INC. All Rights Reserved.
YES, SIR...LOOK AT THE PIANO
THE PIANO?
www.garfield.com
Distributed by Universal Uclick
UM...THE ONE SITTING ON THE BODY?
OHHH, **THAT** PIANO
INSPECTOR OBLIVIOUS, OF SCOTLAND YARD

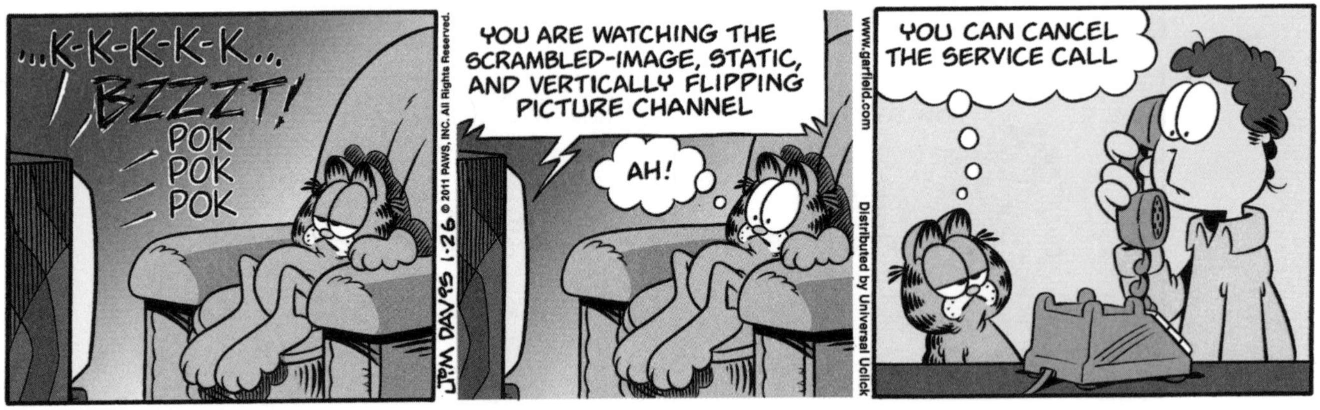
...K-K-K-K-K...
BZZZT!
POK
POK
POK
JIM DAVIS 1·26
© 2011 PAWS, INC. All Rights Reserved.
YOU ARE WATCHING THE SCRAMBLED-IMAGE, STATIC, AND VERTICALLY FLIPPING PICTURE CHANNEL
AH!
www.garfield.com
Distributed by Universal Uclick
YOU CAN CANCEL THE SERVICE CALL

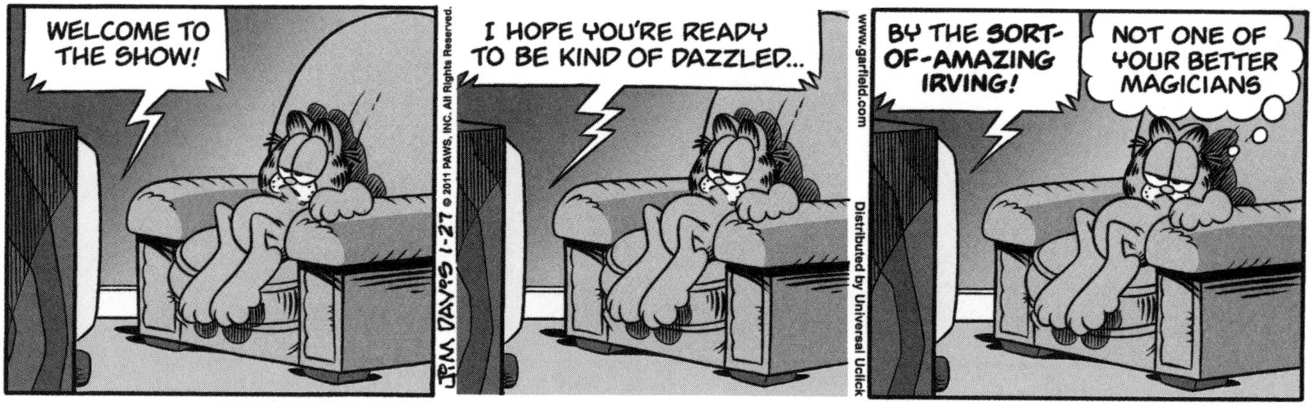
WELCOME TO THE SHOW!
JIM DAVIS 1-27 © 2011 PAWS, INC. All Rights Reserved.
I HOPE YOU'RE READY TO BE KIND OF DAZZLED...
www.garfield.com Distributed by Universal Uclick
BY THE SORT-OF-AMAZING IRVING!
NOT ONE OF YOUR BETTER MAGICIANS

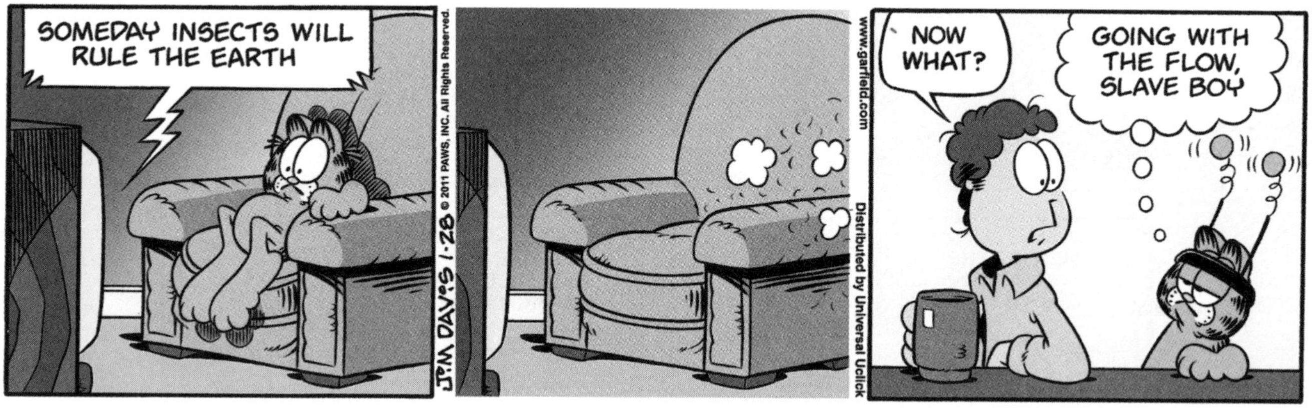
SOMEDAY INSECTS WILL RULE THE EARTH
JIM DAVIS 1-28 © 2011 PAWS, INC. All Rights Reserved.
www.garfield.com Distributed by Universal Uclick
NOW WHAT?
GOING WITH THE FLOW, SLAVE BOY

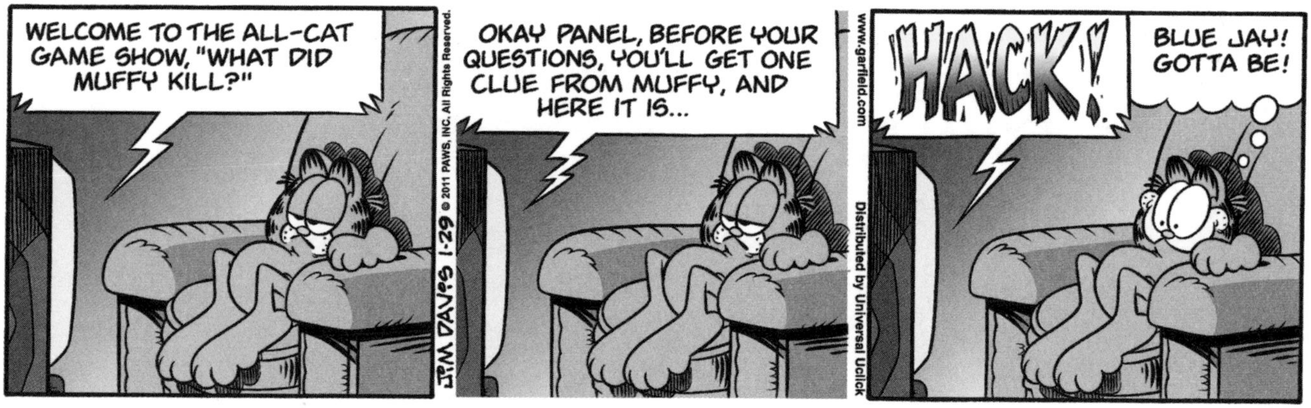
WELCOME TO THE ALL-CAT GAME SHOW, "WHAT DID MUFFY KILL?"
JIM DAVIS 1-29 © 2011 PAWS, INC. All Rights Reserved.
OKAY PANEL, BEFORE YOUR QUESTIONS, YOU'LL GET ONE CLUE FROM MUFFY, AND HERE IT IS...
www.garfield.com Distributed by Universal Uclick
HACK!
BLUE JAY! GOTTA BE!

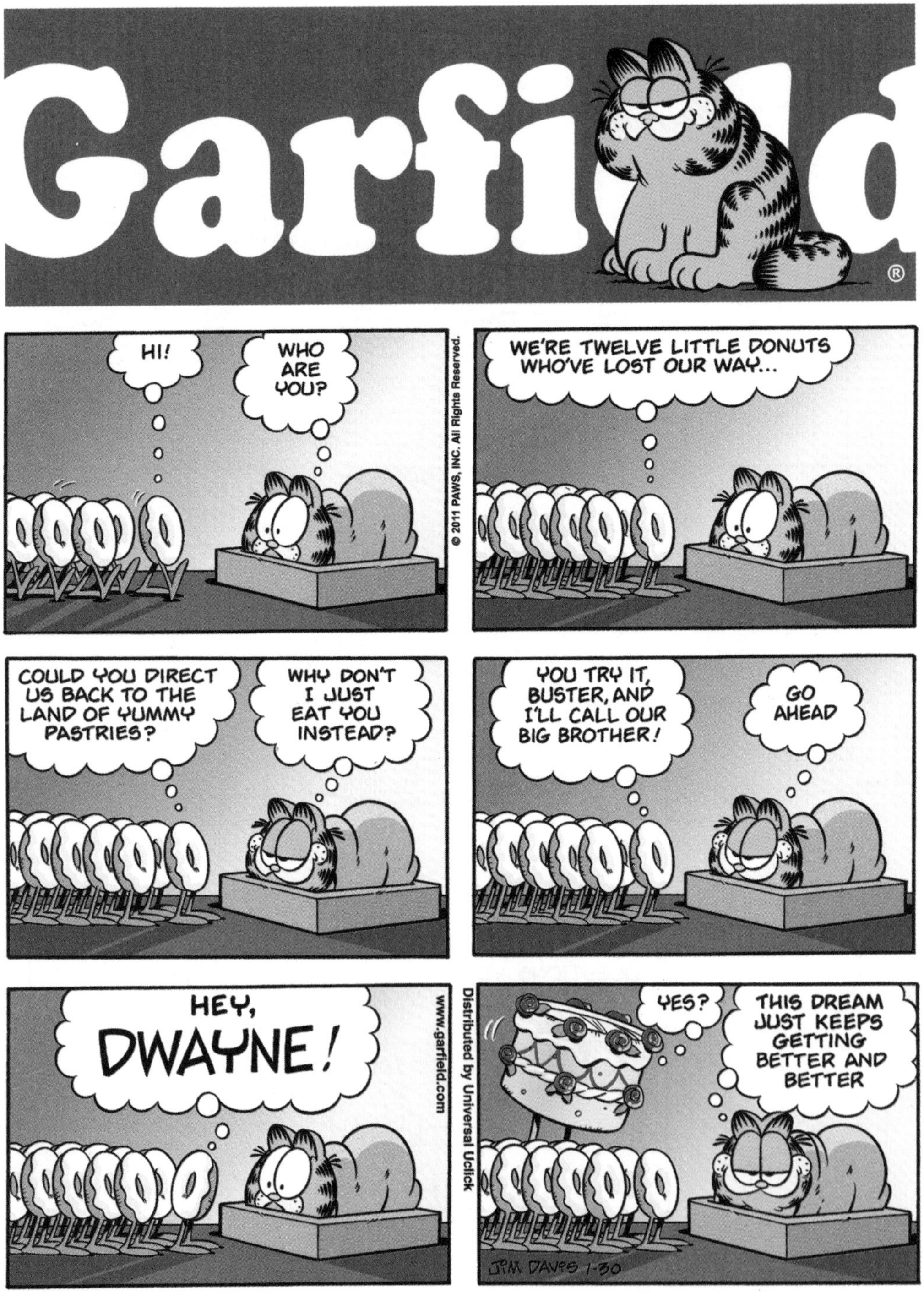
Garfield®
HI!
WHO ARE YOU?
© 2011 PAWS, INC. All Rights Reserved.
WE'RE TWELVE LITTLE DONUTS WHO'VE LOST OUR WAY...
COULD YOU DIRECT US BACK TO THE LAND OF YUMMY PASTRIES?
WHY DON'T I JUST EAT YOU INSTEAD?
YOU TRY IT, BUSTER, AND I'LL CALL OUR BIG BROTHER!
GO AHEAD
HEY, DWAYNE!
www.garfield.com
Distributed by Universal Uclick
YES?
THIS DREAM JUST KEEPS GETTING BETTER AND BETTER
JPM DAVIS 1-30

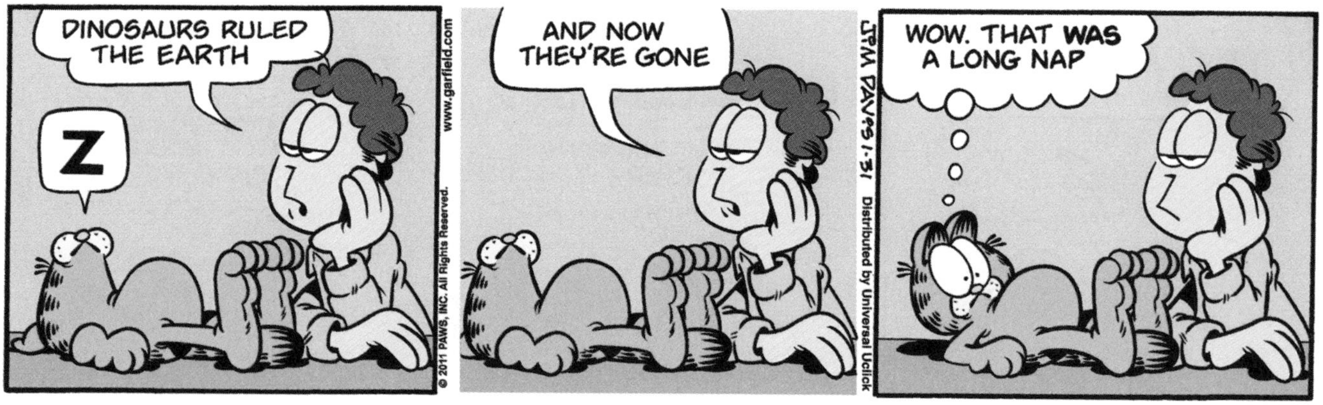
DINOSAURS RULED THE EARTH
Z
AND NOW THEY'RE GONE
WOW. THAT WAS A LONG NAP
JIM DAVIS 1-31
© 2011 PAWS, INC. All Rights Reserved. www.garfield.com
Distributed by Universal Uclick

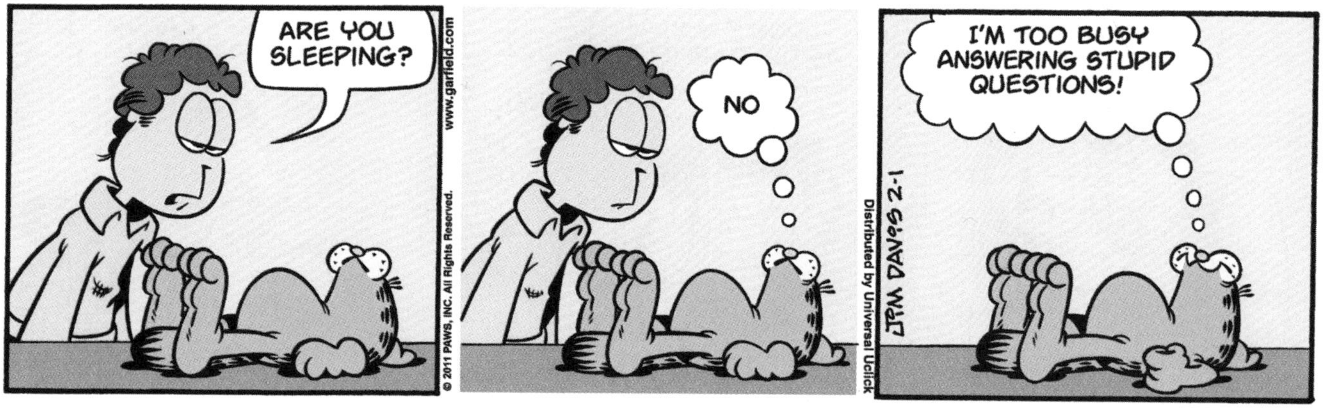
ARE YOU SLEEPING?
NO
I'M TOO BUSY ANSWERING STUPID QUESTIONS!
JIM DAVIS 2-1
© 2011 PAWS, INC. All Rights Reserved. www.garfield.com
Distributed by Universal Uclick

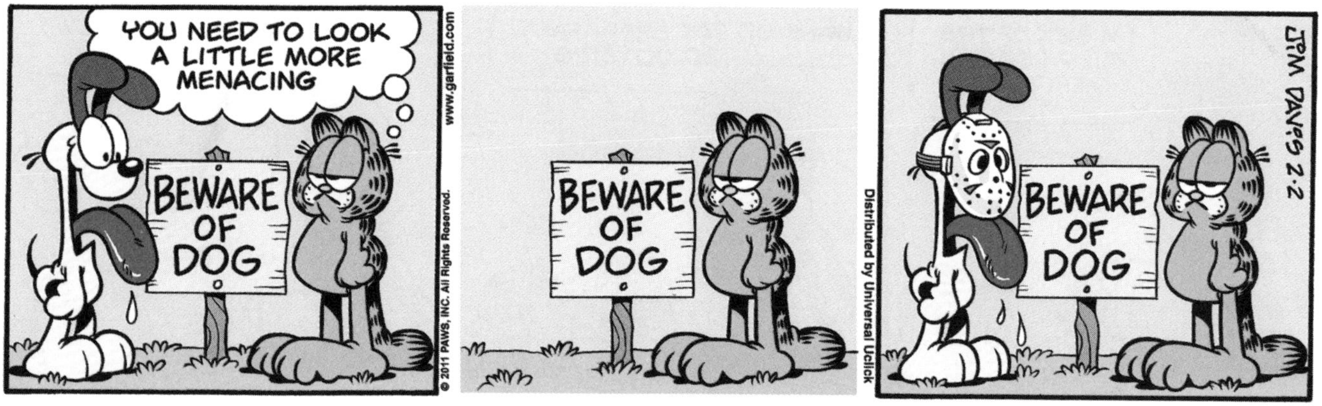
YOU NEED TO LOOK A LITTLE MORE MENACING
BEWARE OF DOG
BEWARE OF DOG
BEWARE OF DOG
JIM DAVIS 2-2
© 2011 PAWS, INC. All Rights Reserved. www.garfield.com
Distributed by Universal Uclick

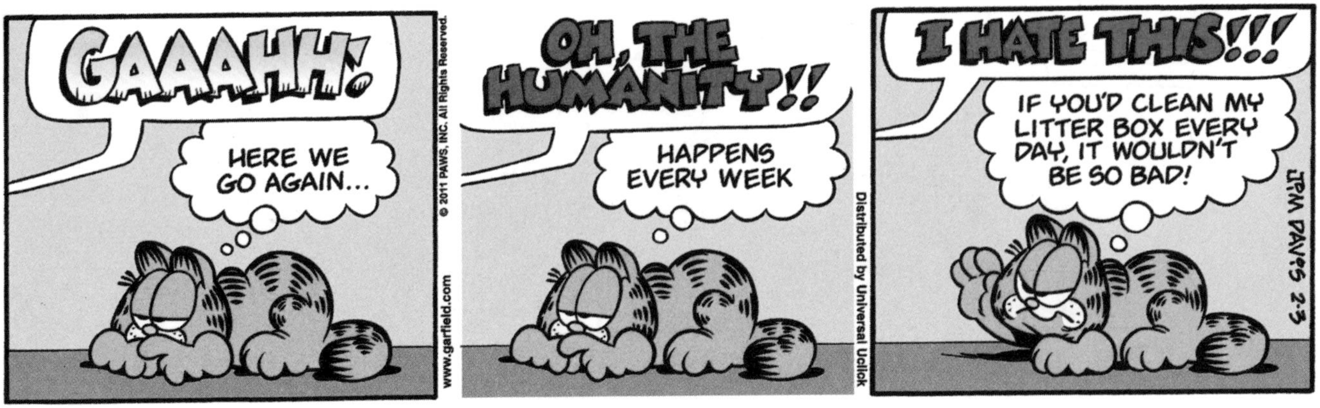
GAAAHH!
HERE WE GO AGAIN...
© 2011 PAWS, INC. All Rights Reserved. www.garfield.com
OH, THE HUMANITY!!
HAPPENS EVERY WEEK
Distributed by Universal Uclick
I HATE THIS!!!
IF YOU'D CLEAN MY LITTER BOX EVERY DAY, IT WOULDN'T BE SO BAD!
JPM DAVIS 2-3

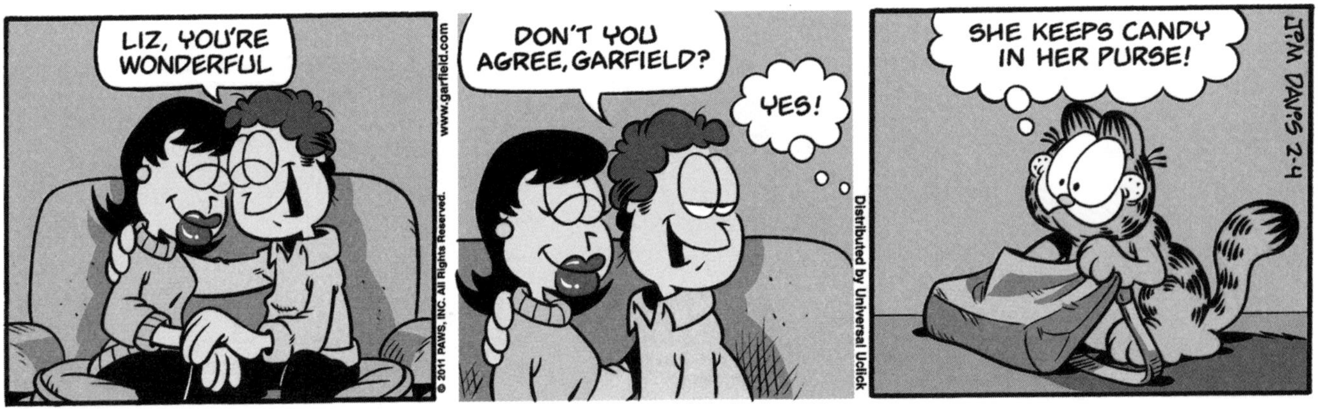
LIZ, YOU'RE WONDERFUL
www.garfield.com © 2011 PAWS, INC. All Rights Reserved.
DON'T YOU AGREE, GARFIELD?
YES!
Distributed by Universal Uclick
SHE KEEPS CANDY IN HER PURSE!
JPM DAVIS 2-4

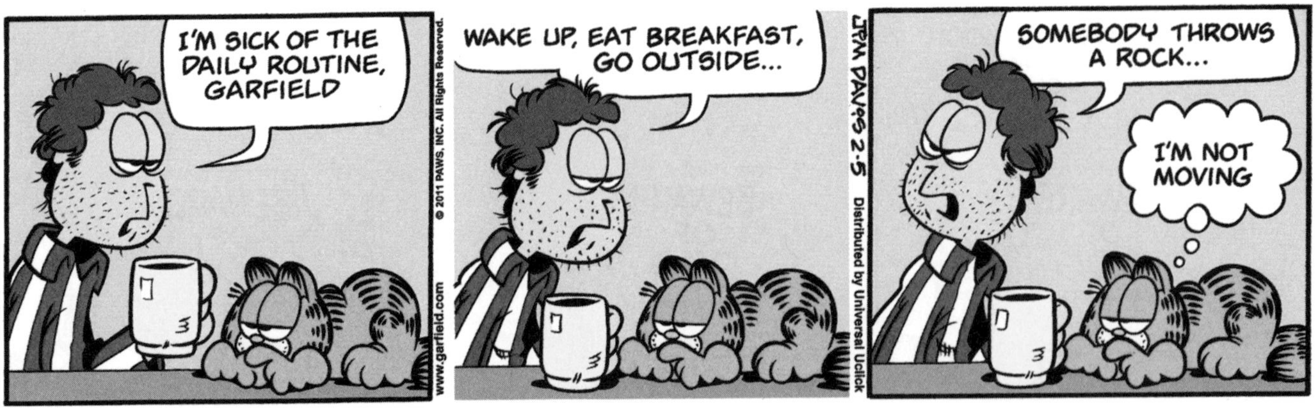
I'M SICK OF THE DAILY ROUTINE, GARFIELD
© 2011 PAWS, INC. All Rights Reserved. www.garfield.com
WAKE UP, EAT BREAKFAST, GO OUTSIDE...
JPM DAVIS 2-5
Distributed by Universal Uclick
SOMEBODY THROWS A ROCK...
I'M NOT MOVING

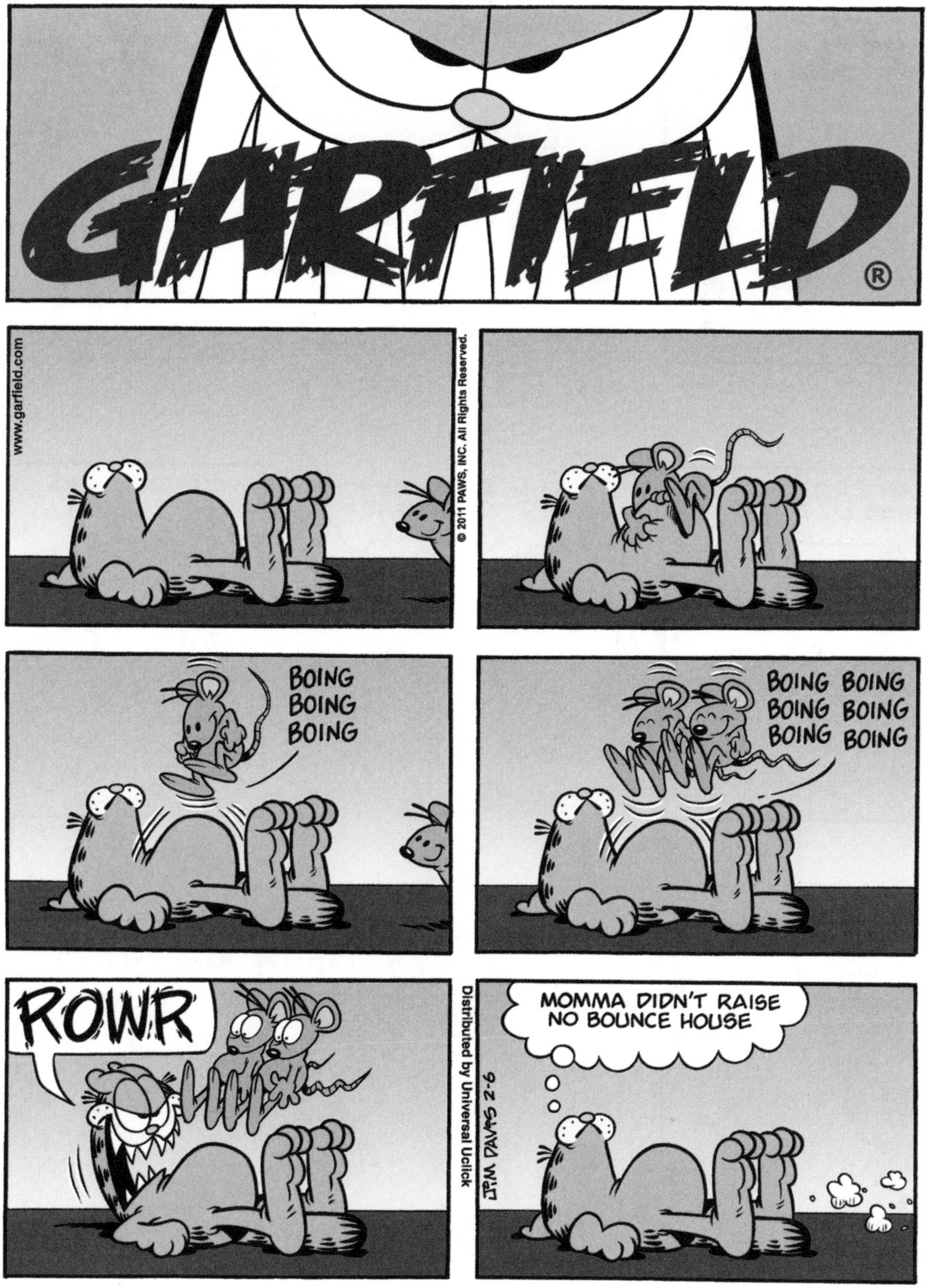
GARFIELD®
www.garfield.com
© 2011 PAWS, INC. All Rights Reserved.
BOING
BOING
BOING
BOING BOING
BOING BOING
BOING BOING
ROWR
Distributed by Universal Uclick
JPM DAVPS 2-6
MOMMA DIDN'T RAISE NO BOUNCE HOUSE

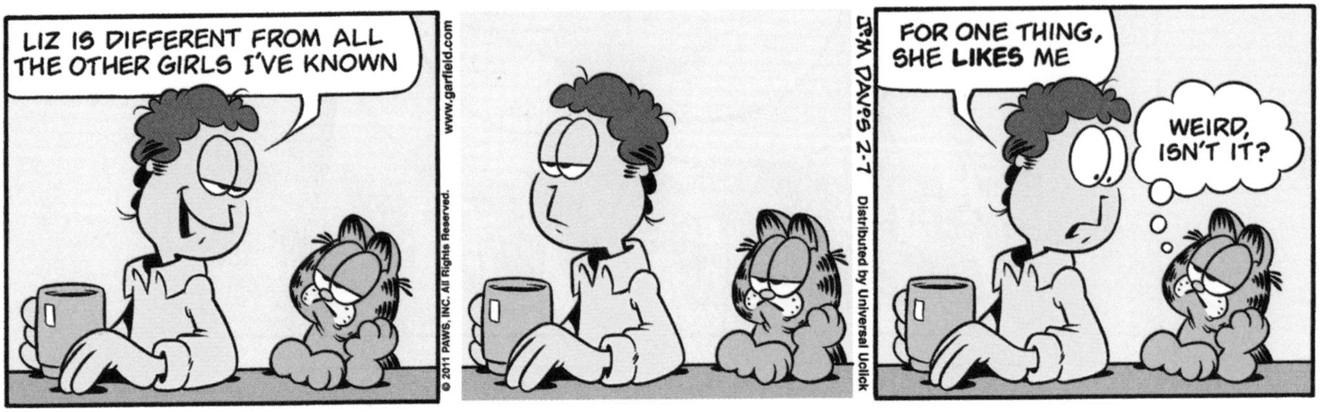
LIZ IS DIFFERENT FROM ALL THE OTHER GIRLS I'VE KNOWN
© 2011 PAWS, INC. All Rights Reserved.
www.garfield.com
JiM DAViS 2-7
Distributed by Universal Uclick
FOR ONE THING, SHE **LIKES** ME
WEIRD, ISN'T IT?

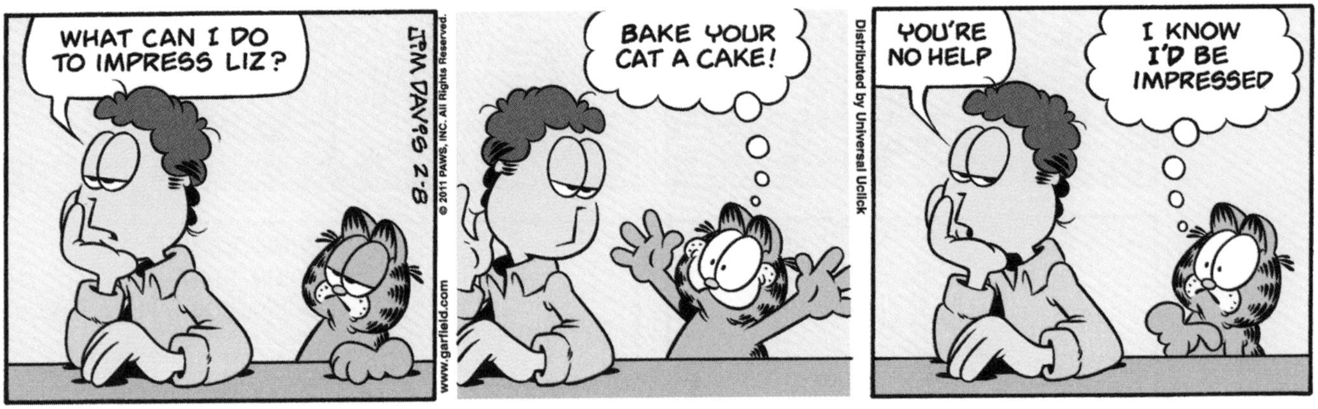
WHAT CAN I DO TO IMPRESS LIZ?
JiM DAViS 2-8
© 2011 PAWS, INC. All Rights Reserved.
www.garfield.com
BAKE YOUR CAT A CAKE!
Distributed by Universal Uclick
YOU'RE NO HELP
I KNOW **I'D** BE IMPRESSED

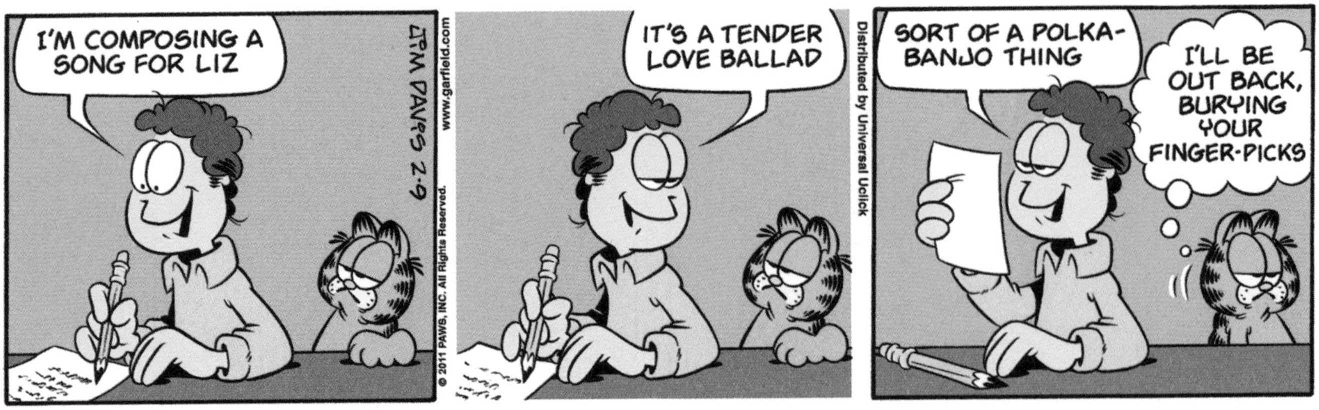
I'M COMPOSING A SONG FOR LIZ
JiM DAViS 2-9
www.garfield.com
© 2011 PAWS, INC. All Rights Reserved.
IT'S A TENDER LOVE BALLAD
Distributed by Universal Uclick
SORT OF A POLKA-BANJO THING
I'LL BE OUT BACK, BURYING YOUR FINGER-PICKS

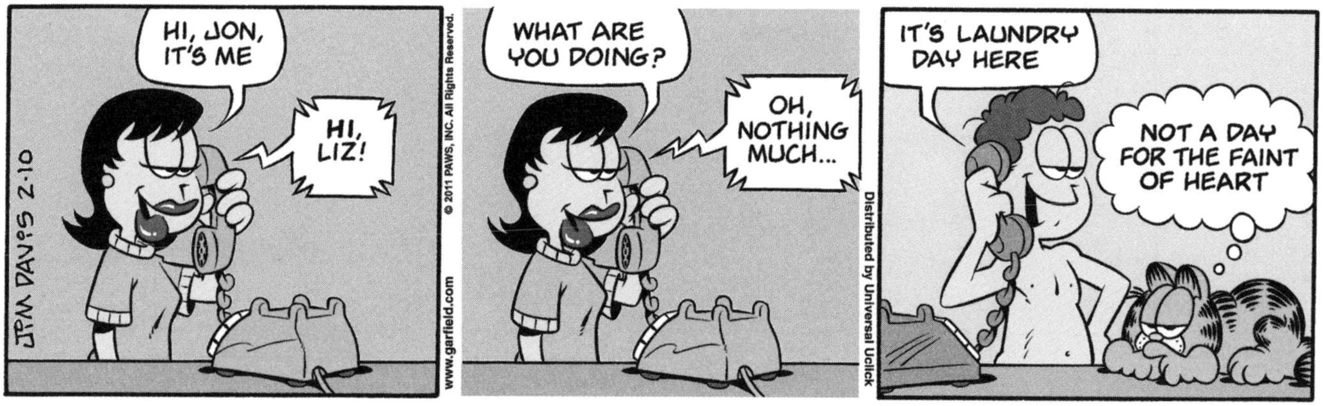
JIM DAVIS 2-10
HI, JON, IT'S ME
HI, LIZ!
WHAT ARE YOU DOING?
OH, NOTHING MUCH...
IT'S LAUNDRY DAY HERE
NOT A DAY FOR THE FAINT OF HEART

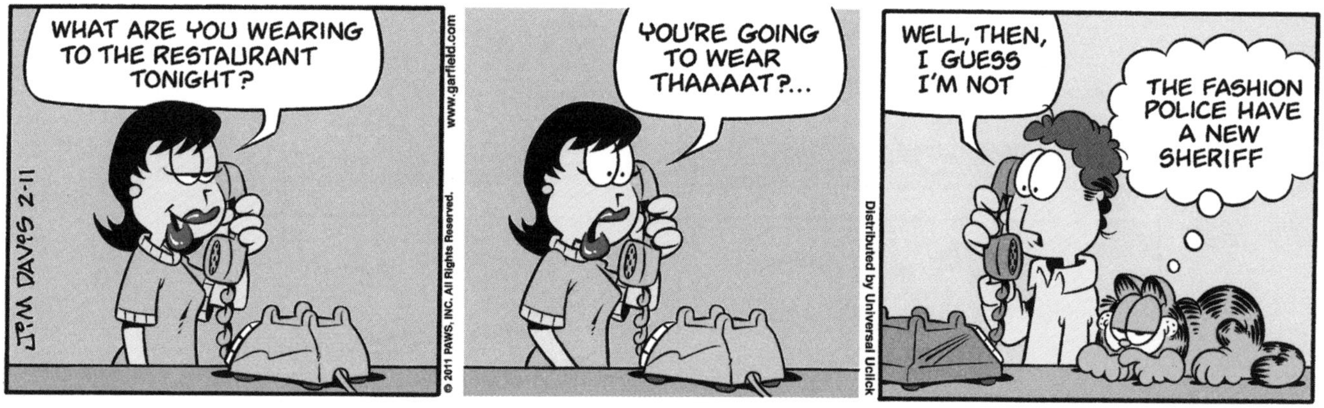
JIM DAVIS 2-11
WHAT ARE YOU WEARING TO THE RESTAURANT TONIGHT?
YOU'RE GOING TO WEAR THAAAAT?...
WELL, THEN, I GUESS I'M NOT
THE FASHION POLICE HAVE A NEW SHERIFF

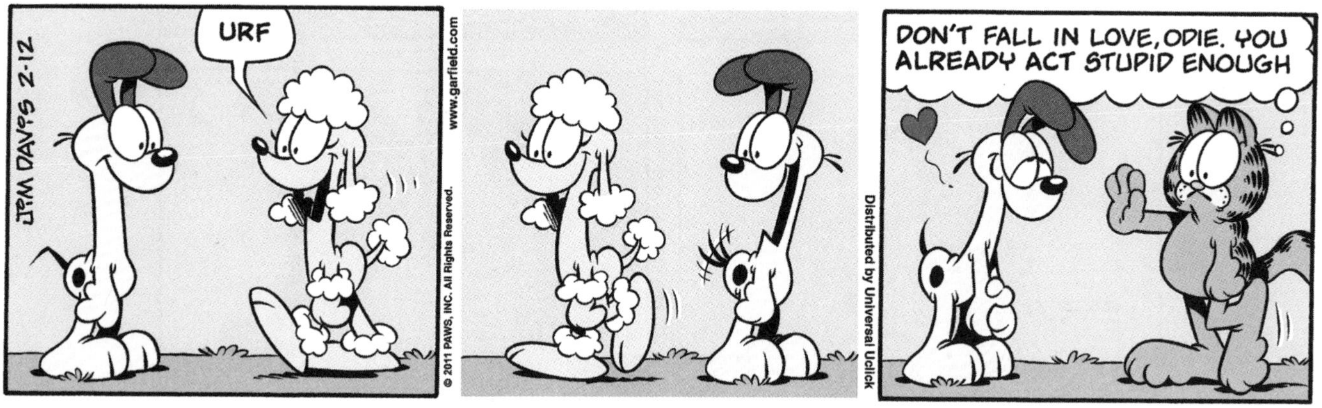
JIM DAVIS 2-12
URF
DON'T FALL IN LOVE, ODIE. YOU ALREADY ACT STUPID ENOUGH

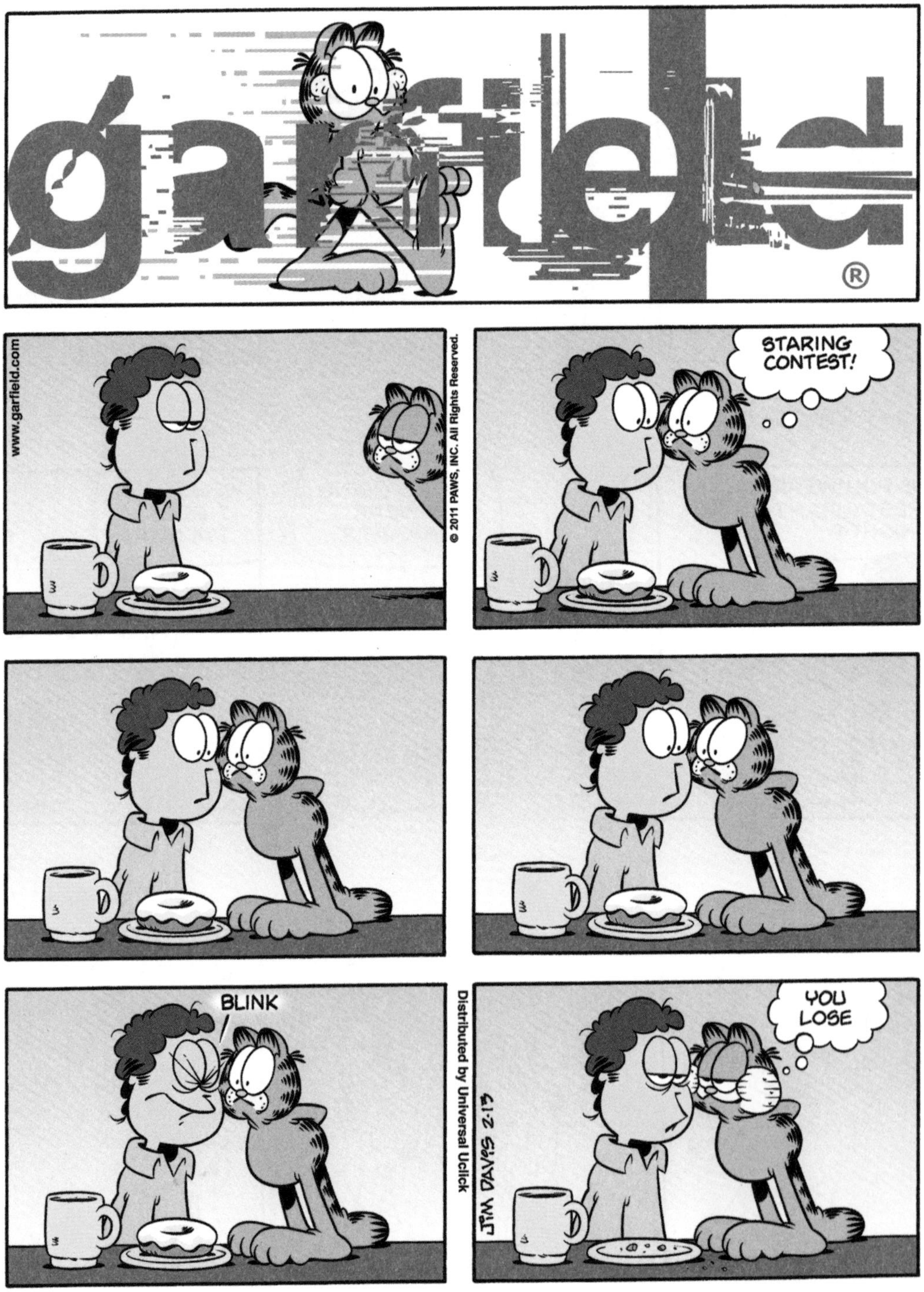
garfield®
www.garfield.com
© 2011 PAWS, INC. All Rights Reserved.
STARING CONTEST!
BLINK
Distributed by Universal Uclick
JPM DAVIS 2-13
YOU LOSE

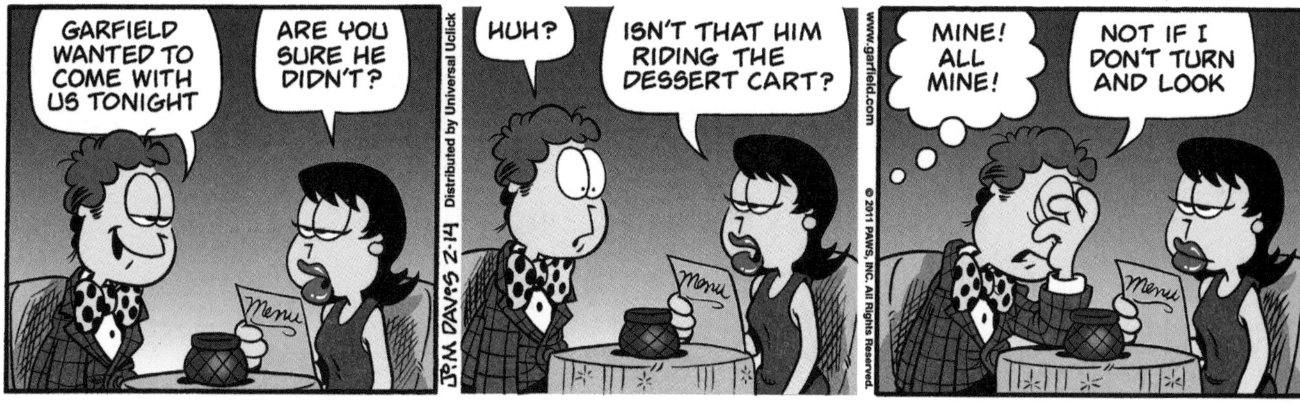
GARFIELD WANTED TO COME WITH US TONIGHT
ARE YOU SURE HE DIDN'T?
JPM DAVIS 2-14
Distributed by Universal Uclick
HUH?
ISN'T THAT HIM RIDING THE DESSERT CART?
Menu
www.garfield.com
© 2011 PAWS, INC. All Rights Reserved.
MINE! ALL MINE!
NOT IF I DON'T TURN AND LOOK

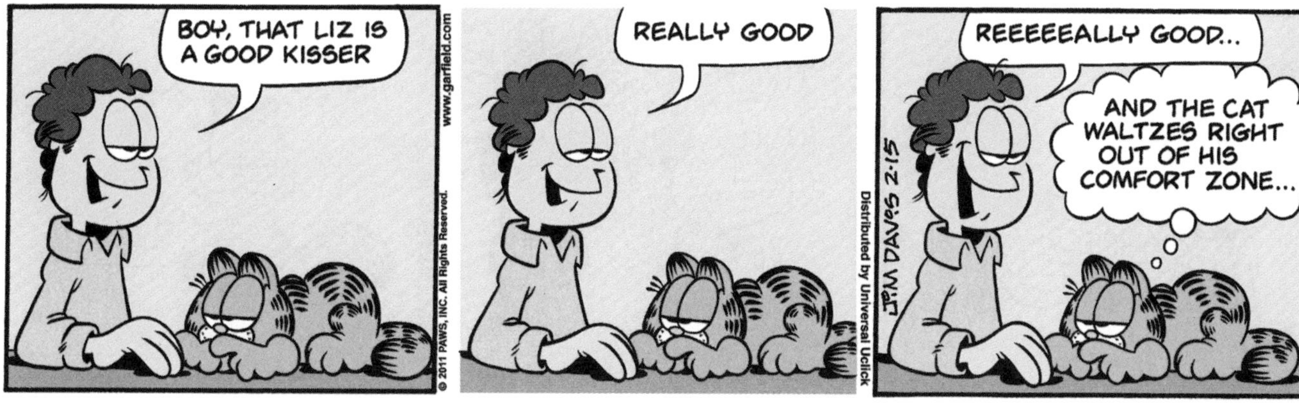
BOY, THAT LIZ IS A GOOD KISSER
www.garfield.com
© 2011 PAWS, INC. All Rights Reserved.
REALLY GOOD
Distributed by Universal Uclick
JPM DAVIS 2-15
REEEEEALLY GOOD...
AND THE CAT WALTZES RIGHT OUT OF HIS COMFORT ZONE...

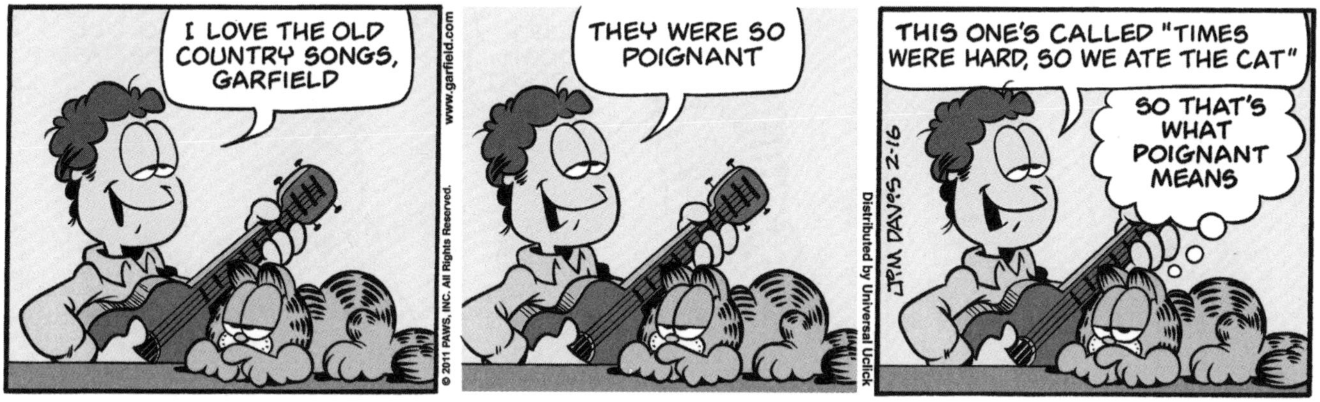
I LOVE THE OLD COUNTRY SONGS, GARFIELD
www.garfield.com
© 2011 PAWS, INC. All Rights Reserved.
THEY WERE SO POIGNANT
Distributed by Universal Uclick
JPM DAVIS 2-16
THIS ONE'S CALLED "TIMES WERE HARD, SO WE ATE THE CAT"
SO THAT'S WHAT POIGNANT MEANS

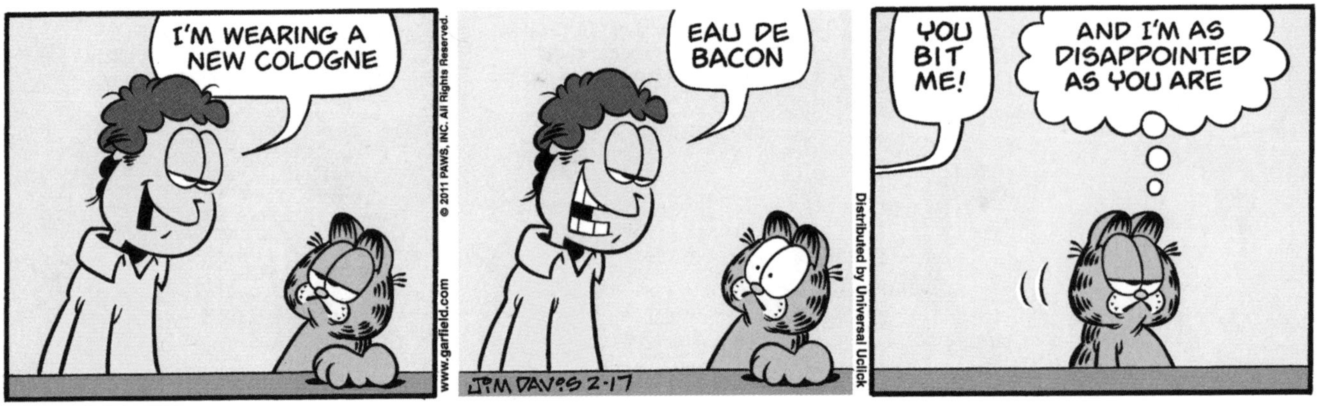
I'M WEARING A NEW COLOGNE
EAU DE BACON
YOU BIT ME!
AND I'M AS DISAPPOINTED AS YOU ARE
JIM DAVIS 2-17

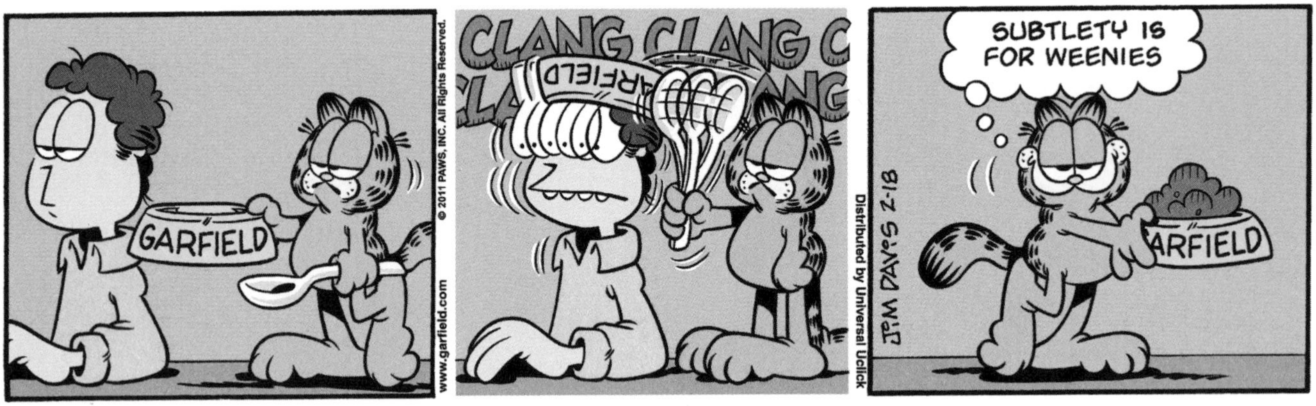
GARFIELD
CLANG CLANG C
CLANG
SUBTLETY IS FOR WEENIES
JIM DAVIS 2-18

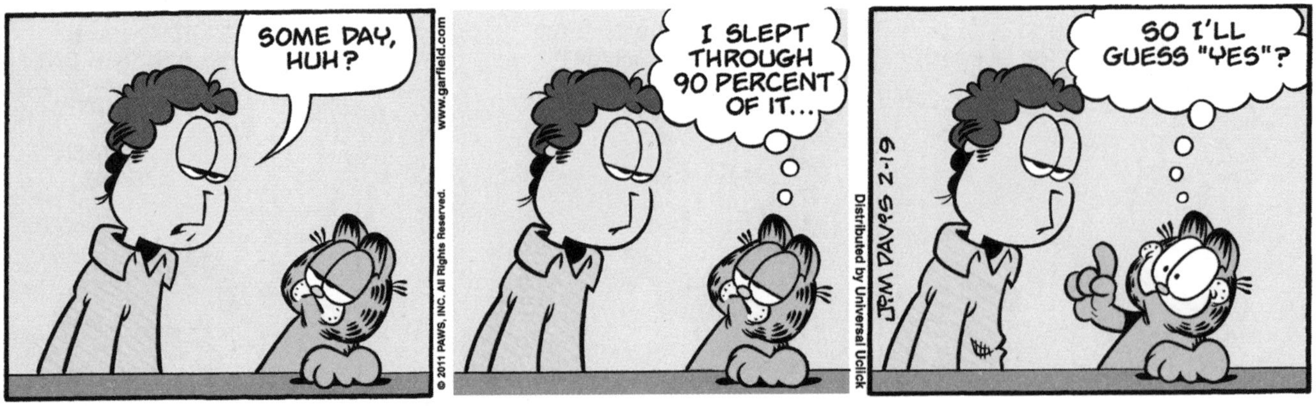
SOME DAY, HUH?
I SLEPT THROUGH 90 PERCENT OF IT...
SO I'LL GUESS "YES"?
JIM DAVIS 2-19

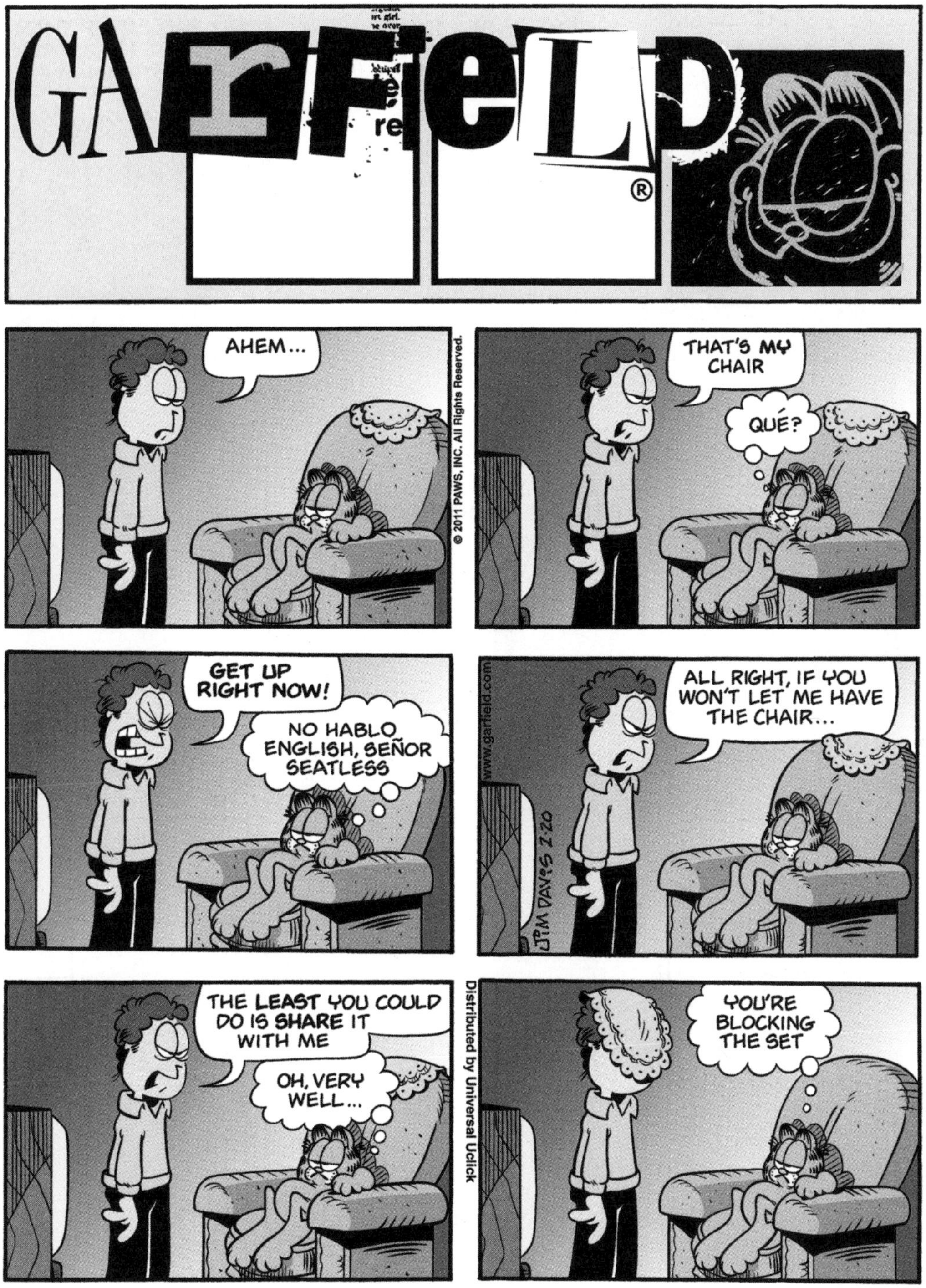
GARFIELD®
AHEM...
© 2011 PAWS, INC. All Rights Reserved.
THAT'S MY CHAIR
QUÉ?
GET UP RIGHT NOW!
NO HABLO ENGLISH, SEÑOR SEATLESS
www.garfield.com
JIM DAVIS 2-20
ALL RIGHT, IF YOU WON'T LET ME HAVE THE CHAIR...
THE LEAST YOU COULD DO IS SHARE IT WITH ME
OH, VERY WELL...
Distributed by Universal Uclick
YOU'RE BLOCKING THE SET

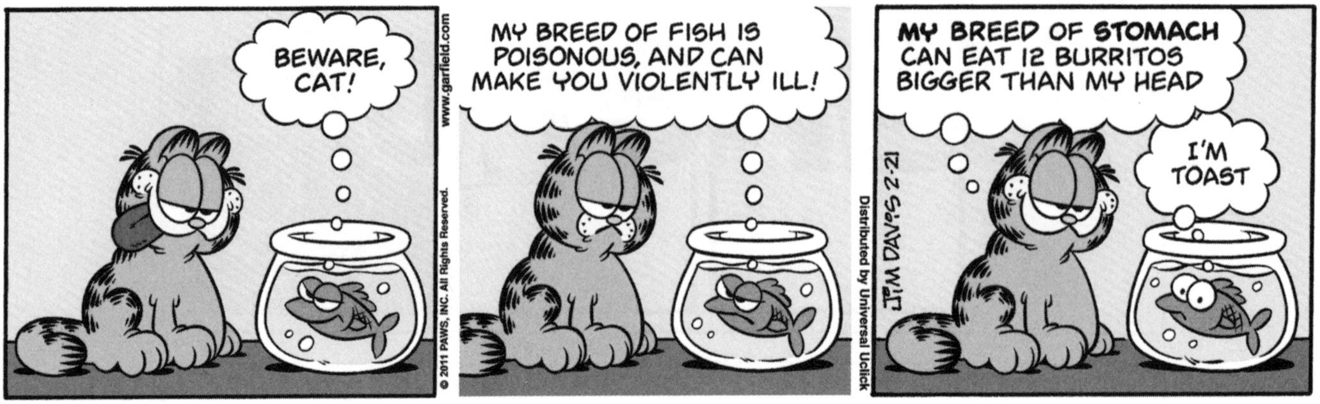
BEWARE, CAT!
MY BREED OF FISH IS POISONOUS, AND CAN MAKE YOU VIOLENTLY ILL!
MY BREED OF STOMACH CAN EAT 12 BURRITOS BIGGER THAN MY HEAD
I'M TOAST
JIM DAVIS 2-21
© 2011 PAWS, INC. All Rights Reserved. www.garfield.com
Distributed by Universal Uclick

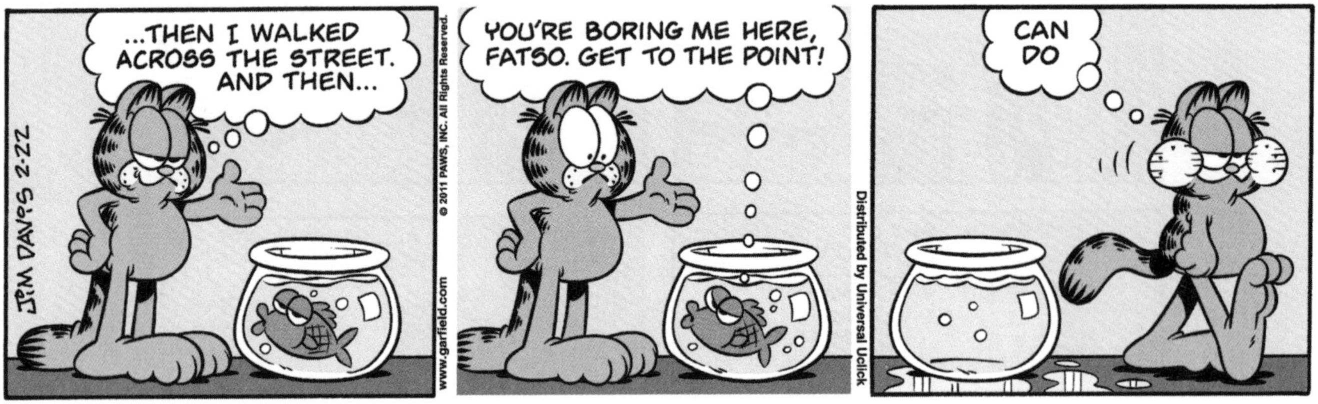
...THEN I WALKED ACROSS THE STREET. AND THEN...
YOU'RE BORING ME HERE, FATSO. GET TO THE POINT!
CAN DO
JIM DAVIS 2-22
© 2011 PAWS, INC. All Rights Reserved. www.garfield.com
Distributed by Universal Uclick

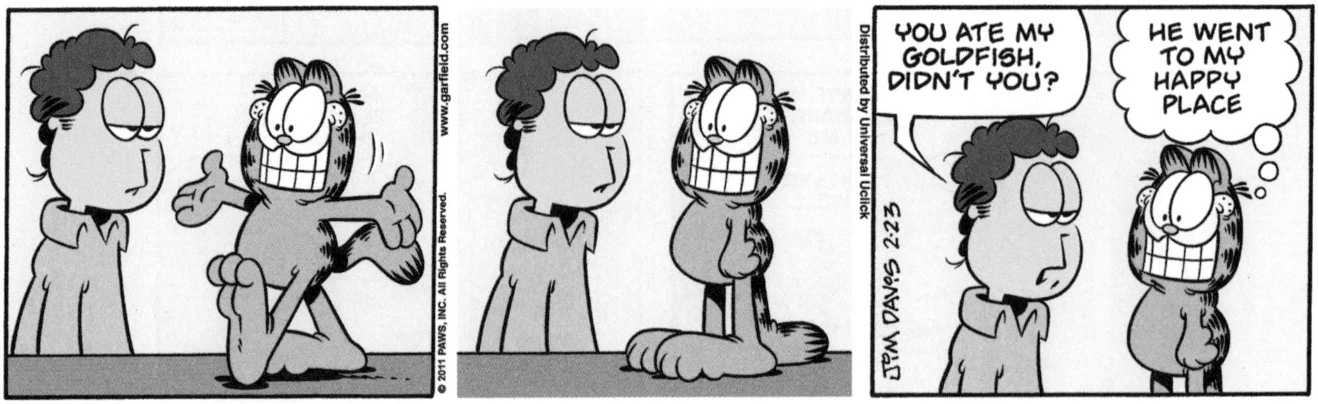
YOU ATE MY GOLDFISH, DIDN'T YOU?
HE WENT TO MY HAPPY PLACE
JIM DAVIS 2-23
© 2011 PAWS, INC. All Rights Reserved. www.garfield.com
Distributed by Universal Uclick

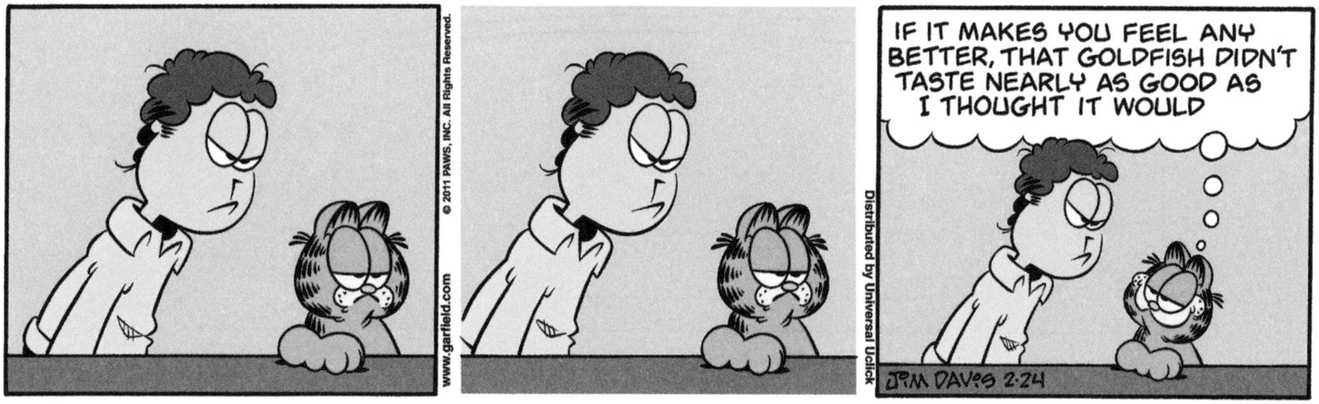
IF IT MAKES YOU FEEL ANY BETTER, THAT GOLDFISH DIDN'T TASTE NEARLY AS GOOD AS I THOUGHT IT WOULD
© 2011 PAWS, INC. All Rights Reserved.
www.garfield.com
Distributed by Universal Uclick
JIM DAVIS 2·24

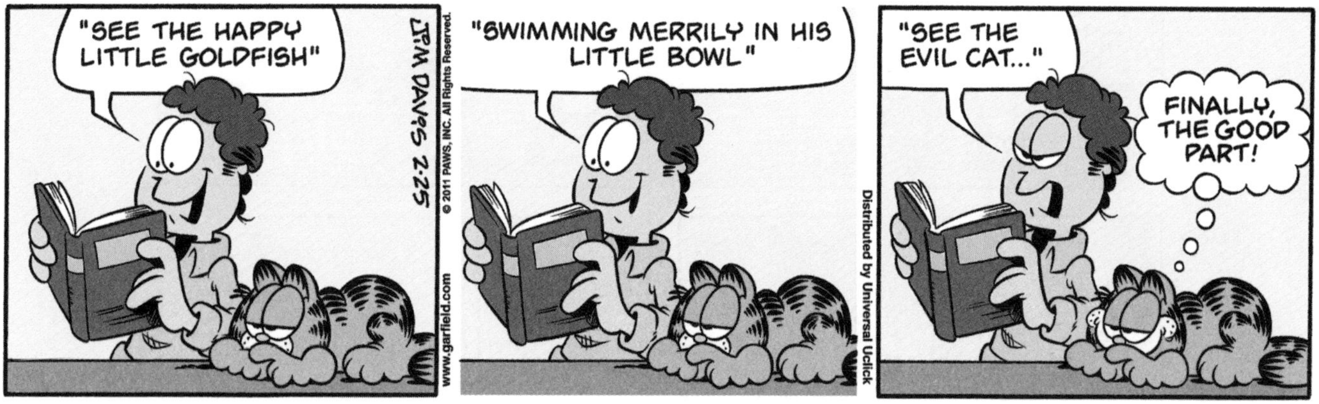
"SEE THE HAPPY LITTLE GOLDFISH"
"SWIMMING MERRILY IN HIS LITTLE BOWL"
"SEE THE EVIL CAT..."
FINALLY, THE GOOD PART!
JIM DAVIS 2·25
© 2011 PAWS, INC. All Rights Reserved.
www.garfield.com
Distributed by Universal Uclick

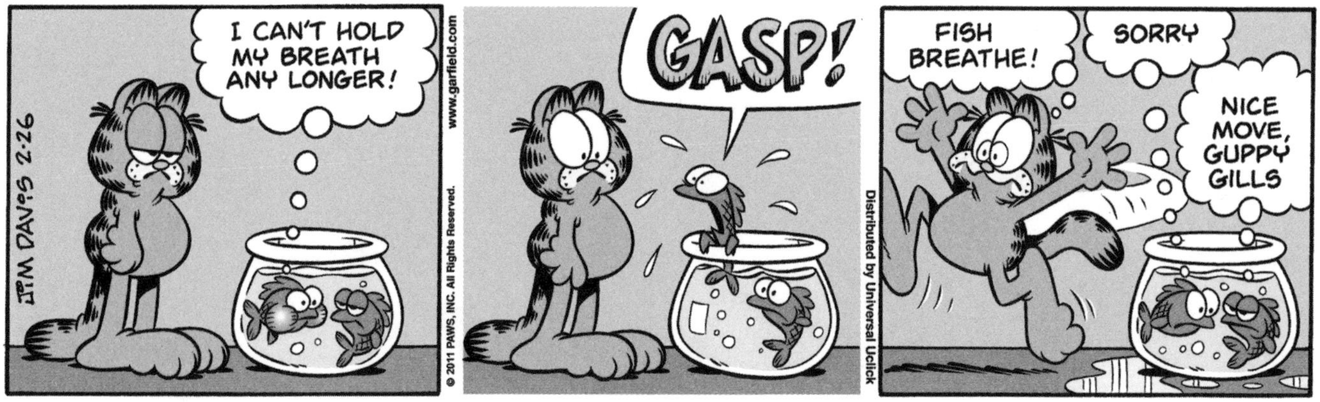
I CAN'T HOLD MY BREATH ANY LONGER!
GASP!
FISH BREATHE!
SORRY
NICE MOVE, GUPPY GILLS
JIM DAVIS 2·26
www.garfield.com
© 2011 PAWS, INC. All Rights Reserved.
Distributed by Universal Uclick

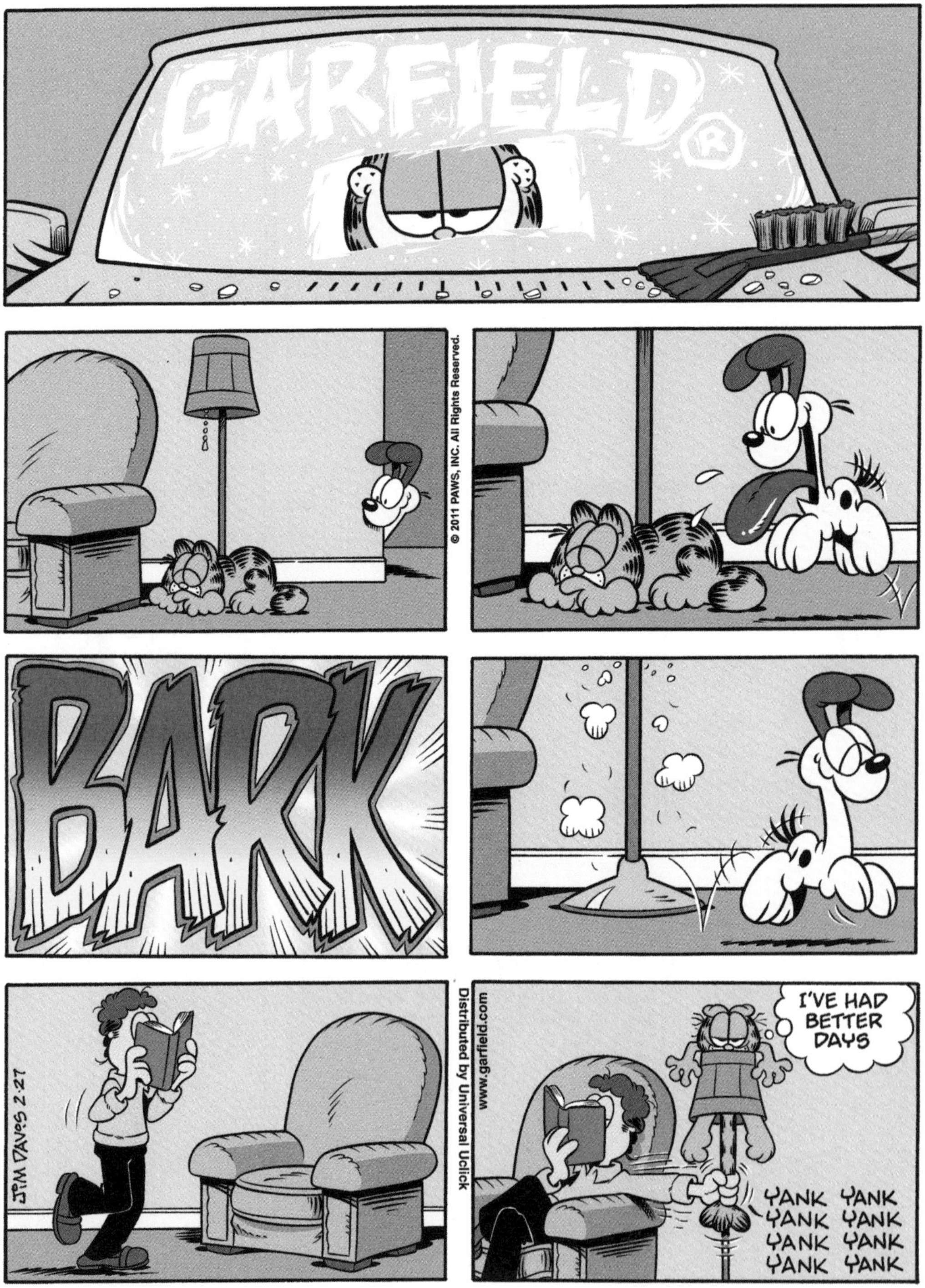
GARFIELD®
© 2011 PAWS, INC. All Rights Reserved.
BARK
JIM DAVIS 2-27
Distributed by Universal Uclick
www.garfield.com
I'VE HAD BETTER DAYS
YANK YANK YANK YANK YANK YANK YANK YANK

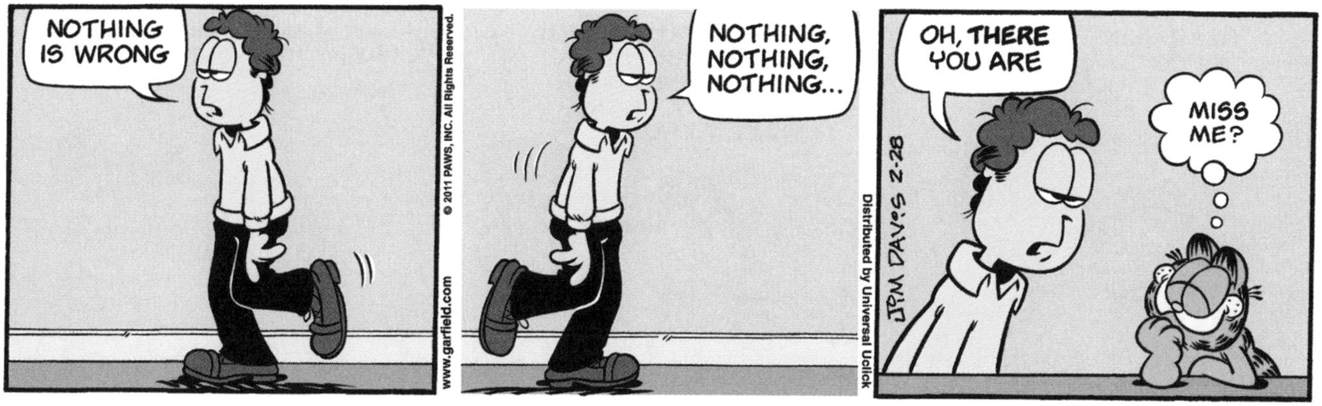
NOTHING IS WRONG
NOTHING, NOTHING, NOTHING...
OH, THERE YOU ARE
MISS ME?
JIM DAVIS 2-28
© 2011 PAWS, INC. All Rights Reserved.
www.garfield.com
Distributed by Universal Uclick

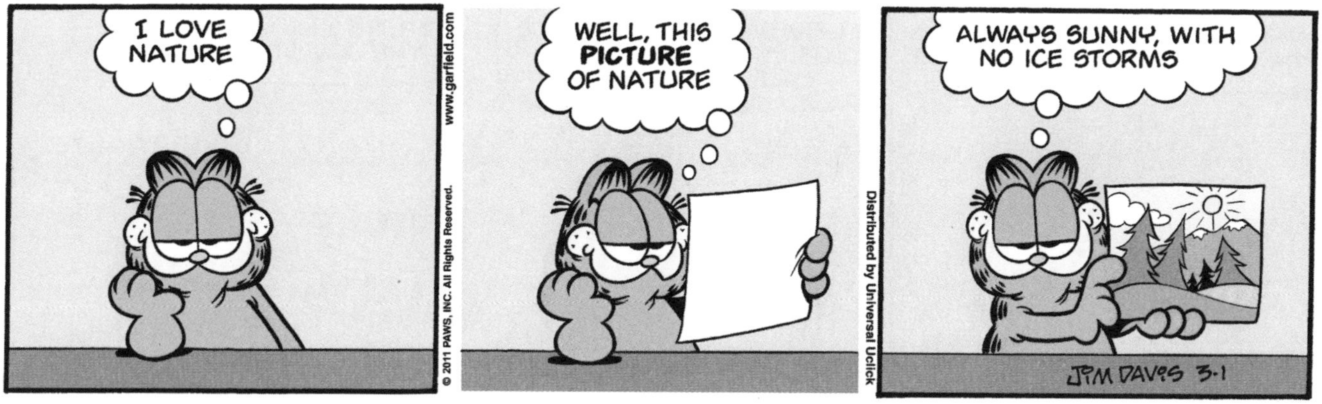
I LOVE NATURE
WELL, THIS PICTURE OF NATURE
ALWAYS SUNNY, WITH NO ICE STORMS
JIM DAVIS 3-1
© 2011 PAWS, INC. All Rights Reserved.
www.garfield.com
Distributed by Universal Uclick

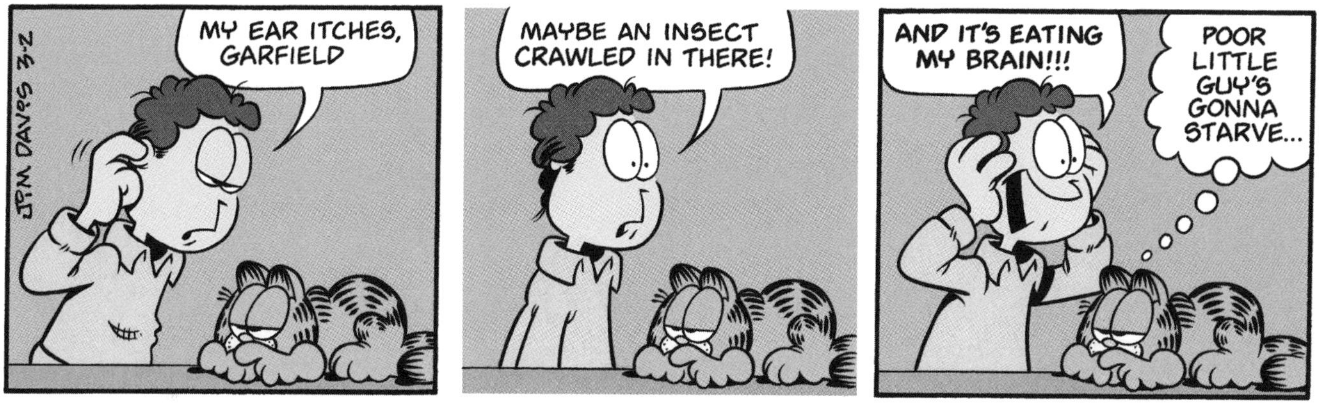
MY EAR ITCHES, GARFIELD
JIM DAVIS 3-2
MAYBE AN INSECT CRAWLED IN THERE!
AND IT'S EATING MY BRAIN!!!
POOR LITTLE GUY'S GONNA STARVE...

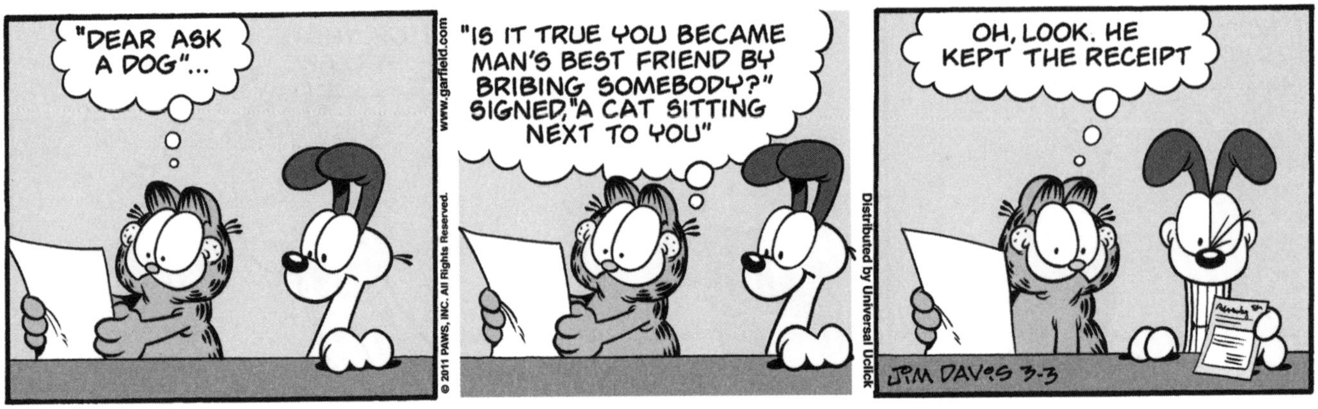
"DEAR ASK A DOG"...
"IS IT TRUE YOU BECAME MAN'S BEST FRIEND BY BRIBING SOMEBODY?" SIGNED,"A CAT SITTING NEXT TO YOU"
OH, LOOK. HE KEPT THE RECEIPT
www.garfield.com
© 2011 PAWS, INC. All Rights Reserved.
Distributed by Universal Uclick
JIM DAVIS 3-3

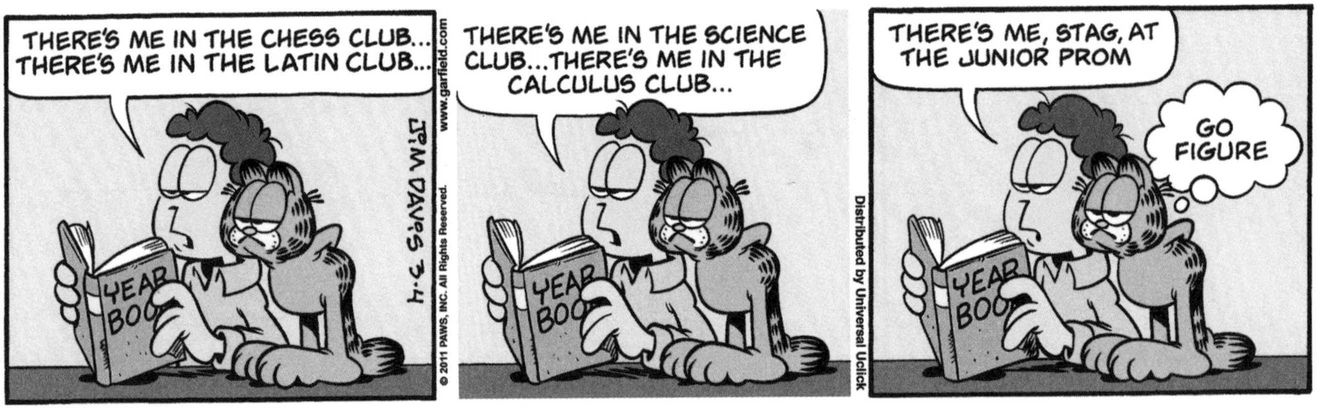
THERE'S ME IN THE CHESS CLUB... THERE'S ME IN THE LATIN CLUB...
YEAR BOO
THERE'S ME IN THE SCIENCE CLUB...THERE'S ME IN THE CALCULUS CLUB...
THERE'S ME, STAG, AT THE JUNIOR PROM
GO FIGURE
www.garfield.com
© 2011 PAWS, INC. All Rights Reserved.
Distributed by Universal Uclick
JIM DAVIS 3-4

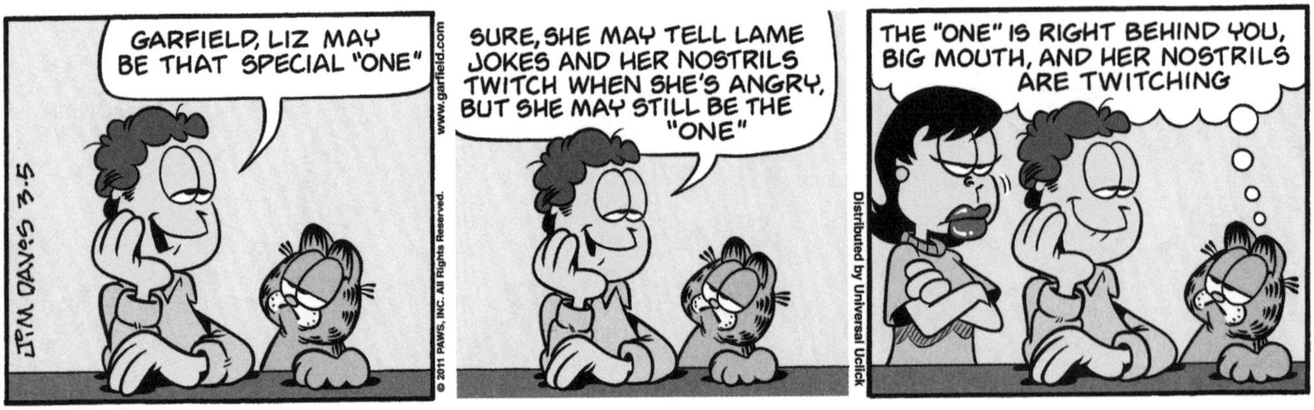
GARFIELD, LIZ MAY BE THAT SPECIAL "ONE"
SURE, SHE MAY TELL LAME JOKES AND HER NOSTRILS TWITCH WHEN SHE'S ANGRY, BUT SHE MAY STILL BE THE "ONE"
THE "ONE" IS RIGHT BEHIND YOU, BIG MOUTH, AND HER NOSTRILS ARE TWITCHING
www.garfield.com
© 2011 PAWS, INC. All Rights Reserved.
Distributed by Universal Uclick
JIM DAVIS 3-5

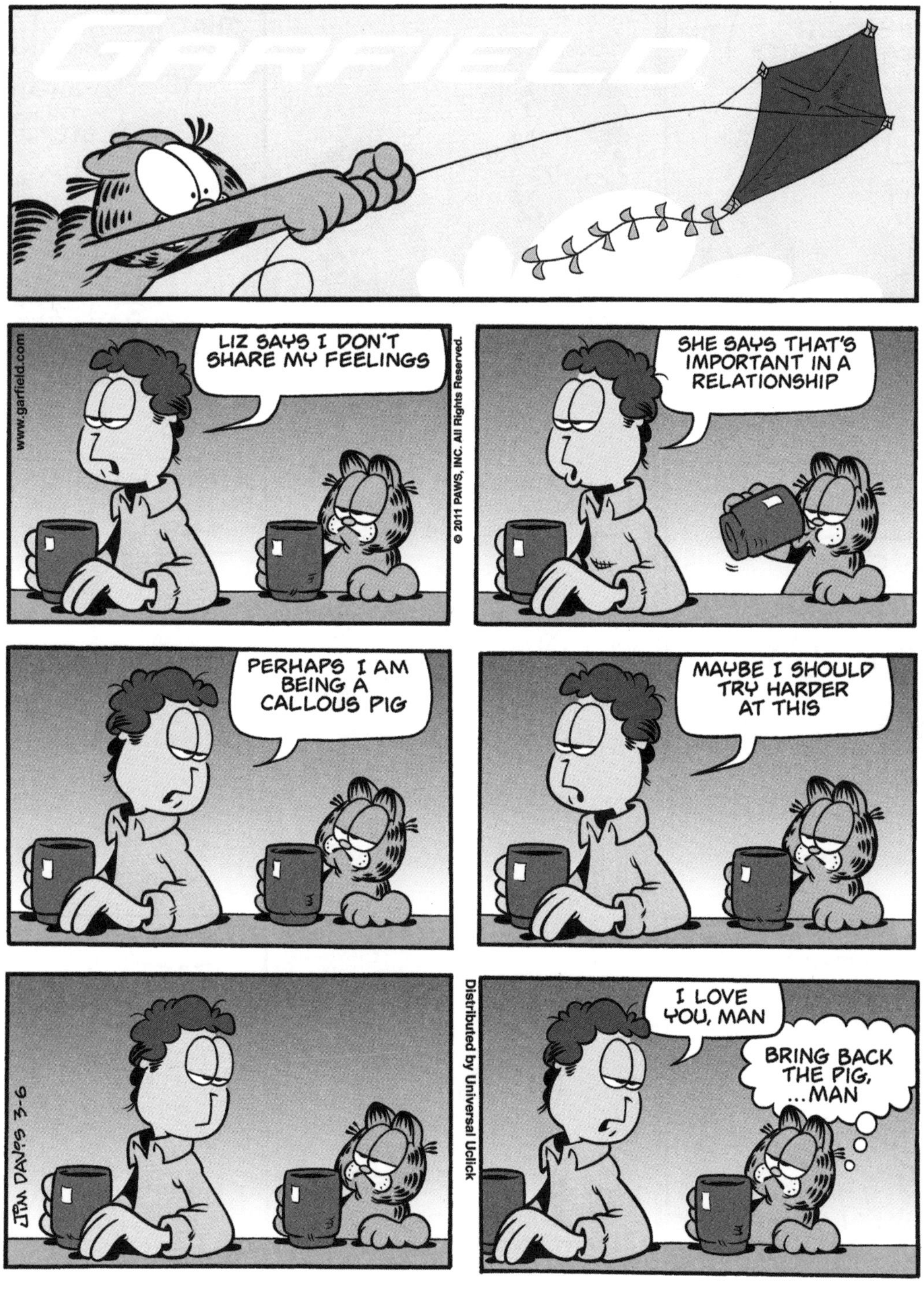
GARFIELD
LIZ SAYS I DON'T SHARE MY FEELINGS
www.garfield.com
© 2011 PAWS, INC. All Rights Reserved.
SHE SAYS THAT'S IMPORTANT IN A RELATIONSHIP
PERHAPS I AM BEING A CALLOUS PIG
MAYBE I SHOULD TRY HARDER AT THIS
JIM DAVIS 3-6
Distributed by Universal Uclick
I LOVE YOU, MAN
BRING BACK THE PIG, ...MAN

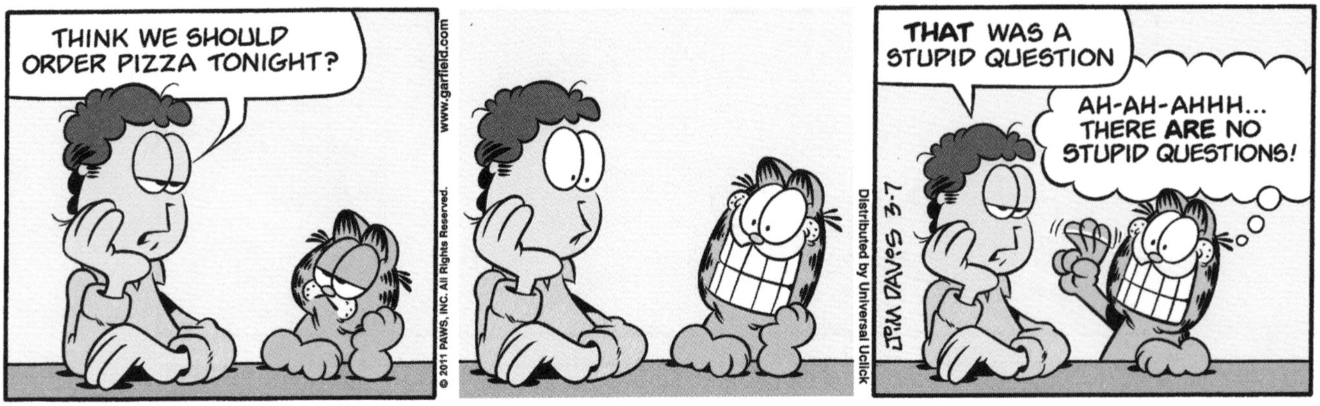
THINK WE SHOULD ORDER PIZZA TONIGHT?
© 2011 PAWS, INC. All Rights Reserved.
www.garfield.com
Distributed by Universal Uclick
JIM DAVIS 3-7
THAT WAS A STUPID QUESTION
AH-AH-AHHH... THERE ARE NO STUPID QUESTIONS!

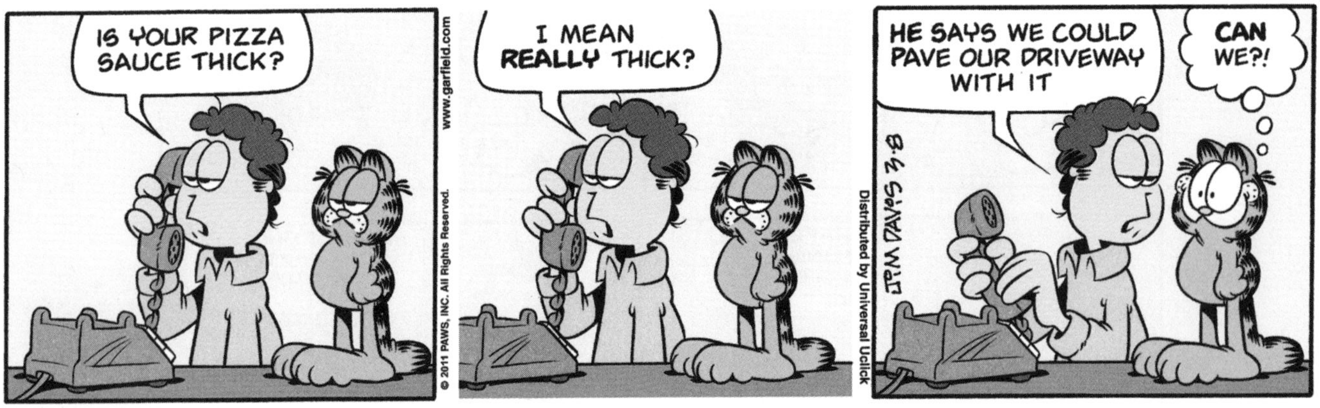
IS YOUR PIZZA SAUCE THICK?
© 2011 PAWS, INC. All Rights Reserved.
www.garfield.com
I MEAN REALLY THICK?
Distributed by Universal Uclick
JIM DAVIS 3-8
HE SAYS WE COULD PAVE OUR DRIVEWAY WITH IT
CAN WE?!

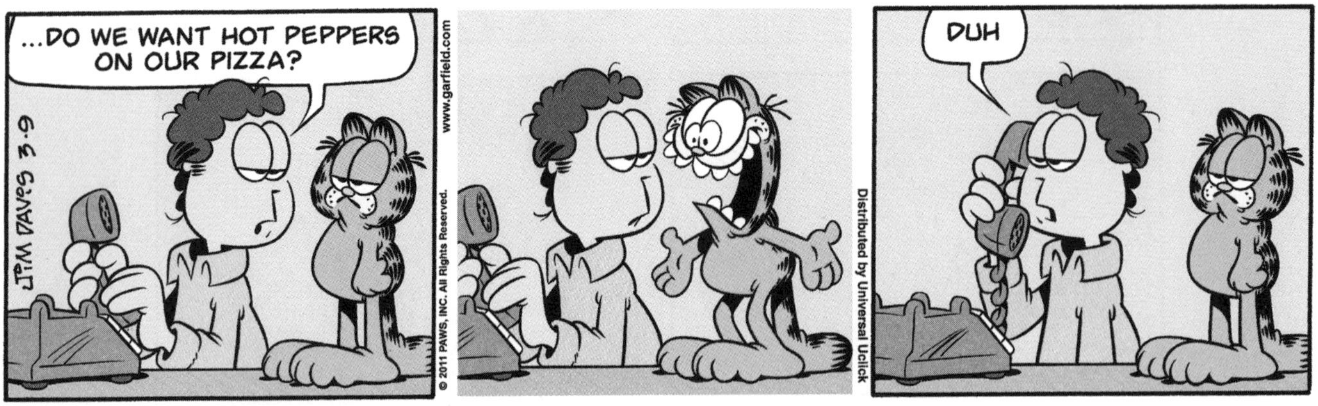
...DO WE WANT HOT PEPPERS ON OUR PIZZA?
JIM DAVIS 3-9
© 2011 PAWS, INC. All Rights Reserved.
www.garfield.com
Distributed by Universal Uclick
DUH

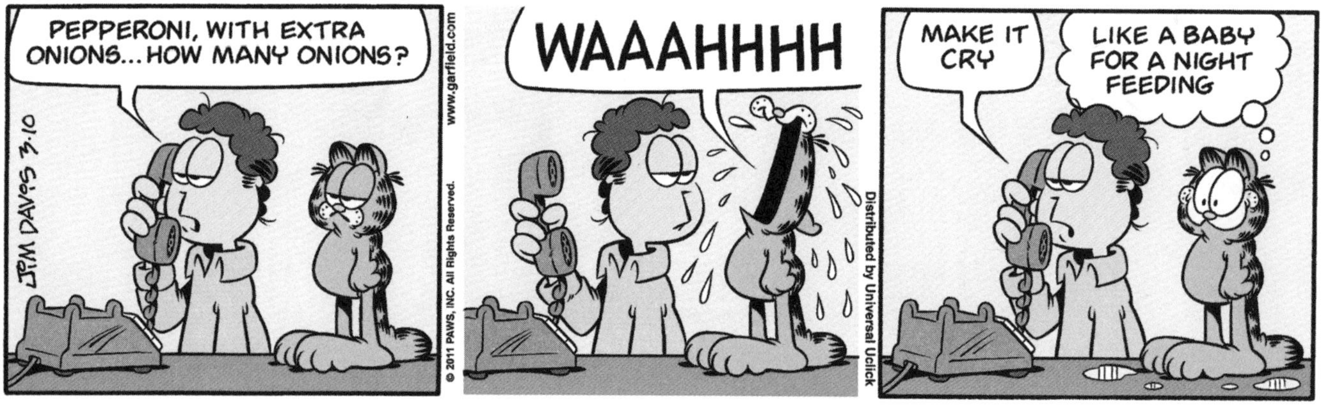
PEPPERONI, WITH EXTRA ONIONS... HOW MANY ONIONS?
JIM DAVIS 3-10
© 2011 PAWS, INC. All Rights Reserved. www.garfield.com
WAAAHHHH
Distributed by Universal Uclick
MAKE IT CRY
LIKE A BABY FOR A NIGHT FEEDING

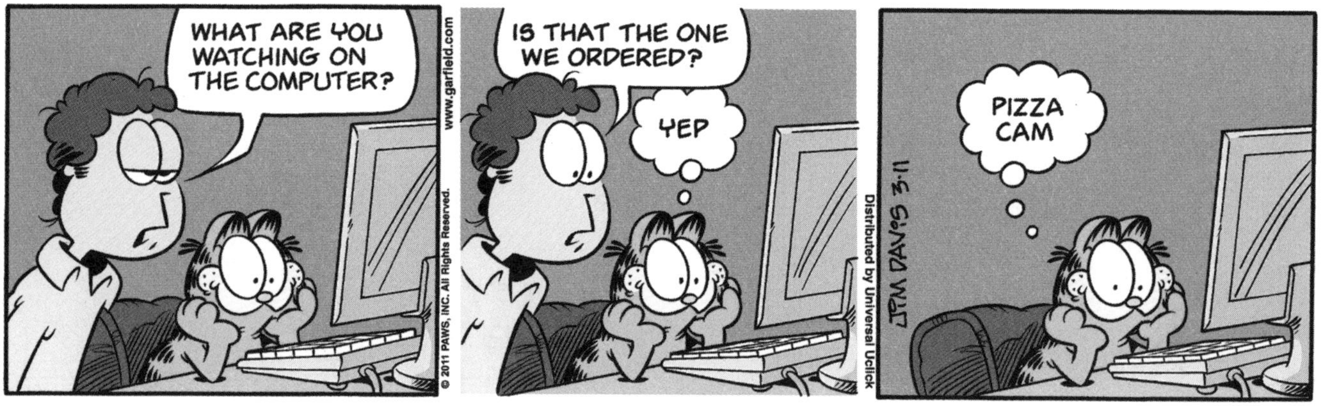
WHAT ARE YOU WATCHING ON THE COMPUTER?
© 2011 PAWS, INC. All Rights Reserved. www.garfield.com
IS THAT THE ONE WE ORDERED?
YEP
Distributed by Universal Uclick
JIM DAVIS 3-11
PIZZA CAM

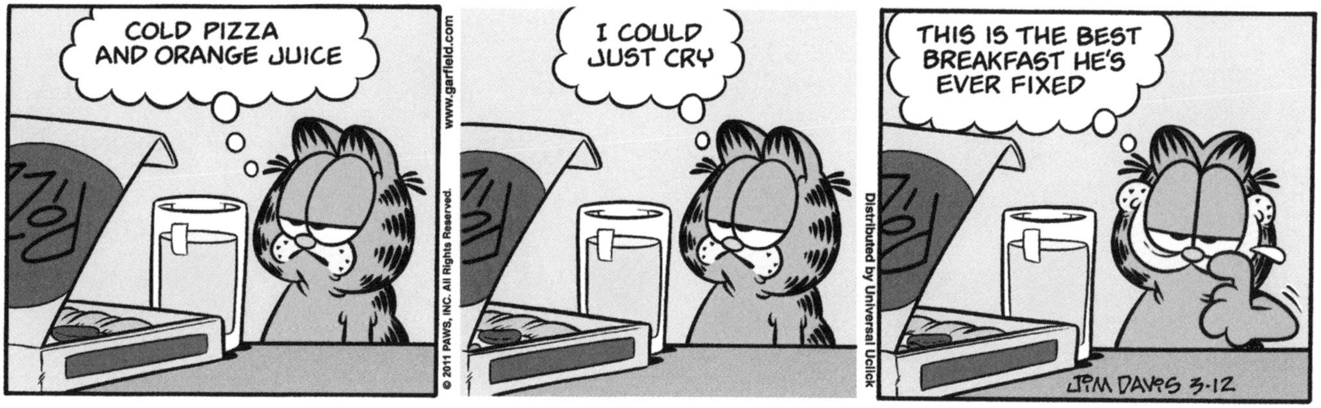
COLD PIZZA AND ORANGE JUICE
© 2011 PAWS, INC. All Rights Reserved. www.garfield.com
I COULD JUST CRY
Distributed by Universal Uclick
THIS IS THE BEST BREAKFAST HE'S EVER FIXED
JIM DAVIS 3-12

NOT-SO-MONSTROUS MONSTERS

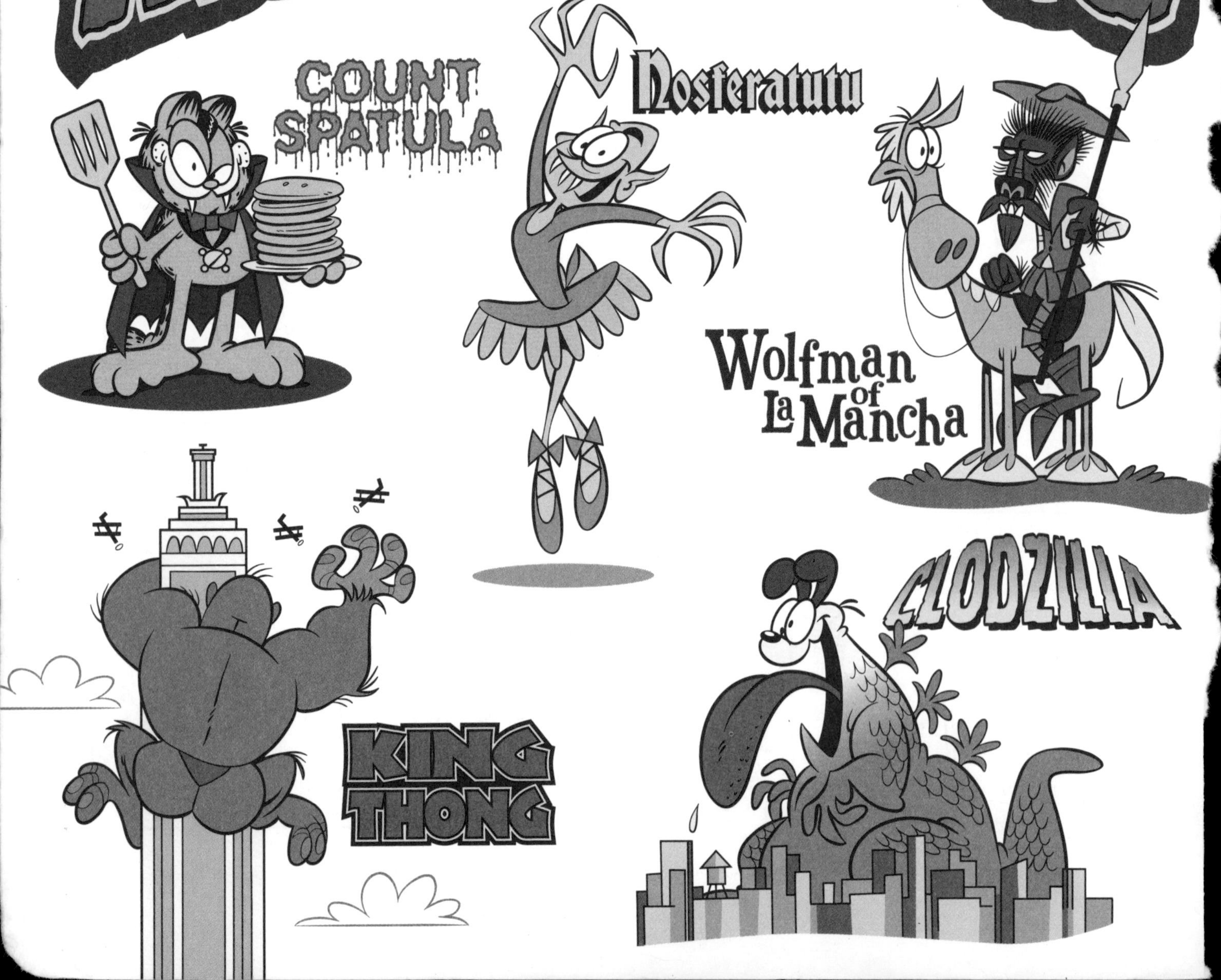
COUNT SPATULA
Nosferatutu
Wolfman of La Mancha
CLODZILLA
KING THONG

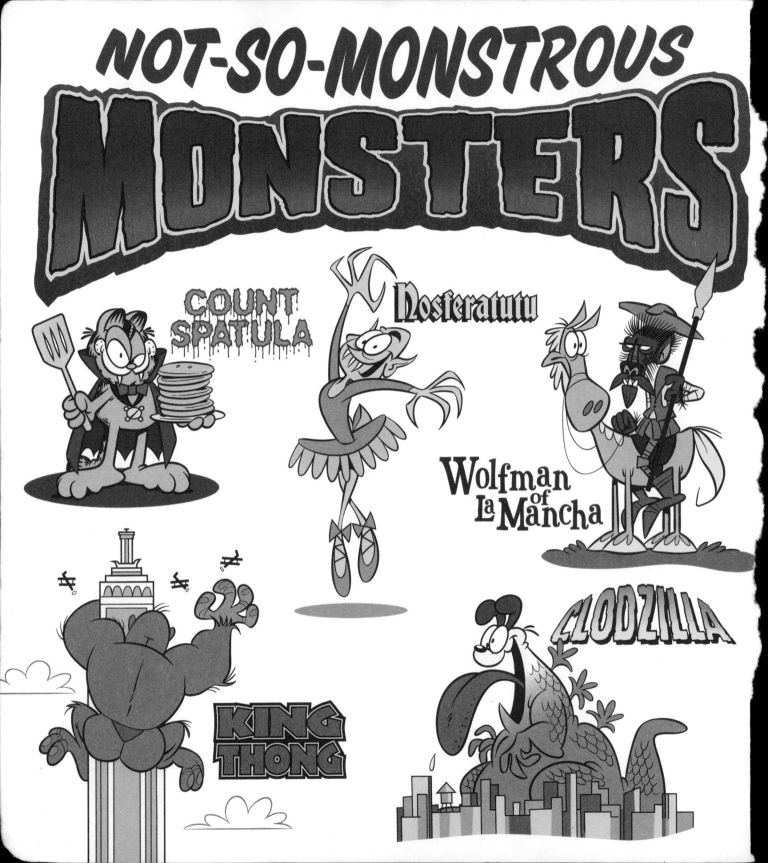

STRIPS, SPECIALS, OR BESTSELLING BOOKS . . .
GARFIELD'S ON EVERYONE'S MENU.

Don't miss even one episode in the Tubby Tabby's hilarious series!

- **New larger, full-color format!**